ENCYCLOPEDIA OF CHINESE ASTROLOGY

TRI LAM

A LIM Book

Published by
Lam Inter Media Corp.
5010 King Edward Avenue,
Montreal, Quebec H4V 2J6
Canada
Tel: (514) 482-6276
http://www.lamintermedia.com

Canadian Cataloguing in Publication Data

Lam, Tri, 1957-
Encyclopedia of Chinese astrology
"A LIM Book".
ISBN 0-9685735-0-9
1. Astrology, Chinese. 2. Divination. I. Title.
BF1714.C5L34 1999   133.5'9251   C99-901159-6

Printed in Canada

This book is dedicated to my children, Duc Thanh, Anne and George, who keep me remembering the past, enjoying the present and dreaming for the future.

FOREWORD

For centuries, the Chinese have been fascinated by everything surrounding the techniques of forecasting the future, whether it is concerning traditional astrology, I Ching, palmistry, the sky chart, Feng Shui, or face reading. These techniques have been developed by observations carried on during hundreds or even thousands of years and they are well rooted in the Chinese culture.

There aren't many books which treat these subjects in such a way that is quite wide and deep and at the same time concise and direct and which can all contain in one volume, therefore I decide to write one myself, I would like to share with you my passion since my youth of this obscure part of the Chinese culture.

I hope that you will have the pleasure to discover or rediscover this art which is the Chinese astrology.

Acknowledgments

I would like to thank all those who have contributed to the realization of this book, especially Stefanie Gude and Eric Galbraith for their excellent editing skills, Judy Isherwood of Shoreline Press for her priceless editorial guidance, Tuan Kiet Sy for the beautiful animals and graphics in the book, and Hélène Rossignol for the pages layout.

About the author

Tri Lam grew up a child of Chinese parents in Vietnam, and received his Master's degree in Computer Science from the Paris-Dauphine University in France. He became interested in Chinese astrology as a teenager, and has studied with several masters in the field. He has also produced a CD-ROM about Chinese astrology.

CONTENTS

1. Chinese Horoscope

Chinese horoscope is based on the movement of the moon, which explains the origin of the term "lunar year". A lunar year does not necessarily last for 365 days - the moon needs 29 days, 12 hours, 44 minutes and 2 seconds to circumnavigate the earth. Therefore a lunar month lasts 29 or 30 days, but never 31 days. Thus, according to the western calendar, the Chinese New Year never falls on the same day from one year to the next. The actual date can always be located at the end of January or the beginning of February.

Chinese astrology has a cycle of twelve years, each cycle represented by twelve animals: rat, ox, tiger, rabbit, dragon, snake, horse, goat, monkey, rooster, dog, and pig. Why have these specific animals been chosen? According to the legend, the Buddha invited all the animals in the world to come to a meeting one day. Only twelve animals answered the invitation and appeared before the Buddha. In order, these animals were the rat, ox, tiger and so on. The Buddha decided to show gratitude for the presence of the animals by awarding each a year in its name.

In addition, there are five elements which have an important influence upon our lives: metal, wood, water, fire, and earth. Our universe consists of these elements. Thus, we assign an element to each sign, resulting in a cycle of sixty years (12 X 5). Each year associated with an element will return only once every sixty years. For example, the year 1989 is the year of earth snake, the year 2001 will be the year of metal snake, and the year of earth snake will reappear only in 2049.

Generally speaking, Chinese astrology plays an important part in the daily lives of all Asians, particularly the Chinese and Southeast Asians. Whether concerned about a marriage, a move or the opening of a business, people consistently look to astrology when seeking a lucky date for these activities. In terms of marriage, people must find a partner with a compatible astrological sign. This is a serious matter which has torn apart many couples. A tradition which has survived for thousands of years is still the current practice.

The Chinese years table

SIGN	ELEMENT	YEAR YYYY/MM/DD
Rat	Metal	1900/01/31 to 1901/02/18
Ox	Metal	1901/02/19 to 1902/02/07
Tiger	Water	1902/02/08 to 1903/01/28
Rabbit	Water	1903/01/29 to 1904/02/15
Dragon	Wood	1904/02/16 to 1905/02/03
Snake	Wood	1905/02/04 to 1906/01/24
Horse	Fire	1906/01/25 to 1907/02/12
Goat	Fire	1907/02/13 to 1908/02/01
Monkey	Earth	1908/02/02 to 1909/01/21
Rooster	Earth	1909/01/22 to 1910/02/09
Dog	Metal	1910/02/10 to 1911/01/29
Pig	Metal	1911/01/30 to 1912/02/17
Rat	Water	1912/02/18 to 1913/02/05
Ox	Water	1913/02/06 to 1914/01/25
Tiger	Wood	1914/01/26 to 1915/02/13
Rabbit	Wood	1915/02/14 to 1916/02/02
Dragon	Fire	1916/02/03 to 1917/01/22
Snake	Fire	1917/01/23 to 1918/02/10
Horse	Earth	1918/02/11 to 1919/01/31
Goat	Earth	1919/02/01 to 1920/02/19
Monkey	Metal	1920/02/20 to 1921/02/07
Rooster	Metal	1921/02/08 to 1922/01/27
Dog	Water	1922/01/28 to 1923/02/15
Pig	Water	1923/02/16 to 1924/02/04
Rat	Wood	1924/02/05 to 1925/01/23
Ox	Wood	1925/01/24 to 1926/02/12
Tiger	Fire	1926/02/13 to 1927/02/01
Rabbit	Fire	1927/02/02 to 1928/01/22
Dragon	Earth	1928/01/23 to 1929/02/09
Snake	Earth	1929/02/10 to 1930/01/29
Horse	Metal	1930/01/30 to 1931/02/16
Goat	Metal	1931/02/17 to 1932/02/05
Monkey	Water	1932/02/06 to 1933/01/25
Rooster	Water	1933/01/26 to 1934/02/13
Dog	Wood	1934/02/14 to 1935/02/03
Pig	Wood	1935/02/04 to 1936/01/23
Rat	Fire	1936/01/24 to 1937/02/10
Ox	Fire	1937/02/11 to 1938/01/30
Tiger	Earth	1938/01/31 to 1939/02/18

Rabbit	Earth	1939/02/19 to 1940/02/07
Dragon	Metal	1940/02/08 to 1941/01/26
Snake	Metal	1941/01/27 to 1942/02/14
Horse	Water	1942/02/15 to 1943/02/04
Goat	Water	1943/02/05 to 1944/01/24
Monkey	Wood	1944/01/25 to 1945/02/12
Rooster	Wood	1945/02/13 to 1946/02/01
Dog	Fire	1946/02/02 to 1947/01/21
Pig	Fire	1947/01/22 to 1948/02/09
Rat	Earth	1948/02/10 to 1949/01/28
Ox	Earth	1949/01/29 to 1950/02/16
Tiger	Metal	1950/02/17 to 1951/02/05
Rabbit	Metal	1951/02/06 to 1952/01/26
Dragon	Water	1952/01/27 to 1953/02/13
Snake	Water	1953/02/14 to 1954/02/02
Horse	Wood	1954/02/03 to 1955/01/23
Goat	Wood	1955/01/24 to 1956/02/11
Monkey	Fire	1956/02/12 to 1957/01/30
Rooster	Fire	1957/01/31 to 1958/02/17
Dog	Earth	1958/02/18 to 1959/02/07
Pig	Earth	1959/02/08 to 1960/01/27
Rat	Metal	1960/01/28 to 1961/02/14
Ox	Metal	1961/02/15 to 1962/02/04
Tiger	Water	1962/02/05 to 1963/01/24
Rabbit	Water	1963/01/25 to 1964/02/12
Dragon	Wood	1964/02/13 to 1965/02/01
Snake	Wood	1965/02/02 to 1966/01/20
Horse	Fire	1966/01/21 to 1967/02/08
Goat	Fire	1967/02/09 to 1968/01/29
Monkey	Earth	1968/01/30 to 1969/02/16
Rooster	Earth	1969/02/17 to 1970/02/05
Dog	Metal	1970/02/06 to 1971/01/26
Pig	Metal	1971/01/27 to 1972/02/14
Rat	Water	1972/02/15 to 1973/02/02
Ox	Water	1973/02/03 to 1974/01/22
Tiger	Wood	1974/01/23 to 1975/02/10
Rabbit	Wood	1975/02/11 to 1976/01/30
Dragon	Fire	1976/01/31 to 1977/02/17
Snake	Fire	1977/02/18 to 1978/02/06
Horse	Earth	1978/02/07 to 1979/01/27
Goat	Earth	1979/01/28 to 1980/02/15
Monkey	Metal	1980/02/16 to 1981/02/04
Rooster	Metal	1981/02/05 to 1982/01/24

Dog	Water	1982/01/25 to 1983/02/12
Pig	Water	1983/02/13 to 1984/02/01
Rat	Wood	1984/02/02 to 1985/02/19
Ox	Wood	1985/02/20 to 1986/02/08
Tiger	Fire	1986/02/09 to 1987/01/28
Rabbit	Fire	1987/01/29 to 1988/02/16
Dragon	Earth	1988/02/17 to 1989/02/05
Snake	Earth	1989/02/06 to 1990/01/26
Horse	Metal	1990/01/27 to 1991/02/14
Goat	Metal	1991/02/15 to 1992/02/03
Monkey	Water	1992/02/04 to 1993/01/22
Rooster	Water	1993/01/23 to 1994/02/09
Dog	Wood	1994/02/10 to 1995/01/30
Pig	Wood	1995/01/31 to 1996/02/18
Rat	Fire	1996/02/19 to 1997/02/06
Ox	Fire	1997/02/07 to 1998/01/27
Tiger	Earth	1998/01/28 to 1999/02/15
Rabbit	Earth	1999/02/16 to 2000/02/04
Dragon	Metal	2000/02/05 to 2001/01/23
Snake	Metal	2001/01/24 to 2002/02/11
Horse	Water	2002/02/12 to 2003/01/31
Goat	Water	2003/02/01 to 2004/01/21
Monkey	Wood	2004/01/22 to 2005/02/08
Rooster	Wood	2005/02/09 to 2006/01/28
Dog	Fire	2006/01/29 to 2007/02/17
Pig	Fire	2007/02/18 to 2008/02/06
Rat	Earth	2008/02/07 to 2009/01/25
Ox	Earth	2009/01/26 to 2010/02/13

THE RAT

The character

Your character is honest and mild. Being sociable and possessing a great ability to communicate, you have many friends. However, such qualities will not interfere with your having a very reserved and private life. You do have a tendency to not reveal your true feelings.

An innovative and imaginative person, you are constantly impressing your friends with new ideas. Although you are skilled in the business world, your excessive caution sometimes hinders your progress. You tend to worry too much about trivial matters.

Lacking patience, you do not like to wait for results. Accordingly, every project must be finished as soon as possible in order for you to launch the next one. Your eagerness to seize all available opportunities may sometimes damage your rate of success. A relentless worker, you are well-equipped to face difficult situations. At times, your intuition may foster unexpected results.

A materialistic person, you enjoy luxury and extravagance. Fortunately, your financial situation makes this possible, allowing you to be very generous with family and friends. You do, however, have some difficulties in your relations with the opposite sex.

The five different types of rat

Rat - metal In order to satisfy your own extravagant tastes, you spend great amounts of money. However, your skill as a financier produces investment results which provide for a comfortable and easy life. As a realistic individual, you never chase impossible dreams. Very cunning, you are able to manipulate people in order to acquire the power necessary for meeting your financial needs. You must nevertheless learn to overcome your excessively cautious attitudes.

Rat - water An exceptional level of intelligence is your most important asset. While your intuition guides you in the making of important life decisions, your eagerness to attain quick results often prompts you to jump into some risky ventures. Your mild manner makes you very popular with others, serving as an excellent key to success in your business enterprise. You are sociable and gifted in the art of communicating, which suggests you may be suited to a successful career in the media.

Rat - wood Your honest and simple personality attracts many friends. You are always sensitive to other people's suffering. A very family-oriented person, you feel a great sense of loyalty towards your partner and relatives. At your place of work, you are very tenacious and once your mind is set, you will persevere until you attain your desired goals. You do not hesitate to persist at all costs if necessary.

Rat - fire You are very energetic and willing to tackle anything. Your abilities to express yourself make you a magnificent orator. You love to attain your goals through deception and trickery, and are fascinated by power. Unfortunately, this undermines your social relations. You strive to display your superiority through extravagant show. Easily provoked, you are often trapped by your own eagerness to prove that nothing is beyond your means.

Rat - earth You worry about everything, even the most trivial of concerns. Your greatest weakness is the excessive caution with which you act, as you dislike to take risks or test new ground. Your financial situation is merely stable, without any great shining successes of which to speak. You are very loyal towards your family and employers, a quality which is greatly appreciated and allows you to gain much support for all your projects.

Compatibility

The signs which you must avoid when seeking a partner:

The rabbit	1927,	1939,	1951,	1963
The horse	1930,	1942,	1954,	1966
The goat	1931,	1943,	1955,	1967

You have nothing in common and any union would result in total failure. This is especially true of the goat and the horse.

You do not share any common interests with the goat and can not withstand his criticism. As far as the horse is concerned, your temperaments are so incompatible that quarrels would surely be your daily meal. Any hope of love shared with the rabbit will prove to be an impossibility.

The signs amongst which to choose an ideal partner:

The ox	1925,	1937,	1949,	1961
The dragon	1928,	1940,	1952,	1964
The monkey	1932,	1944,	1956,	1968

Your admiration for the dragon and the monkey are signs of a love at first sight which will prove to be long-lasting. The talent of the ox is an essential component to your own success.

You will be able to form an union with the dragon which will arouse jealousy in others; and you feel a sense of security in his presence. You can not resist the monkey's generosity and he will make a great effort to please you, displaying his intelligence and talents.

Born under the sign of the rat

Charles Aznavour, George Bush, Jimmy Carter, Benny Hill, Ivan Lendl, Richard Nixon, Mozart, Shakespeare, the Prince of Wales, Louis Armstrong, Nana Mouskouri

THE OX

The character

A solitary person, you tend to be very conservative and reserved. Not very talkative, you find most jokes beyond comprehension. Despite your lack of talent, you are not afraid of working hard to achieve your goals. You can tackle tough situations without complaint and once you have accepted responsibility for a matter, you remain committed.

Once a decision has been made, you are very stubborn and inflexible. It is difficult for you to accept the opinions of others. This may create some friction in your personal relationships. You do not like to make career changes. Even in a low-paying job, you prefer to remain with the same employer, who in turn greatly appreciates your loyalty. You do prefer routine work, as change makes you nervous.

A straightforward and modest person, you never conceal your true intentions. Very sincere and honest when voicing your thoughts and views, it is difficult for you to keep secrets. You prefer to maintain long-term relationships. However, despite your calm nature, you may sometimes display a fearsome temper if things do not proceed according to your expectations.

The five different types of ox

Ox - metal You experience difficulty expressing yourself. Even so, your determination allows you to carry out some very ambitious projects. Once your task is clearly defined, you will take it seriously and make all efforts to achieve your goals. You choose to work alone rather than in a team, preferring not to get advice from others. Your solitude allows you to develop first-rate thinking skills, facilitating your ability to analyze every detail of a problem or project. As a result, you favor giving advice over receiving it.

Ox - water Despite a lack of talents, your tenacity and relentlessness drive you to fulfill all responsibilities and overcome obstacles. You are quite flexible and willing to listen to some practical advice, enabling you to master difficult situations. The sympathy you show towards others is essential for your role as a social worker. You are attentive to details and your determination to supervise all activities can often annoy other people greatly.

Ox - wood You are very stubborn and do not like change. Once you have made up your mind, you will rarely alter your course. For instance, you are able to remain with the same business company for many years without receiving a promotion. You have to overcome your loneliness, as people find it difficult to penetrate your world. You only trust your own thoughts and never heed the advice of others. You feel your ideas must prevail, often ignoring the very existence of others.

Ox - fire You have difficulty establishing friendships with others, as your need for solitude does not make you easily accessible. Very forthright, you do not hesitate to speak out nor do you ever conceal the truth. This may sometimes work against you. A very emotional person, you are easily embarrassed and are constantly seeking a stable and tranquil life. Your superior creative talents may procure you much success in your career.

Ox - earth You are used to working long hours and do more than is expected of you. A very realistic person, you are humble and do not like extravagance. Your tenacity aids you in overcoming any difficult or trying situation. Excessively self-confident, you may follow the wrong path in life. This tendency towards intransigence is a weakness which you should try to overcome.

Compatibility

The signs which you must avoid when seeking a partner:

The dragon   1928, 1940, 1952, 1964
The horse   1930, 1942, 1954, 1966
The goat   1931, 1943, 1955, 1967

You have difficulty getting along with these partners, as your differences are so great.

You are very jealous of the horse's talent and do not appreciate his dominating personality. With the goat, the passion is fleeting. What seems to be love at first sight will never develop into anything real. With the dragon, your extremely disparate personalities make getting along an impossibility.

The signs amongst which to choose an ideal partner:

The rat   1924, 1936, 1948, 1960
The snake   1929, 1941, 1953, 1965
The rooster   1933, 1945, 1957, 1969

You have more respect for the rat than for the snake and you enjoy the rooster's way of thinking.

You have a lot of interests in common with the rat, which is the key to a perfectly joyful life. You admire the snake's leadership talents, as they will guide you through some difficult situations. The rooster always has new ideas with which to save you from monotony. In addition, he can support your financial needs.

Born under the sign of the ox

Bach, Richard Burton, Charlie Chaplin, Walt Disney, Jane Fonda, Gerald Ford, Adolf Hitler, Napoleon Bonaparte, Paul Newman, Renoir, Peter Sellers, Margaret Thatcher

THE TIGER

The character

A very courageous person, you are ready to take risks and accept any challenge. In addition to your innovative ideas and organizational abilities, your leadership helps you to succeed in the business world. A natural leader, you invest all your energy in economic ventures. Your determination helps you to overcome all obstacles and you never lack ambition. Constantly striving to succeed, you do not hesitate to take necessary risks in order to achieve your goals. You do not like to receive orders and your proud nature may create enemies. Your disregard for authority drives you to be the sole master of your own destiny.

Sometimes you can be very indecisive and as you hesitate to make quick decisions, this can create some confusion for others. You care very much for your reputation and dislike criticism. When you are in the wrong, you always seek an excuse for your actions.

Your sense of justice makes you both an incorruptible and generous person. You dare to challenge any authority and remain committed to what you believe. You are especially enthusiastic in affairs concerning community welfare and like to get the attention of others. You never refuse to help those who are less fortunate, as you believe this displays your superiority.

The five different types of tiger

Tiger - metal You are very ambitious and in order to conquer the world, you are willing to confront the unknown. You do not hesitate to challenge a stronger adversary. As the results of your efforts are not always instantaneous, your ensuing impatience may be an obstacle to your success. An endless supply of energy enables you to become involved in countless activities. Your extended and varied interests will ensure the longevity of your company, as well as a colorful life.

Tiger - water While externally you appear to be a tough and intransigent individual, the internal truth is quite the opposite. This dual personality makes you a formidable competitor, as your opponents tend to overestimate your tenacity and thus surrender without little contest. Your excellent leadership is greatly appreciated, although you may find yourself faced with a dilemma when quick solutions are unattainable.

Tiger - wood Your generosity affords you many friends. People appreciate and rely upon your sense of justice and sympathy. You do not fear dangerous challenges when an ill-treated person is in need of your help. Your organizational abilities and creative mind render you an invincible leader. You tend to be overcautious in testing unknown ground, but in spite of this weakness, you attain outstanding achievements in business, thereby creating a very comfortable financial situation for yourself.

Tiger - fire You are very enthusiastic about everything you undertake and are willing to follow your dreams. A talented inventor, you constantly have fresh ideas. Your discomfort with salaried positions suggests you are best suited to become an entrepreneur. Your adaptability and open-mindedness cause you to dabble in numerous careers, in order to fulfill your craving for diversity.

Tiger - earth You do not bow to your opponents and love a great challenge. You do not hesitate to take necessary risks. Your stubbornness is a weakness which you should try to overcome, as your inability to listen to advice results in foolish mistakes. You tend to overestimate your abilities, which actually may assist you in overcoming obstacles from time to time. The incorruptible nature of your character wins the great respect of others.

Compatibility

The signs which you must avoid when seeking a partner:

The snake   1929, 1941, 1953, 1965
The monkey   1932, 1944, 1956, 1968

Your competitiveness is so ferocious that it causes you to hate these partners.

You cannot bear the monkey's arrogance nor his intelligence, which make you feel like an idiot. Also, he will try everything to get ahead of you. You do not accept the snake's hypocrisy.

The signs amongst which to choose an ideal partner:

The horse   1930, 1942, 1954, 1966
The dog   1934, 1946, 1958, 1970

You are the ideal complement to the horse and your passion for him is an inextinguishable flame. He seems to fulfill all your needs. You have much in common with the dog and your shared interests allow you to build an empire together.

Born under the sign of the tiger

Beethoven, Agatha Christie, Charles de Gaulle, Dwight Eisenhower, Karl Marx, Marilyn Monroe, Marco Polo, Jerry Lewis, Stevie Wonder

Chinese Horoscope

THE RABBIT

The character

You are mild, optimistic and joyful, and bring peace to others. Your understanding nature and generosity attract many friends. You enjoy freedom and forbid any supervision of your daily work. You are very loyal to your employer and do not like to make career changes, as variation makes you nervous.

You take a very cautious approach in your business endeavors. You seek security but sometimes you lack caution when making important decisions, which may result in many errors. You also have a tendency to abandon business ventures midway, your enthusiasm fading as soon as something more appealing arises.

An idealist by nature, you tend to live in a dream world which allows you to escape the realities of life and to avoid difficulty. You seek many fashionable possessions and are among the first to try any new product. You do not hesitate to spend a lot to satisfy your luxurious appetite. You can hardly resist the temptation of the opposite sex, which can bring you much trouble in your relationships with other people.

The five different types of rabbit

Rabbit - metal You hate to receive orders from anyone. Thus, your independence brings you the tranquillity and the freedom necessary for fulfilling your dearest dreams. You do, however, tend to retreat into a fog of idealism and often fail to fully reach your intended goals. Eloquence and persuasive power pave the road of success for you, and consequently your enterprises prosper under any circumstance. You also enjoy great popularity amongst your friends.

Rabbit - water A happy and optimistic person, your enthusiasm is very engaging. Wherever you may go, others enjoy your company. You tend to escape from reality by enveloping yourself in unattainable dreams. Your interest and involvement in a great variety of activities may prevent you from completing your tasks. You explore things only on a superficial basis and do not delve deep in any attempt to understand details. Your ambition may exceed your abilities, resulting in occasional failure.

Rabbit - wood A mild and quiet person, you have an easygoing manner and never fight to attain what you want. Your impeccable memory enables you to succeed in your business enterprises. You are an innovator and do not hesitate to search for original solutions. Other people's advice comes second on your list of priorities. You enjoy luxury and are not stingy. Indeed, you are accustomed to extravagance and are able to find money to support this lifestyle.

Rabbit - fire Possessing a joyful and easy-going nature, you often place too much trust in others and rely upon them too heavily for assistance in your own decision-making. Generally you enjoy a quiet and solitary life. You pay great attention to your appearance and your social relationships, being very sensitive to any criticism. Such insecurity may jeopardize your leadership role.

Rabbit - earth Your ambitious endeavors live up to your own expectations, despite their seemingly unrealistic standards. An alert mind acts as the ideal protector of your investments, as at the first sight of potential danger, you will take necessary action to protect your assets. However, this cautious attitude may cost you some very profitable opportunities. A first-rate communicator, you know how to express both your desires and your unhappiness tactfully, making you someone who is respected by others.

Compatibility

The signs which you must avoid when seeking a partner:

The rat	1924, 1936, 1948, 1960
The ox	1925, 1937, 1949, 1961
The dragon	1928, 1940, 1952, 1964

You cannot tolerate the ignorance of the ox and the dragon, and you are not at ease in the company of the rat, making a peaceful relationship seem impossible.

You cannot accept that the dragon is in a superior class, thus a union between you will involve making many concessions. The ox will only think of his work and will not have much time for you, which seems to forecast a monotonous life for both of you.

The signs amongst which to choose an ideal partner:

The goat	1931, 1943, 1955, 1967
The dog	1934, 1946, 1958, 1970
The pig	1935, 1947, 1959, 1971

You have a mutual respect for one another and are ready to accept their shortcomings.

The goat is so mild and so romantic that you can not stop thinking of him. You consider the dog to be the best protector and you trust him with your life. The pig accepts your shortcomings more willingly than others, so you feel at ease in his presence.

Born under the sign of the rabbit

Fidel Castro, Confucius, Albert Einstein, Bob Hope, Roger Moore, Orson Welles, Tina Turner, Edith Piaf, Brian Mulroney, Frank Sinatra

龍

THE DRAGON

The character

You are proud and arrogant, rarely accepting other people's advice. Once you have made a decision, you will stick to it, even if your judgment proves to be in error. You will not be content with a second place achievement and you do not lack ambition. Ready to do whatever is necessary to ensure a leadership position, you are very self-confident and have a lot of energy. You believe you can succeed in anything you undertake and refuse to admit your errors. Fortunately, you have been born under the sign of luck and power, which will allow you the potential to rebuild your empire.

You are not very diplomatic when dealing with other people, which can be a pitfall to your success. You are intelligent and talented. However, owing to your inconstancy and an impatient tendency to act without sufficient thought, you occasionally suffer failures. You can be a winner today and become a loser tomorrow. Fortunately, someone will always be there to save you because you have been born under the sign of luck.

Your feelings of superiority are your most dangerous enemies. You can be very persistent in pursuing your goals and you refuse any questioning of your capabilities.

The five different types of dragon

Dragon - metal You are a forceful and intransigent individual, not taking into account other people's opinions and never admitting to your mistakes. Unsurprisingly, this can create some tension in your relation with others. When deeming it necessary, you do not hesitate to deliver a speech clarifying your position. You represent the most allusive and powerful animal in the Chinese legend, your strong personality making you an ideal leader in any group.

Dragon - water You are mild and temperate, making you a very popular individual. Placing the interests of others before your own, you facilitate a confident climate within your circle of friends. Your ambition is not as great as it appears to be, especially as you tend to surrender when confronted with a difficult situation. This unwillingness to struggle is most prevalent when you are forced to face a situation on your own.

Dragon - wood The wood dragon has a dual personality - on the one hand, you are mild and shy; on the other, you are very critical of yourself. You are also very enthusiastic about everything. An intelligent and gifted person, you sometimes become involved in dangerous ventures as a result of your impatience and eagerness for results. Fortunately, you may overcome difficult situations owing to your tactful manner.

Dragon - fire You are extremely ambitious, with a desire to conquer the world, burn the earth and become master of the entire universe. Your extreme arrogance causes you to laugh at other people's opinions. Rather than wealth, you seek power and will never tolerate being anything but first in command. Thus, your relationships with your superiors are very problematic. You conceal any emotion with an icy facade and this impassive appearance is your greatest weapon in any negotiation.

Dragon - earth Your moderate character makes you a different type of dragon. You seem have your feet on the ground and despite some stubbornness, you are quite willing to receive good advice from others. This affords you necessary support in times of need. You are very enthusiastic and quick to launch new business ventures but are impatient to reap the rewards. Thus, you often quit before finishing and turn your attention elsewhere.

Compatibility

The signs which you must avoid when seeking a partner:

The ox	1925, 1937, 1949, 1961
The rabbit	1927, 1939, 1951, 1963
The dog	1934, 1946, 1958, 1970

Your union will last only a short time, as you do not have any common interests.

You and the ox possess conflicting temperaments and if you attempt a relationship, you will destroy each other. Your relationship with the rabbit will be much like a roller coaster ride. Also, you will be forced to make many concessions, as you wish to dominate the world and believe the rabbit to be docile and obedient. You do not share the dog's interests and each of you wish to be the sole ruler of the world, which will generate constant conflict in your relationship.

The signs amongst which to choose an ideal partner:

The rat	1924, 1936, 1948, 1960
The monkey	1932, 1944, 1956, 1968
The rooster	1933, 1945, 1957, 1969

The monkey's energy arouses you and you admire the intelligence of the rooster and the rat.

The passion between you and the rat is unmistakable. Despite being in a dominant position, you adore the talent of the rat. You will depend greatly on the monkey to help you through the different phases of your life. His energy will revive you during difficult and monotonous days. You are the rooster's eminent guide, which will allow you the unique opportunity to exercise your superior strength and thus feel more useful.

Born under the sign of the dragon

Bing Crosby, Martin Luther King Jr., John Lennon, Francois Mitterand, Bernard Shaw, Jean Drapeau, Christian Dior

THE SNAKE

The character

You are very cautious and rarely make a hasty decision. You analyze problems thoroughly before taking any action and your intuition sometimes helps you to overcome obstacles.

An idealist by nature, once your goals are set you proceed with your plans and never listen to advice. Despite occasional mistakes, your ferocious determination will allow you to succeed in business. You are suspicious and you rarely trust anyone. This may prove detrimental to your business, as you need other people's assistance in order to succeed.

You never reveal secrets, including even the most unimportant matters. You have been born under the sign of wisdom and are a highly intelligent person. You are totally committed to satisfying your curiosity, which in turn makes you a very good researcher.

You become jealous and frustrated at the success of others in your own field. You have a keen eye for beauty, which is vital in any attempt to become a talented artist.

The five different types of snake

Snake - metal Possessing great thinking skills, you are able to analyze and dissect all details of a project before making a decision. This quality is essential in facilitating your success in the business world. You enjoy living in luxury and do not hesitate to make others aware of this. Fortunately, your financial situation can support such a lifestyle and allows you to show great generosity towards your partner. You often use this show of extravagance to hide your loneliness and solitude.

Snake - water An idealist by nature, you desire everything to be perfect. You are blinded by your beliefs, which sometimes go against the current trend. Financially you are very independent and do not hesitate to work diligently in order to climb the social ladder. Your superior intelligence will foster a very bright career in business.

Snake - wood Your superior intelligence enables you to have a career in research, as you are capable of analyzing a problem in great detail. You love discussions and dare to voice your unconventional point of view. You have difficulty forgiving other people's mistakes and will never allow your competitors to excel.

Snake - fire Your ambition is limitless and you climb the ladder of success at any cost. You are capable of great achievements because of your strong willpower and leadership skills. You like to impress people with your extensive and diversified knowledge. You are very suspicious and rarely trust others, never taking their advice seriously. This may be your greatest hindrance to success in the business world.

Snake - earth You like to explore unknown territory in order to satisfy your curiosity. Your own world can sometimes be removed from reality. You are not afraid of dangerous challenges and accept them with great pleasure. A formidable financier, you seem to be beyond defeat in this realm. You are very reserved and do not voice your opinions unless you feel it necessary.

Compatibility

The signs which you must avoid when seeking a partner:

The tiger	1926, 1938, 1950, 1962
The monkey	1932, 1944, 1956, 1968
The pig	1935, 1947, 1959, 1971

You feel insecure in the presence of these partners and are afraid that they will challenge your supremacy.

You lack respect for the tiger because it is you who wear the crown of king of the jungle. The monkey is more cunning than you and you do not approve of his way of doing things. You do not share the same thoughts as the pig and this relationship will cause you more trouble than happiness.

The signs amongst which to choose an ideal partner:

The ox	1925, 1937, 1949, 1961
The rooster	1933, 1945, 1957, 1969

These partners are your only choice for a durable union, as they are the only ones who respect you.

Mutual understanding helps you to build an ideal relationship with the ox and you feel a sense of security in his company. An excellent rapport exists between you and the rooster, as you both respect each other.

Born under the sign of the snake

Charles Darwin, Bob Dylan, Gandhi, Princess Grace of Monaco, Howard Hughes, John F. Kennedy, Abraham Lincoln, Mao Tse Tung, Robert Mitchum, Pablo Picasso, Jean Paul Sartre, Goethe, Jacques Brel

THE HORSE

The character

You are generous, dynamic and always willing to help. This makes you an ideal candidate for the communication. Your sympathetic and likeable nature makes you a welcome presence at any gathering.

You are forthright and frank, with your own way of doing things, and you hate to follow the crowd. You dislike restrictions and regulations. Your reasoning abilities allow you to consider all matters thoroughly and your agile mind is your most formidable weapon.

You can be interested in several things at once and tend to launch many projects simultaneously. Nevertheless, some of these endeavors will prove a waste of time, as you lack the patience required to wait for results. Your eloquence brings you success in most business ventures. However, you can be very impatient when striving to fulfill your dreams, as you want to accomplish everything immediately.

You are impulsive, your emotions sometimes outweighing your logic. This can cause complications in your love life. And even if you generally handle your finances with care, you will not hesitate to spend large sums of money just to please your loved one. Also, you enjoy extravagance and care greatly about your appearance.

The five different types of horse

Horse - metal Direct and frank, you do not conceal your feelings and never hesitate to voice your opinion. Other people are constantly drawn to your many innovative and revolutionary ideas. Active in the milieu of modern art, you are capable of appreciating the finer things in life. As well, your eloquence allows you to dominate discussions and gain personal benefit from them.

Horse - water You are a friendly and tactful person, one who has good relationships with many people and an ability to easily convince and persuade others. Your open-mindedness cultivates interests in many different things at the same time. Your alert mind makes you a formidable financier, while your intelligence and organizational capabilities assist you in achieving a very successful business career.

Horse - wood You are a mild and easily approachable person. You enjoy extravagance and hate to follow the crowd, ignoring the rules of the game in favor of your own ideas. Your words and actions may sometimes contradict each other, a tendency which may harm your social relations. You are ambitious but even though you are capable of excelling, you are limited by your lack of leadership skills.

Horse - fire This horse possesses a thunderous character throughout his lifetime. Being very energetic, you are an overzealous person who commits to numerous things at once. You can be very unrealistic and often even veer toward the extreme. Your emotions override your reason and you are constantly in transition, making change in your life. Loyalty is not a quality for which you are renowned.

Horse - earth Your intuition is a natural gift, one which is most evident if you are a female horse. You do not enjoy analytical decision-making. Instead, your actions tend to be very impulsive and lacking any serious thought. Although this approach may bring quick results and helps you to succeed in the business world, it can also be a pitfall.

Compatibility

The signs which you must avoid when seeking a partner:

The rat   1924, 1936, 1948, 1960
The ox   1925, 1937, 1949, 1961
The rabbit   1927, 1939, 1951, 1963

Your admiration for the rat is fleeting and you merely laugh at the rabbit.

You and the rat are completely different and having a relationship will prove impossible. The ox does not appreciate your talent and your relationship will result only in constant strife and turmoil.

The signs amongst which to choose an ideal partner:

The tiger   1926, 1938, 1950, 1962
The goat   1931, 1943, 1955, 1967
The dog   1934, 1946, 1958, 1970

The tiger understands you and the goat respects you, while the dog is quick to displays his complete loyalty.

You feel a great interest in the tiger because of his superior intelligence. You and the goat love each other passionately, as the goat is so mild and so understanding. The dog is the only one capable of enduring the authoritarian nature of your character.

Born under the sign of the horse

Neil Armstrong, Leonard Bernstein, Leonid Brezhnev, Chopin, Nikita Khrushchev, Paul McCartney, Issac Newton, Franklin Roosevelt, Anwar Sadat, Ingmar Bergman

THE GOAT

The character

A careful and well-organized person, you think twice before taking action. Due to this excessive caution, you occasionally miss out on profitable opportunities. You are an easy-going person whose company other people enjoy, also because they feel you think of their interests before your own.

You are capable of working long hours and never abandon a project midway. You do not hesitate to travel great distances in order to capitalize upon career opportunities. You do not like to make decisions, preferring to leave them for others to deal with. You shun responsibility unless you are forced to take it.

You are very stubborn and hate to listen to advice. This inflexibility may sometimes lead to success in your business endeavors. You are likely to leave your home town early in life, in order to try your luck elsewhere. You make career changes frequently to satisfy your numerous interests. You prefer to have a quiet and lonely life and do not fear solitude.

The five different types of goat

Goat - metal You are mild-mannered and self-confident, allowing nothing to irritate you. You are sure to think twice before making any kind of commitment. Your tenacity and management skills help you to succeed in the business world. As you feel harmony to be very important, you prefer to surround yourself with a small group of high caliber individuals, rather than with a mass of incompetents.

Goat - water Naturally rebellious, you constantly swim against the current because you enjoy the reactions of others. Afraid of falling into traps, your insecurity prevents you from advancing in your career. A lack of resolution hinders the success of your business. You prefer to work alone, knowing that your revolutionary ideas often create more enemies than friends.

Goat - wood You love a peaceful life and seek quiet and tranquil surroundings. You never hurry; you leave competition to the others. You do not easily accept responsibility. Always prepared for the worst, your alert mind is your best weapon. Your friendly nature helps you to establish good relationships.

Goat - fire You experience great frustration at things which displease you, especially another person's failure to abide by your rules. You are a solitary individual and are reluctant to mix with the crowd. You prefer to go your own way when presented with the need to make a decision. Extravagance is evident in all aspects of your life. You enjoy luxury goods, a craving which your financial situation can fortunately support.

Goat - earth You are very caring and also seen as the most scholarly amongst all types of goat. Very analytical, you have the ability to be a very keen researcher. You are particularly renowned for your initiative and people love your revolutionary ideas. You are artistically talented and your multifaceted nature helps you to better combine your professional and private lives.

Compatibility

The signs which you must avoid when seeking a partner:

The rat	1924,	1936,	1948,	1960
The ox	1925,	1937,	1949,	1961
The dog	1934,	1946,	1958,	1970

The love at first sight which you may feel for these partners is fleeting and will only last for a night.

You do not share interests with the rat and cold war will be waged between you. In the case of the ox, it is not love but adventure which attracts you. You will wage relentless war with the dog, as you are too dissimilar to function as a couple.

The signs amongst which to choose an ideal partner:

The rabbit	1927,	1939,	1951,	1963
The horse	1930,	1942,	1954,	1966
The pig	1935,	1947,	1959,	1971

You appreciate the rabbit's mildness and the horse's ability to protect. The pig resembles you more than any other.

You greatly admire the mild and obedient character of the rabbit. With the horse, you are looking for the ideal guide in your common life. You and the pig share the same interests, which make you an ideal couple.

Born under the sign of the goat

Catherine Deneuve, John Denver, Mikhail Gorbachov, Mick Jagger, Mussolini, John Wayne, Michelangelo, Honoré de Balzac, Simone de Beauvoir, Coco Chanel, Tino Rossi

Chinese Horoscope

猴

THE MONKEY

The character

Generous, dynamic, intelligent, eloquent, with a great sense of humor, you are a great leader of any group. Your many talents afford you entrance into almost any domain. Seeking great wealth and honor, you are willing to conquer anything and do not fear competition. You have a tendency to underestimate your adversaries.

Your diplomatic and friendly manner attracts you many followers. You enjoy discussion and do not hesitate to participate in any debate. You have a very good memory and are interested in the world as a whole. You are looking for any opportunity to succeed and generally are able to obtain what you want, thanks to your shrewdness and intelligence.

Capable of focusing upon a problem and finding the necessary solution, you often undertake several projects at the same time, in order to avoid monotony and inactivity. Your creative and agile mind assists you in succeeding in most business ventures. Although your impatience proves a dangerous enemy, you are very cunning and do not hesitate to employ trickery. Your great self-confidence can occasionally result in failure, as you remain unreceptive to the advice of others and insist upon making your own decisions.

The five different types of monkey

Monkey - metal Superior intelligence is your best weapon in any competition. You are also very talented and skilled in the business world, your determination allowing you to overcome all obstacles. You do prefer power over money, finding it to be your main motivation in life. Despite the fact that you are an excellent financier, you laugh at money and would choose to be an executive in a large corporation rather than a millionaire.

Monkey - water You have a wonderful sense of humor and others appreciate the way in which you tackle problems. Nothing is too complicated or difficult for you to handle and you are capable of using humor to solve even the most difficult of problems. You may occasionally be dishonest, but only in order to overcome obstacles. You are very tactful and diplomatic, knowing how to please your partner with your generosity.

Monkey - wood You are the craftiest person in the world and like to attain your goals through deception. You know how to conceal your intentions beneath a crafty appearance, often undermining your credibility. Your eloquence is your most precious weapon and is very helpful in your business enterprises.

Monkey - fire An indisputable leader, your determination frightens away your adversaries and you are willing to battle at every front. Your interests are so varied that you are continually searching for new ventures. You enjoy launching several projects at once and are capable of managing them all simultaneously. You do not fear taking large risks and are a first-rate entrepreneur. You are very ambitious, striving hard to succeed in the business world, as this is your sole motivation in life.

Monkey - earth You are very dynamic and generous, never hesitating to help other people when the situation calls for it. Your generosity is greatly respected by others. You are so stubborn that you remain closed to the advice of others, which can prove detrimental to your business. You enjoy a very comfortable financial position, which helps to support your generous habits.

Compatibility

The signs which you must avoid when seeking a partner:

The tiger   1926, 1938, 1950, 1962
The snake   1929, 1941, 1953, 1965
The pig   1935, 1947, 1959, 1971

You enjoy the tiger's body but this is the extent of your attraction. However, you are not attracted to the pig's body.

The tiger cannot tolerate your superiority. You and the snake lack respect for each other. The competition is so intense that the relationship cannot last. You are very cold to the pig, which soon pushes him away.

The signs amongst which to choose an ideal partner:

The rat   1924, 1936, 1948, 1960
The dragon   1928, 1940, 1952, 1964

You feel great passion for the rat and his mad love, while the dragon's magnetism draws you to him.

The rat is the only one who can tolerate your arrogance. The common interests which you and the dragon share create a perfect union. You are ideal partners.

Born under the sign of the monkey

Bjorn Borg, Julius Caesar, Charles Dickens, Lyndon Johnson, Edward Kennedy, Pope John Paul II, Elizabeth Taylor, Harry S. Truman, Leonardo da Vinci, Diana Ross

THE ROOSTER

The character

A humble and mild person, your responsive and understanding nature helps you to maintain lasting friendships. Even though you may seem too direct and frank, you are very sympathetic. You know when necessary effort is required to fulfill an assignment.

You are very intelligent, your agile mind and meticulousness making you an excellent organizer. You carefully plot your strategies before beginning a project and you possess superior intelligence. A natural expert in communication, you are capable of expressing yourself eloquently. Such skill will help you to succeed in business.

You are extremely ambitious and your goals may sometimes exceed your abilities. Despite the impracticality of your dreams, you will still have remarkable success in life. Financially speaking, you are very well-off, never lacking money to satisfy your needs. Once you have made a decision, you do not change your mind. You seem capable of reading the minds of others, which can be a great help in your career.

You enjoy luxury and extravagance. Fortunately your financial situation allows you to do so, and as well you do not hesitate to work hard in order to maintain your costly way of living.

The five different types of rooster

Rooster - metal Being very eloquent, you are able to present your opinions and persuade others to adopt your position. You do not compromise easily. Your great ability to penetrate the thoughts of others aids you in achieving your goals at opportune times. You are very astute and clever, making manipulation of your opponents an easy accomplishment. This provides you with many opportunities in the business world.

Rooster - water You tend to devote too much energy to trivial matters, and lack a larger perspective on your life. You are very ambitious, wanting to be successful in all endeavors, but your abilities are limited. Nevertheless, your determination may aid you in realizing some of your dreams, allowing you to have quite a successful career in your field.

Rooster - wood Your mild character makes you a very popular person in any group. Moreover, your sympathy for less fortunate people helps you to infiltrate every social grouping. You do not hesitate to help your friends, even if you have to dispense large sums of money. Always ready to prove your determined nature, you are extremely creative and constantly full of innovative ideas.

Rooster - fire Your intelligence is superior to most and you excel in financial and business matters. You have outstanding organizational skills and are an ideal planner of large-scale projects. You include all the necessary details and your determination ensures your success. You are well equipped to cope with seemingly insurmountable difficulties, never retreating when faced with a challenge.

Rooster - earth You are the least determined and focused amongst all types of rooster. You frequently alter your plans in order to accommodate your fleeting passions, your attention seeming to last a mere twenty-four hours. This inability to commit is your obstacle to any genuine business success. You enjoy luxury and extravagance and do not hesitate to spend great amounts in order to satisfy your fancy. You are very fashionable and always among the first to sample new products.

Compatibility

The signs which you must avoid when seeking a partner:

The rooster   1933, 1945, 1957, 1969
The dog   1934, 1946, 1958, 1970

Two roosters together will surely go to war, neither one will accept second place and conflict is inevitable, in business as well as love. You must question whether or not the dog can leave the rooster in peace. You do not share any common interests with the dog and the relationship could be harmful for you both.

The signs amongst which to choose an ideal partner:

The ox   1925, 1937, 1949, 1961
The dragon   1928, 1940, 1952, 1964
The snake   1929, 1941, 1953, 1965

You share the same interests as the dragon and the ox. You respect the snake.

You follow the same paths as both the dragon and the ox. However, you are more dependent on the dragon than on the ox. Even though you have nothing in common with the snake, you compliment him highly.

Born under the sign of the rooster

Princess Caroline of Monaco, Pope Paul VI, Simone Signoret, Robert Bourassa, Andrei Gromyko, Peter Ustinov, Jean-Paul Belmondo, Dolly Parton

THE DOG

The character

You are intelligent and talented. However, you have difficulty expressing yourself and can hardly bear to accept advice from others. You have a very strong sense of justice and responsibility, qualities which are greatly appreciated by those who know you. Always capable of treating people fairly, you are eager to defend a good cause. You have the courage to fight injustice and are always ready to assist the weak.

You are very serious and focused in your work, making every necessary effort to fulfill your responsibilities. Your loyalty is fierce and unconditional, which may sometimes cause you to follow a leader blindly. You can be very direct and frank, offering criticism which is very pointed and blunt, sometimes causing harm to your relations with others.

Anxiety is characteristic of your sign, thus you tend to worry too much, even concerning the most trivial matters. This may hinder your success in business. You always make decisions in accordance with your intuition, believing that your emotions are stronger than your logic. You should learn to devote more time to yourself, as it is futile to believe yourself capable of saving the world.

The five different types of dog

Dog - metal As you place great importance upon loyalty, you never betray friends and rarely even change your job. Consequently, you attain great respect from friends and colleagues. In dealing with people, your frank and open manner can sometimes be misleading. You are a daring individual willing to take necessary risks in the testing of new ideas. However, you are cautious and clever enough to avoid putting all your eggs in one basket.

Dog - water You are very conservative and uncompromising, rarely listening to the advice of others. Your tendency to convince others by force rather than compromise may work against you. You have difficulty expressing your thoughts, which can result in the confusion of others. Your determination will enable you to achieve quite a satisfactory financial state.

Dog - wood You are the most hard-working of all types of dog. Taking your responsibilities very seriously, you do whatever possible to fulfill your duties. Consequently, you are greatly respected by your friends and family. You have a great sense of loyalty which garners exceptional admiration from the opposite sex, amongst whom you are always welcome.

Dog - fire You are very intelligent and talented, the most imaginative of dogs. You are interested in numerous things at once and manage them all simultaneously with great ease. You seek new ideas from other people and impress them with your creativity. Thus, you are capable of outperforming your competitors and conquer them without difficulty.

Dog - earth You are generous and always willing to help, a very popular person amongst your friends and family. You tend to follow a leader without question and base your judgment upon intuition rather than logic, which may harm your career. A redoubtable financier, you are able to accumulate large sums of money with which to satisfy your personal needs.

Compatibility

The signs which you must avoid when seeking a partner:

The dragon	1928, 1940, 1952, 1964
The goat	1931, 1943, 1955, 1967
The rooster	1933, 1945, 1957, 1969

You are so incompatible with these people in both love and business that any union is impossible.

You do not share the same interests as the dragon or the rooster, which prevents you from following the same path. Your excessively authoritarian nature causes war between you and the goat.

The signs amongst which to choose an ideal partner:

The tiger	1926, 1938, 1950, 1962
The rabbit	1927, 1939, 1951, 1963
The horse	1930, 1942, 1954, 1966

You feel a mad love for the rabbit. You are ready to give the horse whatever you have. You and the tiger are a perfect match and your union arouses jealousy in others.

Your relationship with the rabbit is a source of everlasting joy and both of you seek mutual understanding. You and the horse have much in common, as you are perfect life partners.

Born under the sign of the dog

Brigitte Bardot, David Bowie, Winston Churchill, Michael Jackson, Sophia Loren, Madonna, Elvis Presley, Mother Teresa, Voltaire, Victor Hugo, René Lévesque

THE PIG

The character

You are very suspicious and never trust other people, preferring to make decisions without the advice of others. Forsaking the crowds which make you nervous, you enjoy a lonely and peaceful life.

A straightforward person, you can be very stubborn and intransigent. You despise hypocrisy and lies. Afraid of making any irreversible errors, you have a tendency to be indecisive. However, once you have made a decision, you follow through with plans without heeding the advice of others.

Your lack of patience creates a temperament which is easily angered, and you must struggle to control yourself. You are eloquent and dynamic, loving to take part in every debate and discussion. Your cunning ventures bring you great success in business, as does your willingness to work hard. It is only your impatience which may bring you failure.

Generally speaking, you enjoy a financially comfortable lifestyle, one which allows you to satisfy your luxury needs. However, you can not bear to refuse other people's requests for help. This limitless generosity makes saving money difficult.

The five different types of pig

Pig - metal You are an exceptionally honest individual and as a result, people repeatedly attempt to profit from your naiveté and simplicity. You are ambitious but do not approve of power struggles. Politics disgusts you, as does the manipulation of others. Consequently, you prefer to invest your energy in social causes rather than political ones. Your aggressiveness does succeed in scaring off opponents.

Pig - water A naturally eloquent speaker, you are capable of quickly convincing others and this quality enables you to establish good relationships with people. You are quite stubborn and feel frustrated when things do not go according to plan. Once your mind has been made up, you will not be easily swayed. You love a quiet and tranquil life, free of commotion, and you do not fear loneliness.

Pig - wood You are very ambitious and do not hesitate to confront your competitors, even if they are stronger than you. You even intimidate them with your determination. You are used to working hard for your success and your tenacity attracts a great admiration from your opponents. You have a bright future in the business world.

Pig - fire A very hard-working individual, you replenish your energy supply before each new battle. Your eagerness for success is so fervent that you do not hesitate to risk everything in order to overcome obstacles. Consequently, you are highly successful in your enterprise. You have a passion for modern art and know how to appreciate the finer things in life, a taste which is fortunately accompanied by the means to support it.

Pig - earth You seem to have your feet on the ground and are capable of realizing the extent of your ambitions. A very realistic person, you are not deluded about your capabilities. In addition to your total lack of trust in anyone besides yourself, your management talents will bring you success in the business world. Financially speaking, the earth pig always has something to eat. Even if he does not work very hard, he is able to provide for his own needs.

Compatibility

The signs which you must avoid when seeking a partner:

The snake   1929, 1941, 1953, 1965
The monkey   1932, 1944, 1956, 1968

You feel insecure in the presence of the snake, and you hate the monkey because he laughs at you.

Your ideas differ so much from those of the snake that you can never live together. You do not accept the ignorance of the monkey and his superiority is an insurmountable obstacle.

The signs amongst which to choose an ideal partner:

The goat   1931, 1943, 1955, 1967
The rabbit   1927, 1939, 1951, 1963

You share the same tastes as the goat. The rabbit's ardent love stirs a great passion in you.

Your passion for the rabbit is so great that you abandon all others, in order to be lead by him. You share the same interests as the goat, allowing you become the ideal couple.

Born under the sign of the pig

Woody Allen, Ernest Hemingway, Alfred Hitchcock, Elton John, Henry Kissinger, John McEnroe, John Rockefeller, Georges Pompidou, Alain Delon, Ronald Reagan

2. I Ching

I Ching, or the Book of Changes, is one of the most ancient book in China. It contains much wisdom spoken by the Chinese prophets, who have, after observing the changes in our universe for thousands of years, come to certain conclusions about the events occurring in our daily lives.

I Ching is also a divinatory art, allowing you to find solutions to any problems you may encounter. Examples include the following questions:

- Should I divorce?

- Do I have a chance to land this job?

- Will my business be prosperous?

- Will I pass this exam successfully?

- Should I invest in this company?

This art may also offer a means to avoid experiencing a problem in the first place.

The eight trigrams of I Ching

Used to interpret the meaning of Life, the following eight trigrams form the foundation of the I Ching:

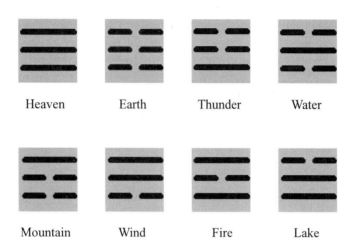

Heaven	Earth	Thunder	Water
Mountain	Wind	Fire	Lake

That is what is known as the method of Pagua, Pa meaning eight in Chinese.

How to consult the I Ching

The I Ching is consulted in conjunction with the throwing of three coins six times, in order to create a hexagram of I Ching, which is itself composed of six lines. For each throw, give a value of 1 to each tails and a value of 2 to each heads, then sum up the total. If the sum is an odd number, it is a straight line; if the sum is an even number, it is a broken line. The first throw constitutes the first line from the bottom up, the second throw represents the second line, again from the bottom up, and so on. Once the six throws have been completed, two trigrams of Pagua are revealed.

For example, if you have two heads and one tail in the first throw, the sum will be 5 (2 + 2 + 1 = 5), which is an odd number, therefore it constitutes a straight line. The second throw might give you three heads; the sum will be 6 (2 + 2 + 2 = 6) which is an even number therefore a broken line. The third throw might yield three tails; the sum will be 3 which gives you a straight line. The fourth throw might be one head and two tails which total 4, a broken line. The fifth throw might give you two heads and one tail which is equal 5, a straight line. And finally the last throw might be two tails and one head again, this will be equal 4, a broken line. Now you obtain two I Ching trigrams:

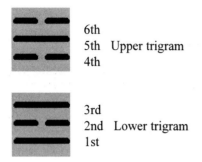

6th
5th   Upper trigram
4th

3rd
2nd   Lower trigram
1st

To find out what this hexagram represents, go to the table on the next page, you see that the lower trigram that you obtained corresponds to the trigram in row number 3 and your upper trigram corresponds to the one located in column number 6, then find the number located at the intersection of the column and the row, this number which is 63 represents the numerical representation for the interpretation of the 64 hexagrams that follow.

Upper→ Trigrams / Lower ↓								
	1	43	14	34	9	5	26	11
	10	58	38	54	61	60	41	19
	13	49	30	55	37	63	22	36
	25	17	21	51	42	3	27	24
	44	28	50	32	57	48	18	46
	6	47	64	40	59	29	4	7
	33	31	56	62	53	39	52	15
	12	45	35	16	20	8	23	2

Numerical representation of the sixty-four hexagrams of I Ching.

Interpretation of the sixty-four hexagrams of I Ching

1. Heaven

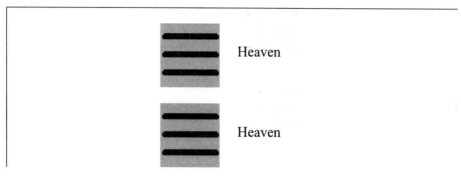

Heaven

Heaven

Interpretation
Heaven represents half of the universe, the other half being represented by the Earth. Thus, you would do well to set your mind at ease, as Heaven exists to protect you. Although any light seems beyond your grasp, it will not be long in coming, serving to guide and provide you with renewed hope.

Hope and luck
Remain hopeful, quiet and self-confident. Do not hurry if you wish to preserve your luck. You will soon achieve your goals - it is just a matter of time. Wait for the right moment to act and remember to follow your spiritual guide.

Business and finances
Any beginning is difficult, especially in the business world. You experience a very slow period, but this is temporary and the future holds much in store for you. Your success will be tremendous. Seek advice from the elders and never refuse the help of others.

Job
This is a very quiet period and there will be no change at the present time. There is no need to hurry, as your opportunity to take action will come soon enough. Wait before making any moves.

Love
Your partner will cause you a lot of trouble. You must not be too hasty and must keep cool. Seek advice from the elders before you make any long-term commitments. Do not travel this road alone.

2. Earth

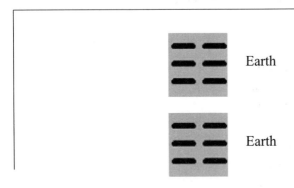

Earth

Earth

Interpretation

The Earth represents half of the universe, the other half being Heaven. The Earth is large and limitless. Thus, it is strong enough to support you and contains the necessary resources to facilitate your success, allowing you to reach your goals. The power of the Earth serves to guide and protect you.

Hope and luck

You must always think positively, so as to chase evil from your mind. Do not hesitate to ask for advice and never venture into anything alone. If you are determined, you will succeed. Maintain a solid spirit, as firm and stable as the Earth.

Business and finances

You will achieve great success in your enterprises. However, you must attempt to maintain a constructive attitude and seek an alternative source of support. With clarity you will be able to overcome any difficulty and by thinking positively, good results will be achieved. Prosperity will be a constant.

Job

Do not act until you have a firm guarantee. You must work consistently, as your current situation does not permit speedy advancement. So, be content with what is yours at the present time and await further opportunity.

Love

Your partner is very hesitant, requiring you to be very patient. Before great success is achieved, a long road must be traveled. Set your mind at ease with the remembrance that you are not the sole competitor.

3. Accumulation

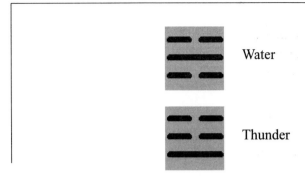

Water

Thunder

Interpretation
Thunder booms but the rain has not yet arrived. Clouds remain high in the sky, gathering at this late moment. Numerous difficulties will arise and things do not run as smoothly as you wish. Although the road is full of obstacles, you must not worry, as rain will eventually arrive to Water your plant. For the moment, perseverance is the essential strategy.

Hope and luck
Maintain your present position and wait patiently. It is a difficult time for you and you must not expect any immediate relief. Remaining tranquil is the best strategy at the present time. Your turn will come eventually.

Business and finances
Business is difficult at the moment. You must try to persevere. Most importantly, keep calm. Any efforts you make to cultivate your land will ensure a brighter future. You cannot accelerate the process but can maintain the present conditions, reserving some fragment of your energy for future use.

Job
There is no change foreseeable in the near future. You take pains to search for opportunities but that which you seek is beyond your present reach. Even if you attain your desires, this will cause more trouble than good. You must be patient and wait. Be content with what you have. This may be more profitable for you at the moment.

Love
Now is not the time to speak of love. Opportunities elude you for the moment, your feelings lacking the depth necessary for establishing any permanent connection. Await your opportunity, as the future holds much in store for you.

4. Uncertainty

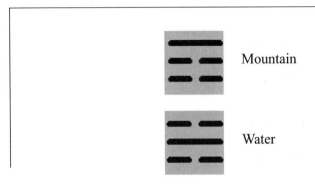

Mountain

Water

Interpretation
The Water vapor remains, as a result of the Mountain, and will not disappear. This morning fog prevents you from seeing clearly, forcing you to await the arrival of a guide. Do not move before receiving the necessary signal. Above all, do not force matters, as this can only make your current situation worse.

Hope and luck
You can neither advance nor retreat - your road is blocked. Unable to cope with this situation, your hope for success has been worn very thin but you must await your turn. Before you the road is shrouded with fog, meaning you risk incurring irreparable damage.

Business and finances
There is a time for work and a time for rest. At the moment, you must choose the latter, as you seem unable to achieve any results, in terms of your business. Your time and money are being wasted and if you force matters, you risk suffering future losses. At present, you would do well not to make any more moves, allowing for the disappearance of the fog before proceeding.

Job
You make many fruitless attempts and your efforts go to waste. Even if you find what you are searching for, disappointment awaits because of your unsuitability for the task. Await new opportunities, as something will present itself soon enough.

Love
Think twice before you commit yourself to this matter. You may fall into a trap because your partner has not yet made a firm decision. People may take advantage of your naïveté, causing you to make some unrealistic promises. Do not be hasty - time will tell all.

5. Need

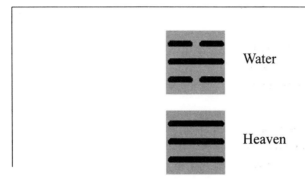

Water

Heaven

Interpretation

You need to Water your garden, your hopes and thoughts. However, Water remains trapped in the skies above. Therefore, you must remain still until the rain washes your path clean. It is pointless to move on without adequate Water supplies for travel in the desert.

Hope and luck

Do not become nervous - that which must happen will do so, regardless of your actions. Remember, everything works to contribute to your good. If you follow the routine, all will proceed on the correct path. You must have confidence in yourself and chase the confusion from your mind. Do not forget that everything will occur in your best interests - it is just a question of time.

Business and finances

Your fear of the future prevents you from making any progress. You must chase this evil away. If you are not too anxious and perform your routine work calmly, you will reach your destination without difficulty. Do not forget that Heaven serves to guide you. You must merely wait for the rain to Water your soil.

Job

Perhaps your present situation is tedious but it is better than nothing. You must maintain it, rather than seeking change. Do not listen to other people's advice, as they may lead you astray. Before taking the plunge, wait.

Love

If you feel hesitant about making a decision, let time do its work. Wait a while, as trying to move more quickly may have regrettable consequences in the future. Be wary of any advice offered to you. This is your business alone and your say is the final word.

6. Conflict

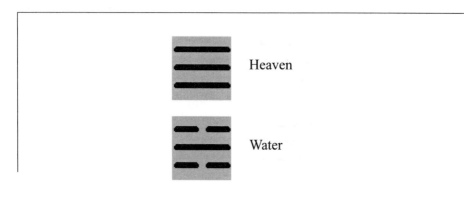

Heaven

Water

Interpretation

There is conflict between Heaven and Water. For the time being, no resolution is possible. However, Water will eventually gain freedom, nourishing your garden and your hope. Remain as you are and all will soon be sorted out.

Hope and luck

An evil force proves to be very strong - do not try to conquer it. Rather, seek advice. Intransigence may harm your chances, so leave things as they are and await the return of your luck. Any attempts made could lead to total failure.

Business and finances

This is not an opportune time to venture into the business world. A negative force within you may cause more harm than good, so postpone all new projects until you have received a favorable sign.

Job

As this is still not the right time, wait for the right opportunity to venture into this area. People will suddenly turn against you, despite your qualifications. They will not include you but be patient.

Love

You are not operating on the same wavelength. Rivalry exists between you and the other person in question. Your feelings are strong but the future holds many bad surprises in store. Differences are too great for a union. Extricate yourself from this matter and you will feel much better.

7. Division of army

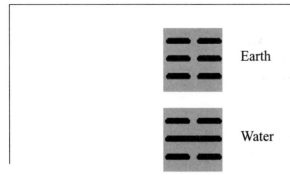

Earth

Water

Interpretation
Water is plentiful beneath the ground. The situation is comparable to an army unit which traverses this vast territory, yet is incapable of achieving anything. Stop running, for you are trapped underground. You have many ideas but they are unusable at the moment.

Hope and luck
Despite great effort, your goal still seems beyond your reach. This is a difficult time for you but that is not a reason to remain still. Increase your activity and an external force will assist you, helping you remove yourself from this situation. God will only help you if you help yourself.

Business and finances
Much difficulty lies ahead on the financial road. Business will take a wrong turn and you must hold yourself responsible for this situation. Seek help from your trusted guides and heed their advice, but do not wait until the last minute.

Job
Summon up your talents, in order to attack the problems and seize all opportunities. If you can not achieve your goals, you may have set your expectations too high. Readjust and start again.

Love
Do not let hatred poison your mind. Seek tranquillity through your spiritual guide, heed his advice, and try to lead a more constructive life. Do not be too hard on yourself.

8. Union

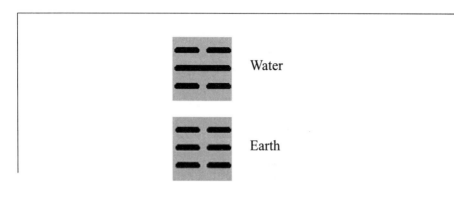

Water

Earth

Interpretation

Water complements the Earth. Without Water, the soil will become dry. The Water which is released by the Earth has various uses - it can help you blossom and can dissolve all your problems.

Hope and luck

Trust your intuition and follow the path you have chosen. Do not stray from your usual routine, as any diversion may lead to nasty surprises. Follow the path of good luck and all will be right for you. If you should encounter difficulty, ask for advice and count on others to help find a solution.

Business and finances

Your success is assured if you remain in known territory. New ground is not suitable for you at this time but if you are desperate to explore, do not proceed without advice. Choose your partners carefully because your success depends on them.

Job

You should not encounter any difficulties here. If you listen to and follow your intuition, a tremendous success awaits you. Your path has already been determined, so follow it.

Love

If your heart has already answered the call, follow your instincts. Do not hesitate any longer or the opportunity will be gone. Share your feelings with your partner and success will follow. Remember, it is your heart which must speak out.

9. Small taming

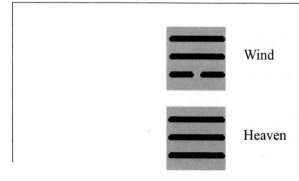

Wind

Heaven

Interpretation
Do not force matters. Let the Wind of Heaven guide you and do not overtake it. If you do rush, your progress will be hindered. If you follow the Wind, all will be well.

Hope and luck
All should go as you have planned, so do not try to change a thing. Leave things as they are and the ultimate success will be yours. Some difficulties may arise but they will disappear.

Business and finances
Have confidence in yourself and your associates. You should not encounter any problems if you stick to your plan. Leave things as they are and all will go well for you, especially if you do your homework. Time will tell.

Job
Achieving your goal is possible but you must wait a little while. Do not try to move faster than planned - it is not worth the effort and may worsen the situation. Be patient and good news will soon arrive.

Love
If things do not work, do not try to make changes. Your path is predetermined. Any additional effort made will be futile and you must leave things as they are. Do not trust the advice of others - decide your future on your own.

10. Step, Walk

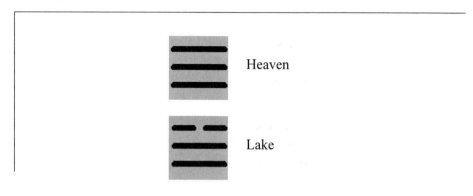

Heaven

Lake

Interpretation
The Lake with a blue sky reveals a harmony of nature which will lead you to success. Even if you seem to be in danger, you will be saved. You must walk cautiously and follow the steps of your guide. Look to the sky for any resources necessary for saving you from your troubles.

Hope and luck
You are faced with great difficulties at the moment. Be honest with yourself - it is you who must face the consequences of your actions. Any obstacle can be overcome, if you stick to a well-planned route. Doing so will ensure that success is yours.

Business and finances
Prosperity can not be attained without smart decision-making. Be logical in your thinking. When in the marketplace, you must follow the rules and remain honest with yourself. An external force will help you to achieve your goals. However, if you try to go it alone and do things your way, your projects are at risk.

Job
A change may bring you better prospects. Be straight with yourself, as lies will quickly be revealed and it is useless to mask your incompetence. If you adhere to such a principle, you will succeed without difficulty.

Love
Results will not be achieved if you proceed too quickly. Speed may cause more harm than good. Regardless of your anxiety, that which must take place, will do so. Remain quiet as emotions run strong.

11. Peace

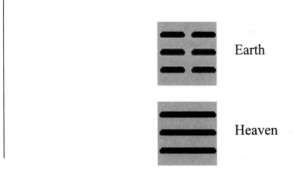

Earth

Heaven

Interpretation

Earth and Heaven form the universe and this union of peace is with you. Everything runs smoothly and no obstacle will block on your path in the future. Joy comes to you from numerous sources and remains for a long time. In business, as well as love, prosperity and happiness lie in store.

Hope and luck

You will be able to realize the most fantastic dreams, as your luck is in its prime period of expansion. Hope appears on every path you encounter and everything important will be by your side, assuring your total success.

Business and finances

Everything prospers in your kingdom. Financially speaking, you will continue to gain for a while. You are assured of your much deserved reward. All partnerships provide complete satisfaction, as long as you respect the rules of the game.

Job

You have great chances for landing a good job at present. All seems to work in your favor and change may bring you increased returns. The future looks brighter should you dare to take a new leap. There is nothing which can prevent your success.

Love

An union must be built on mutual trust and respect. If you can maintain such a foundation, success is assured and you have nothing to worry about. In fact, all will proceed very smoothly.

12. Contretemps

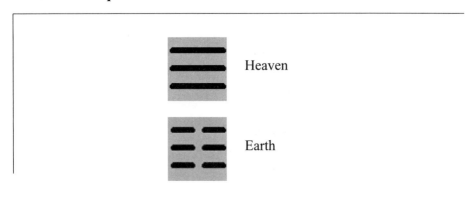

Heaven

Earth

Interpretation

The stagnation of the universe impedes you and obstacles are plentiful. You can not move freely and all your efforts come to nothing. It is your worst moment and if you wish to avoid anguish, you must remain quiet.

Hope and luck

At the moment, many difficulties have arisen. The non-stop pace of your current life is a sign of your anguish. Be calm and achieve harmony within yourself. You will receive assistance in overcoming this difficult period in your life. Deep silence is your best strategy.

Business and finances

If you try to deceive your adversaries through trickery, you will immediately be faced with undesirable consequences. Stick to a basic principle and follow the rules of the game. The fruits of your labor are not yet ready to be harvested.

Job

It is essential to wait and to be patient. Do not force matters - whatever should happen will do so, regardless of you. It is not the right moment for change and there is no point in hurrying. To rush will only harm you, so have patience.

Love

Things should remain as they are, no progress being feasible for the time being or in the near future. Any attempt to speed things up will not help. On the contrary, it will only worsen the situation.

13. Following other people

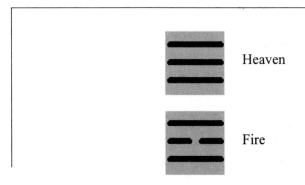

Heaven

Fire

Interpretation

Have confidence in God, remain hopeful and never allow the flame to die. In order to achieve your goal, do not hesitate to ask for the advice of others. Be in agreement with yourself and your reward will exceed your expectations a hundredfold.

Hope and luck

If you trust others, they will trust you. Everyone must work having confidence in each other. Honesty and frankness form the foundation of your success. Be ready to accept other opinions, as they will assist you in opening doors.

Business and finances

Don't be afraid to take positive action, as good will always creates mutual respect and more prosperous relationships. You must assemble a trustworthy team to help you build your empire. Only then is success very likely.

Job

If you want to alter your current situation, attempt to do so without fear. Do not be afraid to cross the ocean to achieve your goal. People will help you take the steps necessary for landing the ideal job. Be ready to assume responsibility.

Love

Hearts speak to one another. You have no difficulty communicating with one another and your common dream can thus be realized. Thanks to a mutual understanding, harmony resides within you. If you heed the voice of your heart, you can obtain desired results.

14. Possession in great quantity

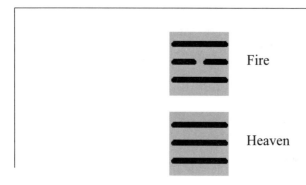

Fire

Heaven

Interpretation
The Fire of Heaven will light your way and all that you seek will be yours in abundance. Any wish can be made. Others will guide you to your final destination and the Fire of Heaven will provide you with light.

Hope and luck
You achieve brilliant success in all realms of life, far exceeding your expectations. Your success is complete and no one can conquer you on the battlefield. You can master and control any situation, forcing your enemies to surrender gradually, one by one.

Business and finances
You will succeed in all your enterprises. Anything you attempt is a success and is achieved by you alone. Your competitors step back in the face of your might. Do not grant power to others and remember that the secret to success is yours alone.

Job
You expect one and receive ten. You wish only to climb one floor and you find yourself on the tenth. What more can you expect? Your luck means any door is open to you. Do not be afraid to make requests, as everyone strives to satisfy you.

Love
Luck accompanies you and allows you to advance. No difficulties lie before you and you should feel free to proceed, taking a giant step forward. This will ensure that love will fall into your arms. You own this world and should advance with confidence.

15. Modesty

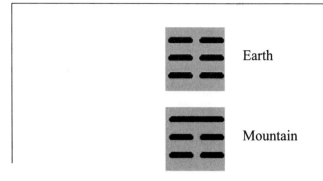

Earth

Mountain

Interpretation

Be humble before Nature, comprised of the Earth and the Mountain. This modesty will guide you on the road to success. Be open to new ideas and accept the advice of others, as they can help you reach your goals.

Hope and luck

This is your greatest period of expansion and prosperity is assured in all realms. You must take responsibilities in hand and success will follow. Everything proceeds as is expected and you will be capable of reaching all your goals.

Business and finances

Be ready to enter a new phase in your enterprise. Be willing to consider new ideas, as expansion beyond your habitual ground will only cause you to blossom. A bird who does not fly is a dead bird - it is as simple as that.

Job

Begin testing the ground but do not rush. If things do not proceed as planned, do not worry, for they will be achieved. It is already written on your path that everything must come together to satisfy your ambitions. It is merely a matter of time.

Love

Learn to open up and welcome fresh ideas. A close relationship requires new horizons. You must learn to accept differences of others, as they can make a contribution to your life. If you can embrace this idea, your success is assured.

16. Giving

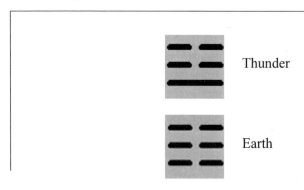

Thunder

Earth

Interpretation
The rumbling of Thunder will clear the path. Remain hopeful, as daylight will not be long in coming. Allow the Thunder to pass and you will regain the strength to resume your journey. Whatever is needed to ensure arrival at your destination will be yours.

Hope and luck
Hope knocks at your door and joy will soon follow. Others wish to give you a weapon necessary for clearing the way. Thus, you will be able to attain your goal without much difficulty. In pursuing your aspirations, you will be shown how to avoid danger and be assured of a prosperous future.

Business and finances
If you think the project is good and feel it to be close to your heart, proceed in realizing your dream. All the resources necessary for building your empire will be provided by the Earth. Nothing can triumph over you except a lack of enthusiasm. If you have great self-confidence, success will be yours.

Job
If an opportunity exists, do not hesitate to seize it. A new venture will provide you with more to do. Others will help you in applying for and securing this job. At the present time, your chances for success are great.

Love
If you do not make efforts to overcome your adversaries, loss is guaranteed. On the other hand, if you take the necessary steps and remain enthusiastic, you will be capable of defeating any enemy and happiness will be yours.

17. Accompaniment

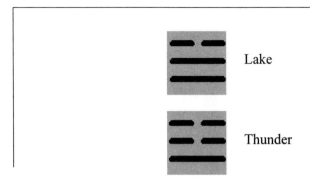

Lake

Thunder

Interpretation
Follow previously planned directions and be determined in your thinking. Thus, glory will come to you. Although it may frighten you at first, the Thunder will provide for you in the future.

Hope and luck
Recover any lost hope. Tenacity is the key to your success and in order to pursue your goals, you must have increased determination. Heed the advice of others, as their help is valuable. Be more flexible.

Business and finances
A lengthy wait is in store before any big game will be caught, but this is worth the trouble. If you seek short-term profit, do not hold your breath. The future does look very bright, in terms of your projects. Shoot for the stars and you will succeed.

Job
Do not give up and remember to heed the advice of others, as they will help you obtain that which you desire. Do not hesitate in getting help because arriving at your destination alone will prove difficult. The journey is mapped out but someone must show you the way.

Love
Listen to your heart and follow its desires. During this difficult time, you must allow it to guide you, thus revealing that happiness can be yours. Strive for the best and that is what you will achieve.

18. Rot

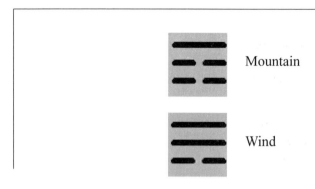

Mountain

Wind

Interpretation
The Wind blows but makes no progress because the Mountain impedes its movement. The road is blocked, making further travel impossible. Persevere, as you will eventually move beyond the Mountain, only to discover your path has been cleared. For the moment, remain quiet and avoid much movement.

Hope and luck
Do not remain in your pessimistic world. You must leave your ivory tower. Thinking of the past and gloom will only rot your being. You must discard such ways and face the world. With such a new approach, your thoughts will provide fresh energy. The fulfillment of your wishes will be followed by Hope.

Business and finances
Everything is moving too quickly for you. Face reality and accept change as something which serves to help you in seizing opportunities. You must learn to increase your speed and to change courses according to the Wind - it is your only chance for survival.

Job
If you want to change your job, do so. Forget the past and proceed in a new venture, as it will bring you greater prosperity. However, you would be wise to take the past as a lesson and to seek guidance from it. Look to the future, as it is more brilliant than you realize.

Love
Hope is a thing of the present, while a love of the future or the past is not productive. Any unrealistic dreams must be discarded, just as you would eliminate all that is rotten. The present is all you can grasp and contemplate, and dreaming of the future will only cause you to miss a precious moment.

19. Approach

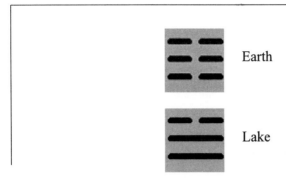

Earth

Lake

Interpretation
You are very close to success and are approaching your final victory. Do not become concerned, as some time still remains before your ultimate goal is attained. The end of the tunnel is very near, lying within your vision, so it is especially important not to abandon your course now. Also, there will be Water enough to nurture your soil.

Hope and luck
Only minimal effort is required, in order for the world to be yours. Opportunities lie so close you can touch them. If an effort is made, you will achieve your goal. Have confidence - all must proceed as you wish it to. Abandoning the situation now will leave you with absolutely nothing.

Business and finances
Success does not come simply by chance, nor without effort. Do not allow your thoughts to be invaded by evil forces. Success is close at hand. A bit more effort combined with concentrated energy, will assure your victory.

Job
You will succeed in hitting the jackpot but it will take time. Not instantaneous, this success is nevertheless not long in coming. Your efforts will soon bring you positive results.

Love
Fill your heart with love, as this will bring happiness knocking at your door. If you do not act, the world will change you. If you want to change the world, you must allow your heart a touch of energy and emotion. All will be for the best.

20. Observation

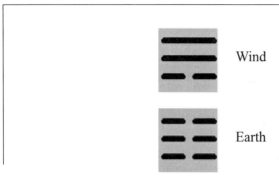

Wind

Earth

Interpretation

The Winds blow above the Earth and do not descend, instead awaiting the right moment. You must not move ahead at the present time, for many obstacles remain on the road. Rather, you would do well to keep watch for the proper Winds.

Hope and luck

Examine reality. Be aware that many things take place and change does occur quickly, often so quickly that you cannot keep up. Do not follow trends, remain firm, and follow your conscience. A state of tranquillity will come to exist in your mind.

Business and finances

If you are not trying to fit in with the crowd, you will complete your projects successfully. Find your own way and remember that Truth will always remain constant. Time is required to build your empire. However, if you observe your competitors and proceed as planned, success will be yours.

Job

That which is good for others is not necessarily good for you. When evaluating the present, make your own decisions and be wary of any advice you may receive. It is your career and you must allow good sense to guide your actions, in order to succeed.

Love

You show great hesitation in this matter. There are too many changes taking place too quickly. Simply, you must control your emotions and trust your spiritual guide. Responses will come in time.

21. Biting

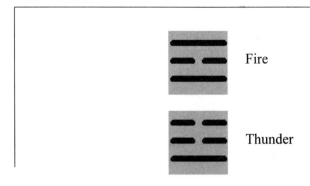

Fire

Thunder

Interpretation
The Fire of Thunder impedes your progress and swallows your thoughts. An anguish within you grows ever stronger but, if you are determined, it will not cause you harm.

Hope and luck
Obstacles constantly impede your progress, causing you great anguish. You must employ force to make progress and if you are determined and tenacious, success will be yours. Power conceals Hope, a force you must exploit.

Business and finances
The road is filled with obstacles and you must use your force to clear the way. If you stray from your usual route, you will encounter great trouble and total failure will take place. Stick to your principles and the end result will be positive. Otherwise, any dreams of the harvest are futile.

Job
Change will be positive but finding a good and satisfying job will be difficult. If you are persistent and increase your determination, chances for success are feasible.

Love
Forget the love troubling you. So many problems exist, making it difficult to continue as you are and the situation will not improve with time. The final decision is yours to make, but you would do well to end things now and attempt to recover your tranquillity.

22. Elegance

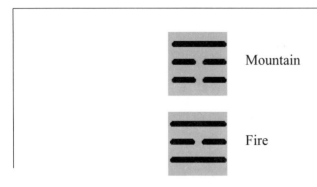

Mountain

Fire

Interpretation
The Fire is violent but the Mountain remains stable and immobile. Be still and calm, and do not allow bad thoughts to poison your mind. You will win in the end.

Hope and luck
The force of evil is powerful and you must not attempt to triumph over it. Instead, seek advice and remain still while the evil Wind blows. If you release your grip, all will return to normal and luck will return to assist you in launching an attack.

Business and finances
It is not the time to launch your business, as negative powers within you may result in failure. Put your plans on hold until the Wind dies down and the fiercely burning Fire is extinguished on its own. Be patient.

Job
You must await good luck, as the time is not right for you to venture forth. Mountains are mighty at the moment and, even armed with your many qualifications it proves difficult for you to find your way. Pause before going on your way.

Love
Be at peace and remember that you have made the necessary arrangements and employed all possible means. You simply are not on par with others. A war is being waged between your various emotions but this must cease at once, as the future has many nasty surprises in store and you should not be wasting your energy.

23. Peeling

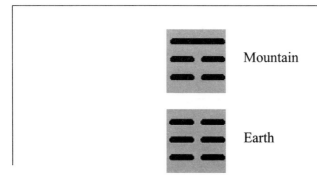

Mountain

Earth

Interpretation
Your soil cannot improve, so you must not proceed. All is blocked by a huge, immobile Mountain. Remain where you are and do not advance, as doing so will mean suffering the greatest loss. Step back and search for another way.

Hope and luck
Remain quiet and calm. In every case, all your efforts will go to waste. You cannot arrive at your destination as planned, so avoid wearing yourself out for nothing. Be still and your problems will soon disappear.

Business and finances
It is not the right moment to launch new ventures. Not only will you be unable to realize your dreams, but you will also have difficulties maintaining your current status. Wait for the evil Wind to pass before you make another attempt.

Job
Stop searching, as there is absolutely nothing which will meet your qualifications. Even if you find that which you seek, results will be poor. It is a difficult period but it will pass. Put your mind at ease and wait for an opportunity to present itself. For the time being, you cannot cultivate the land.

Love
This is a one-way street. For the time being, the other heart does not answer your call and there is absolutely nothing you can do. At present, the situation will remain as it is. Stay quiet and forget nothing. Sooner or later, hard times will come to an end.

24. Turning point

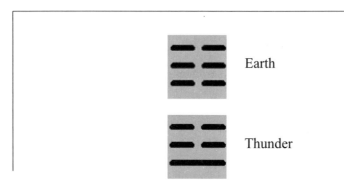

Earth

Thunder

Interpretation
The Thunder will soon return to the sky and the Earth will return to its kingdom. You will retrieve that which you have lost or be granted that which you have been without. Do not worry, as you will be richly rewarded. All should soon return to normal.

Hope and luck
This is a turning point in your life and you are moving in the direction of good luck. Spring will soon return. Flowers will blossom after a long snowy winter. Be prepared for the good news soon to arrive. For the time being, the good Wind will continue.

Business and finances
Begin to prepare for a new venture, as all that you do from now on will result in triumphant success. Although additional time is required in order to reach your destination, you will arrive. Good days are here and you will hear the sound of success drawing near.

Job
A good return on the job market awaits you, whether you are looking for a job or seeking change. All doors are open to you - knocking is not necessary. Simply enter. Good luck.

Love
You are able to renew a relationship which had been cut off. Returning is not easy, but with time, anything is possible. A turning point in your love life is at hand and all should go for the best.

25. No nonsense

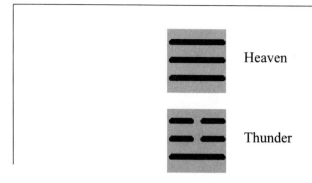

Heaven

Thunder

Interpretation
The Thunder signals a movement of the conscience which guides you. Maintain your current situation and follow this conscience, your spiritual guide. Do not test your luck by charting a new course.

Hope and luck
You wait but nothing happens. You wish, but are not rewarded for the time being. Delays do occur, so you must continue to think and act positively. Everything will go smoothly and as planned.

Business and finances
You want to climb higher but difficulties arise. You have your doubts concerning the feasibility of a project. However, there is no need to seek an answer, as it does not exist. Continue to act normally and prosperity will arrive.

Job
Be content with what you have, as change is not appropriate at present. Be patient and wait for the situation to improve. Eventually, things will get better but now is not the right moment to proceed.

Love
Do not try to progress too far along this road, as advancement is not possible at this time. Thunder booms from the sky and your screams will be drowned out, no matter how loud you are. Remain quiet and await luck.

26. Great taming

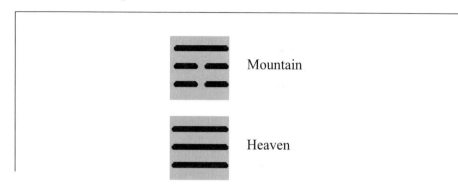

Mountain

Heaven

Interpretation
Be as still as this immobile Mountain, and so will the Heaven grant your wishes. Have no fear, as the power of these two forces serve to assist you. Profit and joy will be with you - allow yourself to feel hopeful.

Hope and luck
The right direction will soon be obvious. At the moment, you can do nothing but simply remain quiet and confident. Harmony prevails in your universe and it will not be difficult to reach your goals. It is only a question of time.

Business and finances
Any beginning is difficult and you must endure a slow period, especially in business matters. The future does promise good things and Heaven will guide you, showing you the way to the summit. However, it will take time and your success will only be great if you make the necessary effort.

Job
Your search requires time but a good position will be found. Do not hurry, as hitting the jackpot demands patience. Follow your routine of work and let time run its course.

Love
You may encounter difficulty in love and all may look bleak and gray. Do not lose heart and decide that the Mountain is too difficult to climb, for you have a skilled and wise guide.

27. Cheek

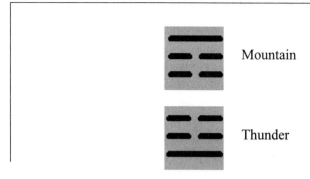

Mountain

Thunder

Interpretation

You hear Thunder emerging from behind the Mountain, but the Rain does not yet fall. Take heart, for it will arrive eventually to Water your garden. You must think positively and nourish your mind. Remain still and do not attempt to advance. You will be granted peace and glory soon enough.

Hope and luck

Hope seems to arise constantly but no results are evident. Several difficulties cause a delayed arrival, but things will happen. Chase terrible ideas from your head and make room for more positive thinking. Wealth and glory await you, no matter what you do.

Business and finances

You must tackle the problem on your own, without any help. By doing so, success will be yours. If others contribute to your venture, further troubles will arise. To assure your success, you must be able to go it alone.

Job

You possess the abilities necessary for acquiring a position in the profession of your desire but you must bide your time, as no offer has presented itself at the moment. Continue to work and remember that your current situation does not allow for rapid advancement. Thus, you should relax and await your opportunity.

Love

It is never too late to make progress, but for the time being, your partner is hesitating. Be very patient. The road to success is a long one and although Thunder loudly proclaims your love, the Mountains continue to muffle its sound.

28. Great superiority

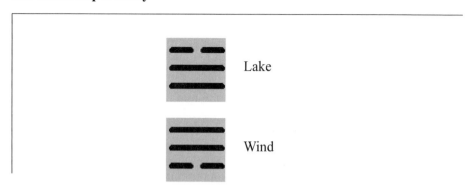

Lake

Wind

Interpretation
The Wind is too strong and creates waves on this quiet Lake. You will have great difficulty finding safe passage for your ship. You do not have what is required and must remain constant, moving at a reasonable speed.

Hope and luck
You set your hopes too high. Be realistic and do not overestimate your abilities. Act appropriately, otherwise you will encounter many problems while trying to realize your dreams. Failure will then be a certainty. Wait for the storm to pass before setting sail again.

Business and finances
It is better to remain in familiar territory and not venture into deep Waters. If your ambitions exceed their limitations, you may be lost. Ask for advice and do not travel this road alone, for doing so may eventually result in a great loss.

Job
Your qualifications do not meet the demands of the task at hand. Stop dreaming and reformulate your plan. Stability will improve your chances. Ask your guide for advice. Be aware of the many boats on the Lake and the strength of the Wind, for you risk bumping into others.

Love
You lack the power necessary for overcoming obstacles, creating difficulties in achieving your goals. Competition is ferocious but if you seek and find assistance, you do stand a chance. Otherwise, simply turn your back and walk away. Remember that your adversary holds a superior position.

29. Water

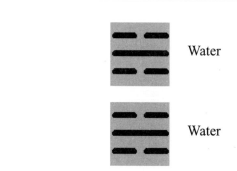

Water

Water

Interpretation
You are submerged in deep Water and find yourself to be completely trapped. Anything you attempt will cause more troubles. Finding a dry, flat road leading directly to your destination proves to be difficult.

Hope and luck
You fall into the Water and no one comes to help you. Avoid dreaming, for you must save yourself. There are many obstacles to overcome on your own. At present, there is little you can do, for Hope is stretched thin and luck is not on your side.

Business and finances
Now is not the time for this game. If you try to play, failure will not be long in coming. Rushing will cause additional problems. The road is filled with holes and is very uneven, creating difficulties during your journey.

Job
Do not search any longer, as you are trapped and powerless for the time being. Your luck has reached a low point and you must await the return of the good Wind. Only then will you be able to move on, so immediate effort is only a waste.

Love
Much greater difficulties have arisen than anticipated. However, if you can solve your problems, your dreams will be realized. Seek advice from your elders - the result will be better than you expected.

30. Fire

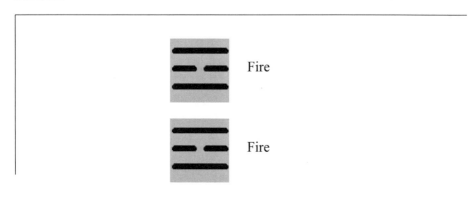

Fire

Fire

Interpretation
Light the flame to reveal the path to success. Remain hopeful and keep the flame lit. Such determination is necessary, in order to reach your goals. Do not be afraid to forge ahead, as the Fire's great light will illuminate your path.

Hope and luck
If you think with confidence, the flame of hope will not be extinguished. Do not hurry; take care to light your Fire slowly. The flame continues to burn and your road remains bright, so that finding your way is not a difficult task.

Business and finances
The Fire you have lit burns like the midday sun and can not be extinguished by one person, except in very special cases. Your enterprise is guaranteed extraordinary success, so carry on according to plan. The road is clear and success awaits you.

Job
Your enthusiasm ensures you a good position. Change may bring increased returns. You may even proceed to a higher level.

Love
Your love is a flame, a burning passion. Do not leave your future in the hands of others. You must proceed and not hesitate to make a declaration of love to assure your future.

31. Whole

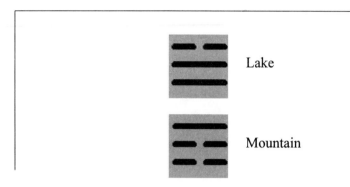

Lake

Mountain

Interpretation
Calm your thoughts. Be as still as this Mountain and this Lake which lie before you. Heaven will shower you with Water sufficient for easing your thirst and replenishing both your garden and an entire forest. At the present time, you will receive everything necessary for obtaining that which you require.

Hope and luck
Tranquillity governs your mind and world. Attempting to silence your emotions, will bring inner peace and a greater chance to see the fruits of your labors. The result will be very good and you will have all that you desire.

Business and finances
If you crave success which is above the average, you must put more enthusiasm into every enterprise. Effort is essential - the more you invest, the greater your harvest will be.

Job
If you make an effort, you will find that which you seek without difficulty. At present, change is risky. Therefore, you would do well to seek advice from others before making a final decision. If you do not rely solely upon your emotions, all will be well.

Love
Harmony prevails in your mind and a spiritual union is very feasible. This union will create near perfect harmony and allow you to walk easily together along the same path.

32. Continuity

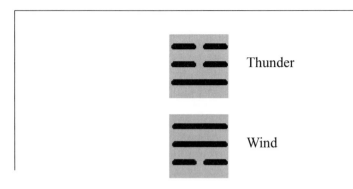

Thunder

Wind

Interpretation
The Thunder serves to frighten and shock you. However, this force cannot reach the Earth, for the tranquil Wind protects you. As long as the Wind remains present, which seems very likely, you may sleep soundly and be assured of long-lasting peace.

Hope and luck
Your luck improves daily. Hope can be found in the tranquillity of the mild Wind. A Wind lies concealed beneath the Thunder. Consequently, you will meet with a very favorable time, in terms of all aspects of life. During this time of continued peace, all hope is welcomed.

Business and finances
The wealth you seek is near, found beneath the blue sky. Your plan can be carried out with little difficulty and goals are easily achieved. Your strength lies in complete self-confidence. If your goals are lofty, more effort is required in order to succeed, but that which you seek will be yours.

Job
That which you seek will easily be found. If you crave change, ask for advice. Remaining content with your present situation, which continues to be strong and full of life, will increase your opportunities.

Love
You are the Thunder and the other is the mild Wind. Your relationship is a marvelous and harmonious union, reaching near perfection. It will prove long-lasting. Also, you are assured arrival at your desired destination.

33. Retreat

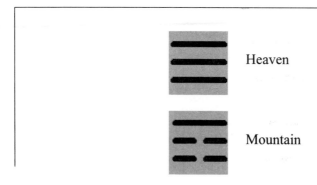

Heaven

Mountain

Interpretation
Return to your universe and familiar domain, where the Mountain of tranquillity provides shelter. Do be aware that the Mountain is high but does not touch the sky. If you advance, you will suffer. Now is not the time to test your luck.

Hope and luck
An urge to retreat becomes apparent. In returning to your former position, you must be prepared to suffer. Advancement is not possible and forcing matters will only create further difficulty. Although this is a difficult time, it will pass.

Business and finances
At present, you must avoid new ventures, for the obstacles you face are as high as Mountains. Remain still, as maintaining your present situation is already difficult. Do not continue new projects.

Job
Many obstacles impede your progress and continuing is not possible. Remain as you are and all will be well. Forcing matters will result in loss for you alone, so you would do better to maintain your present situation.

Love
Your dreams are too euphoric and optimistic. Love is a one-way street, something of which you were already aware. Advancement is not possible for the time being. If you attempt to progress, be prepared to suffer negative consequences. Do not heed the advice of others, as many problems are too discouraging.

34. Greatness

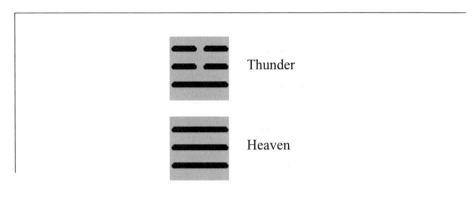

Thunder

Heaven

Interpretation
You hear the Thunder as it becomes gradually stronger. It reveals the power of Heaven for your benefit. You must trust in this great power in order to obtain that which you desire.

Hope and luck
All your dreams are full of hope and seem ready to be fulfilled. Such Hope will grow, as long as you trust in faith. Be aware that although luck is very positive at present, you must not think too big and exceed your limits.

Business and finances
Your project is bigger than expected, as is the degree of success. New ventures will bring triumph, as long as you do not grant power to others and you make your own decisions. Profits will be great.

Job
Gather your forces for an attack. Thunder has announced the arrival of good luck but this has yet to materialize. Do not worry, your victory drum has already begun to sound and it is only a matter of time. All is in place for a triumphant success.

Love
In seeking to conquer the other heart, you must be more flexible. Attempting to initiate discussion will improve your chances. Be prepared to accept the challenge to pave the road for the future. It is you who must take the first step.

35. Progress

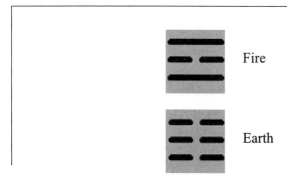

Fire

Earth

Interpretation
At the moment, your luck is clear and hot like the Fire. This light of the Earth will illuminate your progress, your hopes, and your thoughts. This precious guide will allow you to achieve your goals and success is guaranteed.

Hope and luck
The Fire burns on the Earth and lights the way. Your luck is brighter than ever and Hope is everywhere. Much progress will become evident around you and all hopes are allowed during this period of good luck. Be prepared for good news.

Business and finances
Fire will burn obstacles blocking your way and the Earth will provide the resources necessary for nurturing your enterprises, all of which will be very prosperous. Great success greets you everywhere and victory is by your side. Do not be concerned, as everything is yours alone and you will make rapid progress.

Job
All doors are open to you and a light will guide you through the labyrinth. You have little difficulty finding the right door leading out. A speedy promotion is in your future, one which will greatly satisfy you.

Love
Your love will make great progress. You are not left in the dark. A light will shine, guiding you to the correct door, helping you to realize your dreams and to advance your project. Be prepared to fill your heart with love and all will be for the best.

36. Clear and without danger

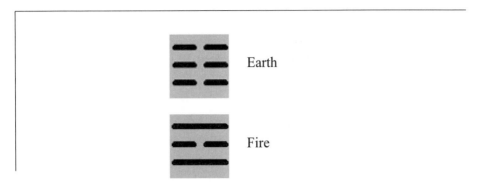

Earth

Fire

Interpretation
The Fire is hidden beneath the ground, its radiance invisible. Do not try to advance on your own, as the darkness prevents you from seeing anything. Wait until the light of Fire shines brightly enough to lead you from danger.

Hope and luck
Morale is very low at the moment and everything seems to move in the wrong direction. Difficulties arise constantly and everything is in a terrible state. Nevertheless, you must be patient. A light will appear to save you and hope does already exist. Have you noticed? The road before you is well-lit and flat, free of obstacles which could impede your progress.

Business and finances
If you encounter any difficulties in realizing your plans, remember that no condition is permanent. Once a light appears, your problems will disappear. You are on a terrible road at the moment but this will end. Just be patient.

Job
Do not try to change - it is not the right time, as you have now entered a difficult phase. Make applications everywhere but be aware that it will not be easy to find something which suits you. Await your turn and you will receive guidance.

Love
You follow the wrong road and everything seems to conflict with your feelings. You are in a dark tunnel, but be patient and someone will lead you from this place. Peace and happiness lie at the end of the tunnel and complete harmony will be yours.

37. Extended family

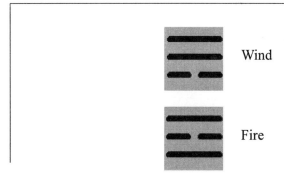

Wind

Fire

Interpretation
Harmony reigns in your universe and the light of Fire will guide you in everything you do. Although you will not have any great success, you will not be left alone in darkness. You will be helped by the Wind.

Hope and luck
Your luck travels in an upward trajectory and runs smoothly. Hope is ever-present. There is no spectacular progress but you are traveling on a flat road and no danger exists. As harmony reigns in your universe, what more can you ask for?

Business and finances
You will have wealth, even though it is not great. Business is quite good for you at present and good results will soon be yours. Consult your family before making any attempts and do not go it alone. In the end, success will be yours.

Job
If you search, you will have little difficulty finding that which you seek. For the time being, change is somewhat risky. Consult your circle, especially family members, before making the final decision. You are taking a risk if you walk the path alone, so you would do well to seek the advice of elders.

Love
Family is very important to you. Love is peaceful and harmonious. Marriage is in your future - allow this union of well-being and prosperity to guide you.

38. Difference

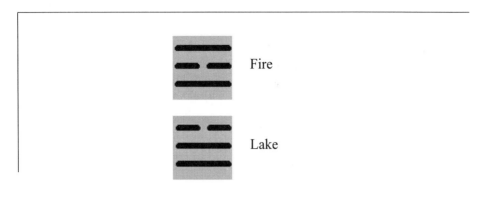

Fire

Lake

Interpretation
The opposition of Fire and the Lake causes you difficulty in life. You swing between Fire and the Lake just as you vacillate between success and failure. Try to remain in the middle and await the return of your luck.

Hope and luck
Luck always works against your wishes. You seek peace and are faced with war. You desire success and failure awaits. Obstacles constantly impede your progress and good luck remains out of reach. Remain where you are, be patient and await your turn. It will come eventually.

Business and finances
All your efforts are gone with the Wind. You make many attempts to plan your route but many unexpected events await you. Your projects will meet with much trouble and may result in failure. Greater difficulty is a certainty if you do not cease your current activity. Take care and be cautious.

Job
At present, nothing exists for which your qualifications are suited. When you search on the left, opportunity appears on the right. When you alter your course, luck flees. Do not waste your efforts - the timing is wrong. Maintain your current position and await the arrival of good luck, for it is on its way.

Love
Your current situation resembles Water and Fire. These elements can never combine and your attempts to breach the gap are unsuccessful. At present, there is little you can do, for the law of Nature is at work.

39. Obstacle

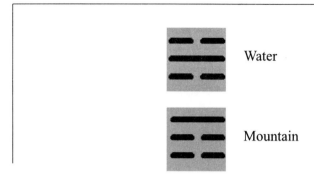

Water

Mountain

Interpretation
There are many obstacles to be faced on your journey. You are caught between the Mountain and the Sea, prevented from moving forwards or backwards. Your only choice is to wait and luck will eventually clear the road.

Hope and luck
Faced with great difficulty on the road of luck, you find many obstacles impede your progress. When trapped in a dead end, you must be patient. Do not struggle to escape, as your efforts will be in vain. Remain quiet and still, awaiting the return of luck before following the path once again.

Business and finances
Difficulties arise everywhere, approaching you from all directions. There is nothing to be done for the moment. The time is not right for expansion or the launching of a new business. Instead, remain where you are and do not move, as attempting to advance will only cost you dearly.

Job
If you search, you will not find. If you desire change, the situation will worsen. It is not worth wasting your energy, so do not test your luck at present. Maintain that which you have and be patient, as luck will soon smile on you again.

Love
They will try by all means to impede your progress. Great difficulties will force you to give up quickly. Be patient, as now is not the time to speak of love. Perhaps the moment will come.

40. Solution

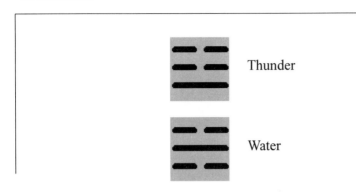

Thunder

Water

Interpretation
You have just heard the Thunder and rain is sure to follow, that much is certain. Water will rain down, offering solutions to the problems which have long bothered you.

Hope and luck
Thunder and Rain always come as a pair. Solutions to your problems, be they big or small, will become apparent, and obstacles will disappear. A cloudy period is followed by the rain, bringing an end to your troubles, as well as great prosperity.

Business and finances
Relief from a period of difficulty has finally come. Rain will wash the path clean and you must quicken your pace before luck disappears. Solutions appear at every street corner. Attack your problems immediately and proceed faster than anticipated, as time is of the essence.

Job
If you seek a job, be aware of the guide who is available to help you open the door. Be prepared to begin your search. If you anticipate a career change, take action quickly, as no one will wait for you. The new career will prove brilliant, opening up new horizons.

Love
The solution you find has existed for some time. The rain relieves some tension between the two of you and brings long-awaited, refreshing relief.

41. Decrease

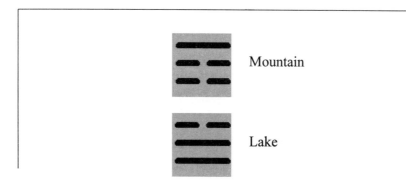

Mountain

Lake

Interpretation
The Mountain of Forest hanging over the Lake will dry up your Water and gradually empty the Lake. Do not challenge the law of Nature. Seek an alternate source for your needs and your future will be brighter.

Hope and luck
You are in a period of transition. Everything is at a standstill for the moment and development is unforeseeable. This is normal, as you prepare the road for a brighter future. Be patient and know that in time, you will obtain that which you seek. Nice weather will soon be here.

Business and finances
Your business experiences a quiet phase but this is not cause for alarm, for an expansion will soon take place. A transition is occurring, in order to help you climb the hill and take everything in hand once again. If you attempt to advance immediately, you risk suffering loss, decreasing future chances of success.

Job
Although it may not be a very good position, you will be able to advance to great heights in this organization. Everything depends upon your attitude towards your daily work. You are the only one responsible for your career. If you make a small effort, the future will look bright.

Love
The more love you give, the more you will receive. If you are unable to give or cease giving altogether, do not expect joy from others. This is a reciprocal affair.

42. Profit

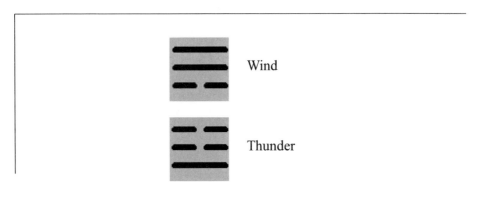

Wind

Thunder

Interpretation
The Thunder signals big news. The good Wind will soon arrive and provide precious support to all your projects. Profits can be increased but you must move forward quickly.

Hope and luck
At present, your luck shines very brightly. In any case, you will be able to achieve your goals. Hope is guaranteed and no obstacle will interfere with your dreams. All should run smoothly and you will have nothing to worry about.

Business and finances
Even if you have not begun to cultivate your soil, profit already exists. At the moment, all is in your favor and if you want to launch a venture, proceed without fear. The result will be better than expected.

Job
You will obtain that which you seek. If you want to make a career change, proceed. The choice is yours but be aware that it will bring more than expected. The present is good and the future looks even better.

Love
This love will bring only good things. You have nothing to lose in this affair. Whether or not you wish it, people will approach you with propositions. Seize the opportunity, as you will not come to harm.

43. Resolution

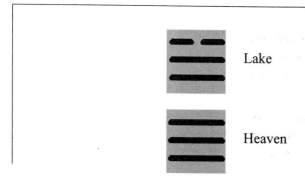

Lake

Heaven

Interpretation
You will have great difficulty drawing water from the Lake of Heaven. It is beyond your reach and you will encounter many obstacles. Do not continue in your attempts, for they are futile. Remain in your current position and do not advance too far, as it will simply be a waste of time.

Hope and luck
You reach the end of the road of good luck. Signs of weakness are emerging, so do not try your luck. Several attempts only bring the same results. Do not force matters and remain where you are, in order to avoid ruining your chances.

Business and finances
Bad luck threatens you and your enterprise. Do not play with Fire, for you will lose. Monitor every step, as one miscalculation will destroy all your efforts. Reformulate your plan and await the return of luck.

Job
You have difficulty finding what you seek, as luck is not on your side. Stick with what you have and do not venture forth immediately. Avoid the back door - such an entrance will only complicate matters.

Love
You face great difficulty at the moment and must constantly control your emotions. Surrender your search, if possible, as you seek the unsuitable. Nurse your wounds and choose a new path.

44. Interaction

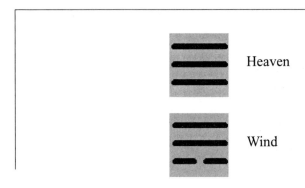

Heaven

Wind

Interpretation
The Wind of Heaven will cause you much trouble and you will encounter many difficulties. The Wind will blow ever stronger and take all your dreams away.

Hope and luck
You must face unexpected obstacles. You may fall into a black hole, one which will prove very difficult to escape. By and large, hope does not shine brightly. Do not count on it, as you will only be disappointed with the result.

Business and finances
All partnership propositions must be rejected. You should not form an alliance with anyone. The Wind is strong enough to blow away all your resources. Do not take pointless risks, as loss is guaranteed. Problems within your social relationships will occur, the consequences of which you must then risk suffering.

Job
Every approach is a failure at present and it is pointless to test your luck. Hope remains an illusion and fighting with the Wind of Heaven is futile - you must allow it to pass before beginning again. Only then will your chances for success improve.

Love
If anyone should spark your interest, you must disregard that person. You cannot function together and any attempt will end in disaster. You must make a choice immediately, before it is too late.

45. Gathering

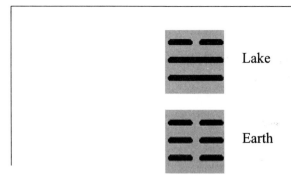

Lake

Earth

Interpretation
The Lake is comprised of many particles of Water. A drop of Water can accomplish little of consequence but a Lake will nurture your soil. Forces will combine to provide you with complete success.

Hope and luck
All the good things in this world assemble to push you in the right direction. Hope is protected by this marvelous gathering. Not only will joy and money be yours, but happiness and glory as well. You will have all the resources necessary to reach your destination.

Business and finances
Good luck protects the future of your enterprise and all the elements necessary for success are already in place. The future looks rosier than ever. Everything is in the bag: money, honor - all is yours.

Job
If you have decided to make a career change, proceed. Your new career will be even more interesting than you can imagine. It will bring an increase in salary and prestige. You have absolutely everything sewn up.

Love
Two hearts join together under the same roof, a place where love is protected. Once you enter into this century union, all other competitors will be out of the running. Harmony prevails in your universe.

46. Going upward

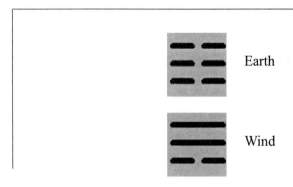

Earth

Wind

Interpretation
The Wind of the Earth will eventually return to the sky and encourage you to rise into its universe. This force works to assist you in reaching your goals. Be without fear - this Wind brings glory, profit, happiness, and many other good things.

Hope and luck
The Wind of the ground will push you to the top, rising continuously. Hope is strengthened as a result of this rise. At the moment, nothing can defeat you and all is yours and yours alone. Your future luck appears absolutely remarkable.

Business and finances
All your projects will progress at a spectacular pace. If you have an idea, do not hesitate to proceed. Tremendous success will be yours, thanks to the help of others. Launch your plan without delay.

Job
Your career continues to advance. You will very quickly climb even higher. Thanks to this Wind on the ground, a good position in an interesting field is easily obtained. Continue to search and you will receive good news.

Love
Love walks beside you, accompanying you everywhere and always watching out for you. If you welcome this marvel, joy will surely arrive. Be more attentive and do not miss your chance.

47. Surrounding

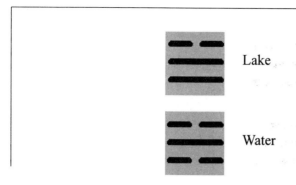

Lake

Water

Interpretation
Water and Lake combine forces to destroy you. Wherever you go, Water surrounds you. You will get wet, so do not act or move. You need not try to escape, instead remaining calm and waiting for the Water to subside.

Hope and luck
You are trapped in a room without an exit. You cannot move. If you become nervous, your situation will only worsen. Keep quiet and remain hopeful about your escape. A solution does exist, so reformulate your plan and await the arrival of luck.

Business and finances
Numerous problems arise, preventing you from continuing as you have done. The situation may become worse, so find an exit as soon as possible to avoid incurring loss greater than you anticipated. Be cautious.

Job
You are in the middle of a Lake and cannot swim. You cannot find the solution on your own, so you must seek help. Remain where you are and keep calm. Should you panic, it will all be over. Most important is to maintain your current situation and be patient.

Love
Your game is that of a child, as it leads nowhere. Stop dreaming, as you simply cannot achieve your goals in the face of so many discouraging problems. Moreover, you are not really in tune. It is useless to force matters. Better to stop this game immediately, rather than allowing it to continue without purpose.

48. The well

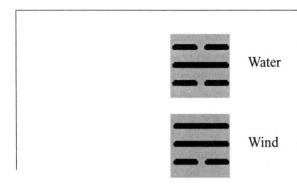

Water

Wind

Interpretation

You must remain as still as the surface of the Water, for the Wind below is very strong. If you make a mistake, a whirlpool will carry you far away. Remain where you are, keep calm, and wait for the Wind to disappear before you travel on.

Hope and luck

Hope lies in a well. Great effort is required to attain it, as is true of all desirable things hidden in this well - power, money, happiness, etc. Nothing will come as easily as expected and much work is called for.

Business and finances

You seek profit, especially in terms of business. However, you are successful only at gradually accumulating small amounts. You will achieve your goals by taking this approach, that of drawing Water from the well one bucket at a time.

Job

Your well is not dry, so you have no cause for concern. As long as you are not too demanding, that which you desire will be yours. Simply by using your competent retrieval skills, you will always collect enough Water from the well. In order to reach the top, you must climb one floor at a time.

Love

Happiness is hidden out in the world and it is a star in your heart which will guide you to the treasure. Do not take everything at once, but instead, leave something for future use.

49. Revolution

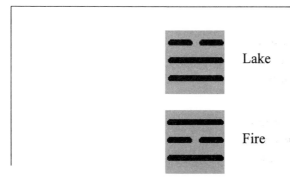

Lake

Fire

Interpretation
You must destroy all your bad ideas. Seek change, as the traditional way is no longer suitable. You must undergo a radical transformation in order to find your road to success. Revolution will lead you to your final destination.

Hope and luck
A Lake of Fire burns and you must rid yourself of all evil, hatred and despair. Although you are not aware of it, the revolution has already begun and if you follow it, your chance will come when peace returns.

Business and finances
Starting a business will make your future appear profitable. If you wish to improve results, any old projects underway require a change in work strategy and tactic. You must be revolutionary in your methods, in order to stand out.

Job
If you seek greater satisfaction and more responsibility, a career change is essential. At present, your work is dull. If you take drastic measures, you will be assisted in making a revolutionary move. A good place under the sun does exist for you.

Love
A change in tactics and thoughts will ensure happiness. Fill your heart with love in order to experience a genuine revolution. Difficulties exist but you can make them disappear. It is your turn to play the game.

50. Cauldron

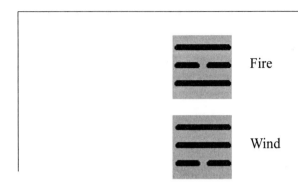

Fire

Wind

Interpretation
With the help of the Wind below, the Fire will burn stronger. Thus, success approaches and exceeds your expectations and desires a hundredfold. As long as the Wind remains, your luck will persist and you should have no concerns.

Hope and luck
With the help of the Wind, everything should now go as planned. The Fire will burn stronger than ever. Hope exists eternally and you will always be protected by a powerful star helping you to attain great heights.

Business and finances
The future for your business looks bright even though difficulties still exist. They can be resolved with external assistance, thereby allowing the road to be paved for you alone. Money will pour in from all possible sources and every undertaking will meet with great success.

Job
If you want to find a good position, seek help. You will be led to the correct door. Just as a Fire blown by the Wind burns more brightly, your career advancement will be made possible by the assistance of others. Even though things may initially seem uninteresting, the future holds good things in store. Thus, do not be afraid to proceed.

Love
Smoke comes from somewhere. In your relationship, a triangle is forming and your competitor is quite strong. You can not beat him alone, so seek help. Armed with love, you can change anything, even the world. Have confidence in yourself.

51. Thunder

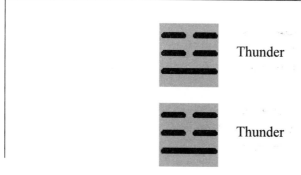

Thunder

Thunder

Interpretation
The noise of Thunder frightens you, apparently coming from all sides. The shock is great but Rain will soon follow, bringing great profit. Remain where you are and have no fear. You must wait for the Thunder to pass and all you have long sought after will be yours.

Hope and luck
The sound of Thunder frightens you but remember that Rain will follow, watering your garden and cultivating your soil. This will bring hope and a sense of rebirth. Your chances will be greatly improved. Do not be afraid to make wishes, as you will attain your desires.

Business and finances
Development will take place quickly, faster than a clap of Thunder. The Rain will arrive to water your plant and cause it to grow faster. Great expansion is at hand and if you wish to be on the ball, prepare yourself to follow on time.

Job
A good position in the labor market will be yours, your message having already been transmitted. When an opening occurs, you will be the first one to know. Do not worry - nothing will escape you.

Love
Do not try to progress too far along this road, as advancement is not possible at this time. Thunder booms from the sky and on the Earth, your screams will be drowned out, no matter how loud you are. Remain quiet and await luck.

52. Mountain

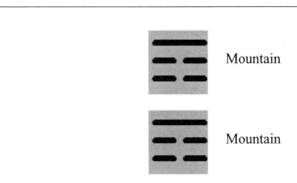

Mountain

Mountain

Interpretation
Remain quiet, just as these two Mountains of silence are still. Most important is not to proceed, for you will encounter many difficulties on your way. You are trapped between two Mountains and cannot move. Stay where you are and keep calm, for any movement could cause greater damage. For the time being, there is nothing you can do.

Hope and luck
Everything seems to go against the flow at the moment and you cannot seem to find an escape route. Do not panic, as life is simply in a rut for the time being. Things will soon improve and you must remain calm and patient. You are trapped between two Mountains and there is little you can do - the future shines brilliantly, so take heart.

Business and finances
If you want to launch new projects immediately, you would do well to think carefully before you proceed. The road looks bumpy and the obstacles many. You cannot move the Mountain, but rather must wait for help from others. This will come soon enough, as will your opportunity for success.

Job
Do not attempt to change your current situation, as there are no positions available for which you are qualified. The doors will remain closed for a while and you would do well to maintain your current status. Simply bide your time.

Love
Things look bleak and gloomy in your love life. The love which you seek does not seem to heed your call and the good Wind still does not blow. It is blocked by two Mountains and you may wish to change your course - the choice is yours to make.

53. Progressive

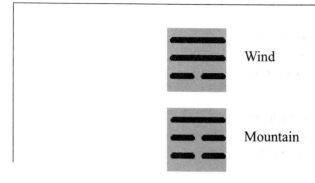

Wind

Mountain

Interpretation
The Wind has finally passed over the Mountain and the road is no longer blocked. Things will progress faster and your dream will be realized. Your success will progress and advance, quietly but definitely.

Hope and luck
Your chances have improved and hope is increasingly present. Everything will continue in the right direction. Do not be anxious, as the Wind has been slowed somewhat by the Mountain, but it will gradually make its presence felt. Remain quiet and await good news. The near future will mean rapid progress.

Business and finances
All profits will not come at once but rather in several small packages. You will make progress in your enterprise gradually, rather than in one big leap. This will allow you to better manage your expansion. Prepare your way now, for the Wind will blow ever stronger and your expansion will be great.

Job
If it is a job you seek, a good one will come your way. If it is change you desire, it is unnecessary, as your current job allows for progress. Your situation will soon improve, so why seek change?

Love
An empire cannot be built in one day, a principle which applies to everything. If you want a long-lasting relationship, you must invest much love. In order to realize this dream and build your empire, add some love each day.

54. Marrying woman

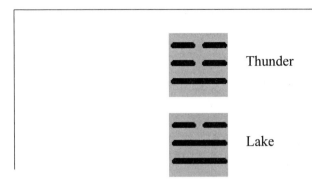

Thunder

Lake

Interpretation

The Thunder makes itself heard on this quiet Lake, signaling the approach of a storm. Dock your ship to avoid difficult passage. Do not move unless you are prepared to suffer loss. Wait until the storm has passed before setting sail again.

Hope and luck

Your luck is unproductive and you seek a good Wind to stir up the clouds, resulting in rain. There is little you can do, as luck is nowhere to be found. Await the arrival of the good Wind, which will guide you on your way and remain quiet for the time being. All will be well.

Business and finances

If you wish to begin a business venture immediately, be cautious, as failure is a real possibility. Luck will not assist you and you must travel this road alone. Rain will soon fall and you must be patient in order to avoid an enormous loss. It is no time to be playing games.

Job

Do not search, as your qualifications do not meet the requirements. Do not dream. Instead, readjust your plans and remain in the same domain. Do not alter your course at this time, as it is too great a risk. Your competitors are more powerful than you and you would be better off limiting yourself to your own territory. If so, luck will soon be yours.

Love

A project proves difficult, as you lack the necessary skills to overcome obstacles. Competition is ferocious, but with help you may have a chance. Otherwise, look elsewhere, as this love is not to be yours.

55. Abundance

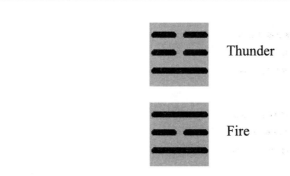

Thunder

Fire

Interpretation

As has been announced by Thunder and Lightning, the Fire of Hope is near. This means much food, a bountiful harvest and assured success. You will have everything you need to nourish your hope, glory and wealth. Heaven will give you everything about which you dare to dream.

Hope and luck

You have plenty of hope with which to move forward on the future journey. Your luck is in its greatest expansion period and everything should run smoothly. Whichever road you take, it will be a royal one. Advance without fear and realize your dream.

Business and finances

Thunder and Lightning have long been announcing that the Fire of Hope is near. Your company achieves a position of affluence, whether or not this is what you desire. Money pours in from all sources and your harvest will be excellent, in preparation for any projects, now or in the future. Prosperity is written in your company's book, so you have nothing to worry about.

Job

If you are looking for a job, one which suits you will be available at a later date. On the other hand, changing a job you already have is unnecessary, as your current position suits you well and allows for rapid advancement. You will profit greatly from this job.

Love

Don't be afraid to give your love. The more you give, the more you will receive. Your love is plentiful and you must remember that a union without love will not last. If you are sincere, your reward will be great.

56. Traveling

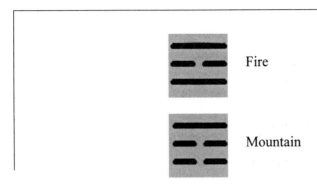

Fire

Mountain

Interpretation
The Fire escapes from the Mountain to make a great journey, allowing it to travel around the world. It will destroy everything it meets, so do not remain where you are. Your traditional route is no longer suitable and you must seek an alternative to avoid the Fire and rediscover hope.

Hope and luck
Things do not work as well as you wish them to. There are too many obstacles blocking your way and change is too frequent for you to keep up with, especially in terms of the evolution of your business. Hope is present at the moment. Move forward to catch it before it is too late.

Business and finances
Your business luck is like a traveler, as it comes and goes. The same can be said of your money, which does not remain anywhere for long. Now is not the moment to test your luck, as this would be a waste of energy. In any case, you will profit greatly at first, but proceed to lose it all soon enough. Do not wear yourself out without reason.

Job
You make a great effort to conduct a search but it continues to escape. You believe it to be in the bag but the next day finds it gone. Do not waste your time, as opportunities will present themselves eventually. For the time being, wait quietly.

Love
This love game will only last several nights. You are playing with Fire and the volcano can reactivate at any time. When it explodes, disaster occurs. You must stop the game and look elsewhere for love. It is fruitless to penetrate this forest.

57. Wind

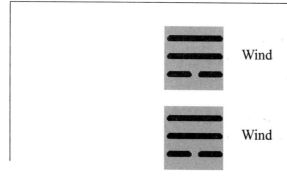

Wind

Wind

Interpretation

Winds blow in from everywhere, from all sides, creating whirlwinds. Your luck will fluctuate incessantly between good and bad. You must follow the Wind but wait until all is calm before resuming your journey. For the time being, remain where you are. Everything will be all right in the end.

Hope and luck

Your hope is like the Wind blowing in all directions. Whether from the east or from the west, it changes quickly. Difficulties constantly arise and to correct the situation, you must remain calm. Seek the advice of your elders. Everything will return to normal in the end but do not go against the grain.

Business and finances

Your luck in business matters seems to fluctuate greatly and this is also true for matters of finance. You are caught in a whirlwind and must wait until the Wind has calmed before finding solid ground. For the time being, you have little choice but to be carried by the Wind.

Job

You knock at the back door but luck resides at the front of the house. However, your knock at the front door comes too late, as luck has already moved. This is a game of hide-and-seek. The Wind is too powerful at the moment and you must wait a while before being able to land on the ground. Once you do so, anything is possible and everyone will try their hardest to satisfy you.

Love

A whirlwind tosses you in all directions and you are completely disoriented. You feel a deep void inside you and simply follow the flow without accomplishing anything. Allow the Wind to blow and remember that luck looms in the future, to bring you total satisfaction.

58. Lake

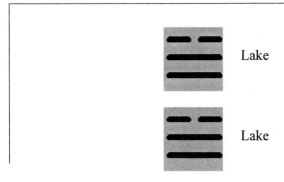

Lake

Lake

Interpretation
Joy fills your universe and accompanies you on your journey. Everything goes as you wish. You receive glory in exchange for glory, wealth in exchange for wealth - what more can you expect? These Lakes of joy bring you great success.

Hope and luck
People will only bring you great joy - in life, at work and home. Hope is everywhere. You can enjoy your life. At present, there is nothing to worry about.

Business and finances
Everything is running as you expected, whether the projects be old or new. Well-deserved rewards should be yours and large ones at that. You must spread joy throughout your business, thereby creating greater opportunities for yourself.

Job
Whether you are seeking a job or merely want a change, this field offers a good position. You have little difficulty being admitted into the labor market. You will have help achieving your goal, as all the necessary resources lie in this Lake of joy. Be prepared to assume responsibility.

Love
Harmony prevails in your universe and joy is everywhere, as love is eternally present. There is nothing to worry about. The currents of the two hearts intermingle, like the water of these two Lakes.

59. Dissolution

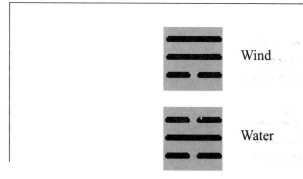

Wind

Water

Interpretation

Wind can create some waves on the surface of the Water but nothing more. There is no danger and the waves will soon calm down. A safe return is possible. All your problems will soon go away. You have reached a turning point and things will move in the right direction. If you seek good results, continue in your present efforts.

Hope and luck

All should go as planned and altering your course partway is not a good idea. Relax and allow the Wind to carry you to success. Do not give up, as the future holds much in store for you. Focus your energy on forging ahead to regain lost hope.

Business and finances

Trust the Heaven's good Wind, as it will bring happy news. If you seek to launch new projects, do not allow your forces to disassemble and go ahead with your assault. Otherwise, your harvest will not be bountiful. If you stick to your plan, you will encounter little difficulty.

Job

Water removes all obstacles from your path and, with the help of the Wind, it washes the dust from your sight. You are able to accomplish everything as long as you are patient and a guide will arrive to lead you to glory.

Love

Do not force matters of the heart, and if things do not work out, do not try to change things. The road is cluttered at the moment and your efforts will not prove effective. If you seek to improve your chances for success, leave things as they are and look elsewhere.

60. Limitation

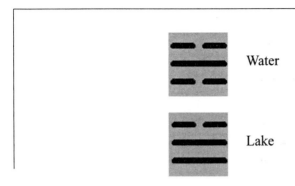

Water

Lake

Interpretation

A Lake contains a limited amount of Water from the sky. You are also limited in your capabilities. You cannot do everything or have everything you desire. Remain within your personal bounds and do not push things too far. In any case, your resources will not permit this. As problems arise, do not forget the limits of your energy.

Hope and luck

There is a limit to everything you do but you believe yourself capable of anything. Be careful and evaluate your own abilities honestly before beginning anything. If success is your goal, do not exceed your limits. Within your own domain, all hope is permitted.

Business and finances

Seize any opportunity which arises before it disappears. Remember to consider all possibilities before commencing a journey. Analyze your talents and be aware of your limitations. Going beyond your limits will make achieving your goal difficult.

Job

You feel your talents are not being put to use in your current position and this must change. You will have difficulty fulfilling your great expectations, as your ambitions are too lofty. Set more moderate goals and you will have a better chance for success.

Love

Limit your search to avoid wasting time, as you lack the resources to have it all. Decide upon a specific direction if you hope to succeed, otherwise you must forget this beautiful love which awaits you.

61. Truth

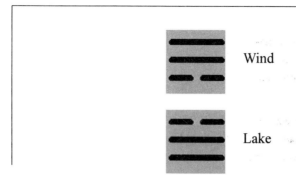

Wind

Lake

Interpretation
The Winds will create a few waves on the surface of the Lake but do not worry. You do not put anything at risk and the waves will soon cease. In no time at all, you will be able to surface. A mild Wind is merely passing, bringing good news of the future.

Hope and luck
Do not become agitated, as you must face whatever is in store for you and your actions will not affect your destiny. The Wind is strong at the moment but it will die down soon enough and the sea will become quite calm. All will go according to plan and you must simply have confidence in yourself and empty your mind of tension. Everything will be yours, it is simply a matter of time.

Business and finances
You dare not proceed, as you fear the future. This is an evil you must chase away. Do not be too hasty or rush, continue to work steadily and you will achieve your goals without great difficulty. Remember that Heaven exists to guide you and will send the Wind to clear the obstacles from your path. Once the Wind has died down, you will be alone on your journey.

Job
Your current position may bore you but you must be satisfied with what you have, not seek a change. Most importantly, do not heed the advice of others, as they may guide you in the wrong direction. Pause before you take the plunge.

Love
If you hesitate before making a decision, you must learn to let time do its work. Do not act, distrust all advice, and remember that the final decision must be yours alone.

62. Small superiority

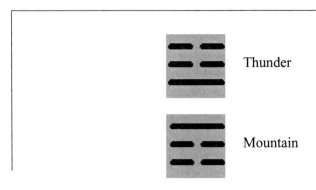

Thunder

Mountain

Interpretation
You hear the noise of Thunder on the Mountain, which shocks you somewhat. It is there only to frighten you and nothing more. You must infuse your mind with positive thoughts and remain quiet, not trying to move forward. You will attain peace and glory at a later stage.

Hope and luck
Be realistic and remember what any attempt to build castles with sandy soil will bring. Settle upon something solid, otherwise your dream will be a mere illusion and all will disappear midway without a trace. Stop dreaming and keep your feet on the ground.

Business and finances
If you want to construct an empire, build it on solid ground. Maintain a clear idea of your purpose. Set your sights on something you can make happen. Otherwise, it would be better to stop now, as failure is guaranteed and danger already looms over you.

Job
End your search, as it will be difficult to find a suitable offer. Even if you take great pains, hope is now at a low and the doors remain closed. As the future will certainly be brighter, you must be patient and wait.

Love
You try to talk loudly, so as to be heard by the other heart. However, it is busy listening to others and as loud as you may scream, your voice goes unheard. You must wait until things calm down, remain quiet and still. Your time will come.

63. Help is gone

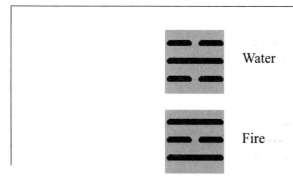

Water

Fire

Interpretation
Water will extinguish the flame representing your progress, desire and tenacity. A difficult road lies ahead and every possible obstacle will appear. Your determination will be put to the test as you strive for the ultimate success.

Hope and luck
The road of hope has come to an end. Although everything has worked faultlessly until this day, things will now go downhill. Do not be too active; continue at a slower pace. Thus, you will avoid a free fall.

Business and finances
You have already made a profit, haven't you? You should know that you cannot always do well. Prepare for a difficult time ahead, as damage will be less devastating if you have taken necessary preventative measures.

Job
If you feel the need for a career change, pause for a moment and think. It is not advisable if you wish to avoid moving from good to bad. It is not the right time to play such a game. If you are seeking a job, have patience - your dream will come true.

Love
The future holds some nasty surprises in store for you. All seems well at the moment but cracks are appearing in your relationship. If you want to save this love, act in a constructive manner.

64. Help is not coming yet

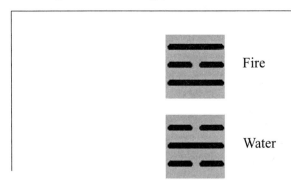

Fire

Water

Interpretation
Fire easily penetrates the territory of Water. However, Fire burns beyond the reach of Water. With tenacity and determination, a successful attempt may occur. Be patient - good luck will eventually lend a helping hand.

Hope and luck
Hope does exist but you have difficulty getting your hands on it. Seek help, as you will be unable to do it alone. Otherwise, you will be forced to wait. Heaven has granted you resources but these will not prepare you adequately for the journey of life, so you must choose between waiting and getting help.

Business and finances
You have the opportunity to begin an exciting project but you must not move too quickly, as something is still missing if you are to realize your dream. You must wait for luck to assist you and avoid walking the path alone, as you will have great difficulty proceeding on your own.

Job
If you wish to change your job, now is not the time to do so. You lack the necessary qualifications required for all currently available positions and luck is also not on your side. Therefore, you should wait before seeking something more suited to your capabilities.

Love
You try to make happen a love which you have sought for a long time. This is not, however, the right moment to do so, as the path is treacherous and the other heart remains closed to your propositions. Only luck will make a true difference to your situation.

3. Palmistry

Lines of the hands can reveal your character and help to predict your future. They can also guide you to the road of success. The principal lines studied in Chinese astrology are the Life line, Head line, Heart line, Fate line, line of Success, and lines of Marriage.

If you are a right-handed person, contemplate the right hand. If you are a left-handed person, the left hand is your active hand.

The Fingers and the Mounts

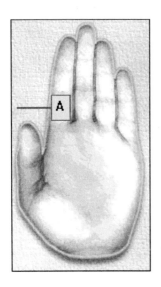

Thumb: Represents leadership, power, determination and faculty of reasoning. Its normal length reaches the middle of the "A" area.

Longer: You are a talented person who is very intelligent and possessing of great reasoning power. At a very young age, you will have already experienced success in your life. It is not uncommon for you to become a leader in society.

Shorter: You have difficulty adapting to society. You suffer many failures and most of your dreams will never be realized because you lack the determination necessary for achieving your goals.

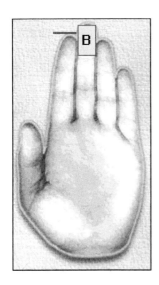

Index: Represents leadership, desire for power, confidence, self-esteem. Its normal length should reach 3/4 of the "B" area.

Longer: Authoritarian, a genuine tyrant, you enjoy giving orders and refuse the advice of others. You believe your method of working to be the best. You have an intense desire to take control and reign over the entire world.

Shorter: You are a very ambitious person but lacking a fighting spirit and determination. You have difficulty being a leader and seldom complete any task. You have a tendency to step back in the face of challenge and also tend to refuse responsibility.

Middle finger: Represents vigilance, concentration, attention. Its normal length should reach 3/4 of the palm's length.

Longer: You are very melancholy and unstable in your thinking and your actions. You waver in any definitive decision-making. At the first sight of difficulty, you change your approach without a thought and this anxiousness may cost you unnecessarily.

Shorter: You are a quick-tempered character and very impatient in your work. If you do not achieve quick results, your enthusiasm fades. You are very vigilant and focused, which may bring some business success.

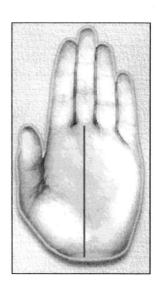

Third finger: Represents your abilities in artistic and technical matters. It can also indicate social success. Its normal length should reach the middle of the "B" area.

Longer: You will play an important role in the business world. Success has been yours from a young age. You are capable of managing your finances. You have an extraordinary sense of the fine arts.

Shorter: Very realistic and honest, you know when it is time to seize an opportunity and launch an attack. You do lack some of the necessary elements for success in the business world.

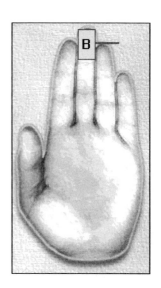

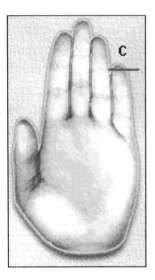

Fourth finger: Represents intelligence, talents in scientific and technical fields, capability in the business world and an ability to express yourself. Its normal length should not extend beyond line "C".

Longer: You are very astute and vigilant. With a superior intelligence, you quickly seize any available opportunities and reap the benefits. You have a great aptitude for business and are an unshakable leader in this area.

Shorter: Reveals a difficulty expressing yourself and a lack of energy in all your undertakings. Very enthusiastic at the beginning of a project, your lack of determination can cause you to abandon it midway. You have very few talents in the business world.

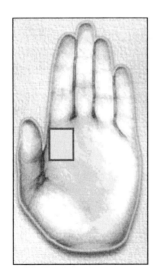

Mount of Jupiter: Represents leadership, power, ambition, and fame.

A well-developed Mount indicates your ability to reveal your talents and to take a leadership role in society. You enjoy scientific research and are very open to exploring new ideas. Having great ambition, you are somewhat authoritarian and arrogant. In order to realize your dreams, you will try by any means to seize power.

A less-developed Mount indicates your lack of fighting spirit and your passivity. Your ambitions are not compatible with your abilities.

Mount of Saturn: Represents determination, judgment, and vigilance.

A well-developed Mount indicates your tendency to be excessively prudent and cautious in everything you do. You never venture into unknown waters. Always in search of profits to be gained, you see money to be very important and it even acts as the focus of your social relationships.

A less-developed Mount indicates your tendency toward pessimism and suspicion. Thus, your social relationships are under-developed and you live a lonely life.

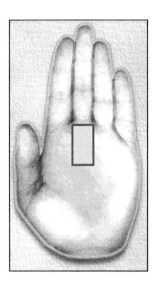

Mount of the Sun: Represents creativity, artistic talent, and financial luck.

A well-developed Mount indicates your artistic and scientific talents and intelligence. Your social relationships are well developed and your optimism will make you a natural leader, especially in the business world.

A less-developed Mount indicates your inability to lead a normal social life. Incapable of dealing with responsibility, you have little chance for financial success. You frequently have poor judgment, which leads you to failure.

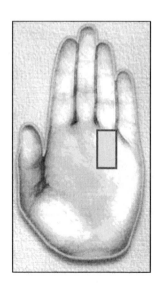

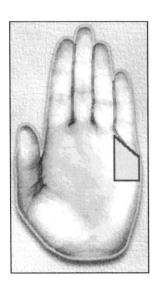

Mount of Mercury: Represents abilities in business and commerce, as well as the ability to form relationships.

A well-developed Mount indicates your great eloquence and skill in public relations. A fearsome competitor in the business world, success will follow you almost everywhere.

A less-developed Mount indicates that you are not really prepared to enter the business world.

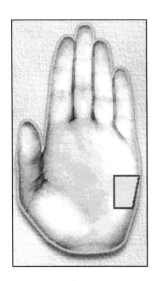

Mount of Mars (negative): Represents resistance, and quiet.

A well-developed Mount indicates your resilience, shown in difficult situations, and your refusal to display your temper. Rough conditions do not ruffle you, as you always manage to remain calm.

A less-developed Mount indicates a lack of perseverance and a tendency to abandon undertakings before they are completed.

Mount of the Moon: Represents creativity, artistic and literary talent.

A well-developed Mount indicates your very romantic and impatient character, your tendency to often fall into an endless reverie. Possessing great imaginative capabilities, you are creative and gifted in the realms of art and literature. Additionally, you constantly seek an easy means for making a profit.

A less-developed Mount indicates your lack of firm beliefs and ideology. Also, it reveals a tendency to wait passively for others to present you with structure, rather than any ability to take the initiative or to act on your own creative instincts.

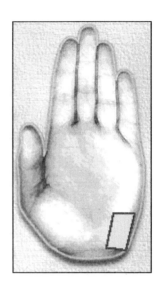

Mount of Venus: Represents vitality, wealth, and love.

A well-developed Mount indicates your extremely energetic and friendly character, which allows you repeatedly to go beyond expectations. Your financial opportunities are excellent and you will have little difficulty providing for your needs. You are drawn to the opposite sex and sexual pleasure.

A less-developed Mount indicates a lack of vitality and a tendency to experience difficulty in love, as well as a precarious financial situation.

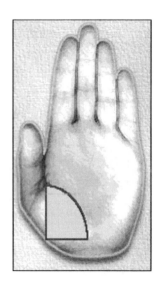

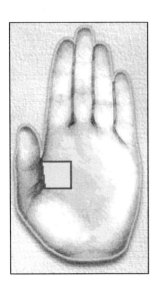

Mount of Mars (positive): Represents competitiveness, resistance, and aggressiveness.

A well-developed Mount indicates your ability to overcome all obstacles in order to reach your goals and the strength which enables you to face any difficulties. You love to fight with those stronger than you, frequently winning as a result of your tenacity.

A less-developed Mount indicates your pessimistic, easily discouraged character. As you lack the strength to overcome difficult situations, others find it easy to triumph over you.

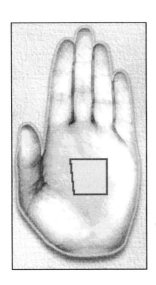

The Plain of Mars: Located between the two Mounts of Mars, this is your battlefield. It can increase the influence of the two Mounts of Mars.

If the positive Mount of Mars and the Plain of Mars are well developed, your competitiveness and your fighting spirit will grow.

If the negative Mount of Mars and the Plain of Mars are well developed, your ability to resist will increase.

If the two Mounts of Mars and the Plain of Mars are well developed, quite a dangerous situation may arise. Your competitiveness and your ability to resist will both increase, creating in you a person who is always able to resist, is willing to fight on all fronts, and will never back down.

The Life line

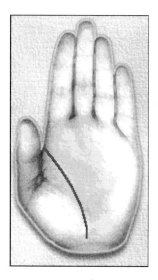

The Life line indicates your general health, as well as important events in your life, such as accidents and sickness. It reveals your vitality and your forces of resistance. The starting point of the Life line is located between the thumb and index finger, going around the Mount of Venus and ending at the base of the hand.

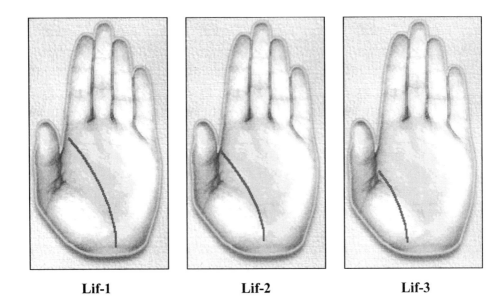

| Lif-1 | Lif-2 | Lif-3 |

Lif-1. Your Life line originates near the index finger and is very lengthy, the latter being an indication of longevity.

You are a very active person with much energy to expend. Very ambitious, you will achieve great success in your life. You do not hesitate to make the effort necessary for achieving your goals. Very generous and friendly, you are very passionate about many different things in life. The curve of your Life line is lengthy, which indicates longevity of life.

Lif-2. Your Life line originates between the thumb and index finger.

This indicates that you are full of energy and vitality, a joyful character who is open to new ideas. Your life is filled with success. Generally speaking, you are in good health - longevity is written in your hand.

Lif-3. Your Life line originates near the thumb and characterized by its narrow curve, the latter being an indication of a potential for numerous health problems.

You are very passive by nature and do not seek to conquer the world. Instead of taking the initiative and pursuing your goals, you wait for others to issue orders. A very quick-tempered and undisciplined person, you lack the ability to resist temptation. As well, you are cold in your relationships with others on a social level.

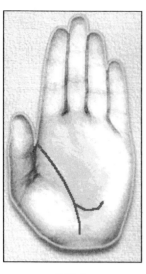
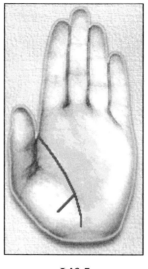
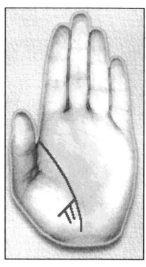

| **Lif-4** | **Lif-5** | **Lif-6** |

Lif-4. Your Life line is characterized by a termination in fork slanting upward.

This indicates health problems and a diminished vitality. This can also mean frequent changes of job and career. You continually attempt to launch new projects before completing ones already begun.

Lif-5. Your Life line is characterized by a termination in fork slanting downward.

You have a lot of energies and vitality, even after the age of 50. For you, life does not end with retirement and you try your luck in a new field. In general, you are in good health.

Lif-6. Your Life line is characterized by a termination in many lines.

Facing many health problems, your vitality is diminished at the age of 50. Prior to this, your physical strength weakens and you have no desire to do anything, preferring a quiet life. Your familial relationships are complex and difficult, as you do not get along with your next of kin easily.

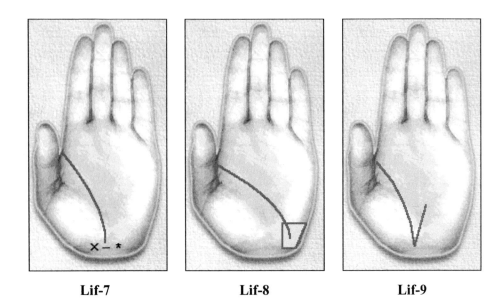

| Lif-7 | Lif-8 | Lif-9 |

Lif-7. Your Life line is characterized by a termination in a cross, a crossbar or a star.

This can mean acute illness or meeting with an accident.

Lif-8. Your Life line meets the Mount of the Moon.

A very hard-working and determined person, you do not hesitate to work alone, in order to achieve success. You are able to work long hours to achieve your goals. You have a lot of financial luck, seeking profit and material pleasure beyond anything else. In your love life, sex is the most important thing. Generally speaking, you are in very good health and longevity is written in your hand.

Lif-9. Your Life line is characterized by a termination returning to other fingers.

You will experience very good luck in your career or business, which will allow you to be very financially comfortable, as well as renowned. Near the end of your career, success may be yours.

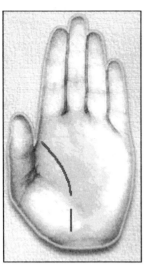 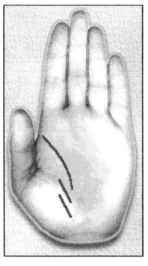 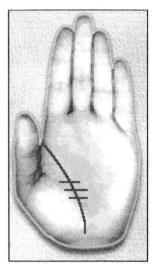

| **Lif-10** | **Lif-11** | **Lif-12** |

Lif-10. Your Life line is characterized by a break.

This indicates obstacles or dangerous situations, especially the disruption of your life by illness or accident.

Lif-11. Your Life line is characterized by a ladder-like break.

Your health is very fragile. Serious and repetitive illness may arise throughout your life.

Lif-12. Your Life line is characterized by multiple breaks.

You may experience numerous minor failures or illnesses, causing you great worry throughout your life.

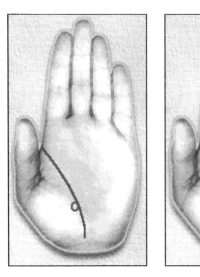
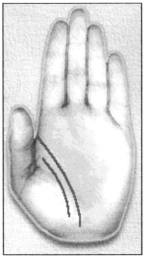
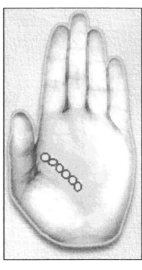

| Lif-13 | Lif-14 | Lif-15 |

Lif-13. Island on your Life line.

This indicates chronic disease. Your resistance to disease or any difficulty is poor. You are very prudent in your actions and feel the need to contemplate all actions. You have great patience.

Lif-14. A double Life line.

This indicates that you are in very good health and also possess great resistance against all illness and difficulty. This is also called the line of vitality. Thus, people have difficulty fighting you and you are always able to recover after suffering failure. This aids in the quest for success in your career.

Lif-15. A chained Life line.

A lack of vitality will disrupt your health and sickness surrounds you. Your willpower is weak and you quickly abandon ship when faced with difficulty. You are very impatient and must learn perseverance in order to achieve success. Your resistance is weak.

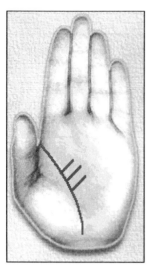
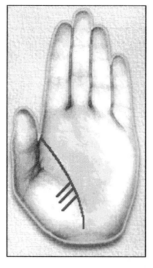
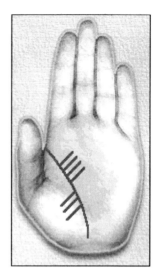

Lif-16   **Lif-17**   **Lif-18**

Lif-16. Your Life line is characterized by small rising lines.

This indicates you are filled with ambition and glory and find success in your life. In general, you are able to realize your cherished dreams. You make great efforts to advance your career and are never short of energy. You have success written in your hand.

Lif-17. Your Life line is characterized by small falling lines.

You experience a complete loss of ambition and energy. You have no desire to change your situation or your career. Your vitality decreases, your physical and mental capacities decline, and you lack the enthusiasm to realize your dreams.

Lif-18. Your Life line is characterized by small rising and falling lines.

Early in life, you are filled with ambition and energy. You make much effort to develop your career and in general, you are able to fulfill your dearest dreams. However, near the middle of your life, you will begin to feel a lack of energy and enthusiasm. You no longer possess the will to overcome obstacles. This important moment will lead to a downward turn in your life, the reality of which you must be ready to accept.

The Head line

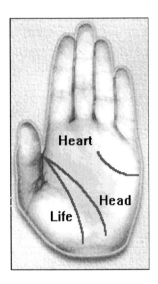

The Head Line is located in the middle of the palm, between the Life line and the Heart line. It is the most important line, indicating your thoughts and mental power, your intelligence, and your talents. It can also depict the evolution of your career.

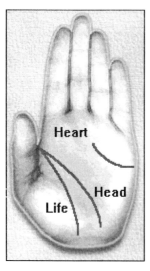 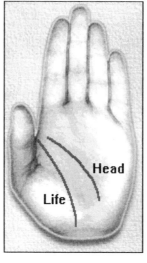 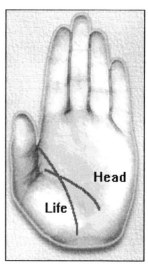

Hea-1   **Hea-2**   **Hea-3**

Hea-1. Your Head line begins at a starting point on par with the Life line.

You are very cautious and possess a great capacity for understanding. Your vision is geared to the future and you never act without careful consideration. Once you have begun, you will continue with great effort to succeed. You can always arrive at a solution to your problems because of your great intelligence.

Hea-2. The starting point of your Head line is detached from the Life line.

You possess great judgment and the ability to comprehend matters quickly. You prefer to make decisions based upon your own judgment, rather than upon the advice of others. You have your own way of doing things and a stubborn approach which may cause you to suffer great failure. You dare to take risks, even dangerous ones, as your courage overrules your reason. This is especially true if the distance between the two lines is great.

Hea-3. The starting point of your Head line is inside the Life line.

You are a very nervous person and are quickly discouraged by any complication. The future scares you and you prefer to live from day to day. Whenever you encounter difficulty, you will change your direction. Therefore, you have little success in your life. You are always picking fights, over even the most trivial of matters.

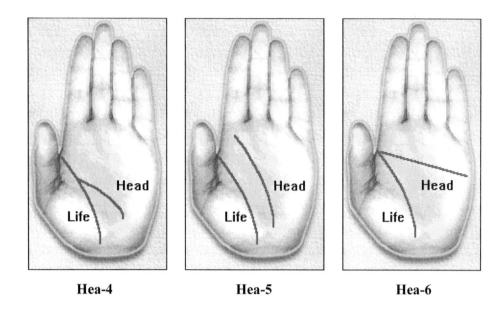

| Hea-4 | Hea-5 | Hea-6 |

Hea-4. The starting point of your Head line is on the Life line.

Without fail, you are armed with a plan. You rely on others for help. You are able to concentrate for a long time on a particular subject and upon finding a way to achieve your goals. With your superior intelligence, you hesitate to act hastily.

Hea-5. Your Head line begins under the index finger.

You are able to fulfill your ambitions and your leadership allows you to manipulate people easily, in order to reach your goals. You will experience great success in life.

Hea-6. Your Head and Heart lines converge and become one.

This new line is very special, indicating that you possess superb concentration skills. Having set your sights on something, you employ all means necessary to reach your objective. You are also very realistic. A very independent person, you prefer working alone to being on a team, employing your own particular methods, never listening to the advice of others.

Your emotions are ruled by reason. You crave power and pursue it at any cost. Your business career will be extremely successful and you will enjoy a comfortable financial standing. Starting from scratch, you more or less build your empire single-handedly. Your very rational approach to life causes you to be quite cold when relating to others and disturbs your marital happiness. Thus, your success is destined to be solely in business and society, rather than in familial relationships. If both your hands possess the same lines, your chances for success will be much greater.

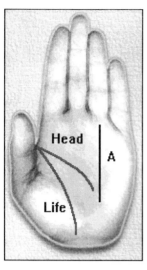 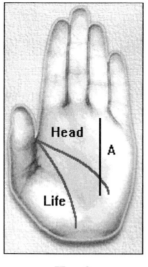 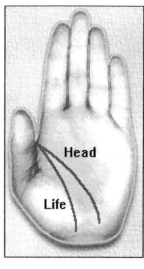

Hea-7   **Hea-8**   **Hea-9**

Hea-7. Head line stops before line A.

A short Head line is generally a sign of weak intelligence and your reasoning power is less than average.

Hea-8. Head line goes beyond line A.

A long Head line means you have a lot of imagination and are creative in everything you do. You have superior intelligence and are very successful in activities which require strong intellectual concentration.

Hea-9. Your Head line is characterized by a termination occurring after downward movement. Sometimes, it may enter the Mount of the Moon.

You possess a strong propensity for spiritual life and also a joyful character. A great imagination and an extraordinary capacity to comprehend are written in your hand. Your life is greatly influenced by your imagination. Thus, it is this type of line which can be found on the hands of most writers, artists and musicians. If the downward slope is severe, your imagination is excessively powerful, giving you difficulty with solving problems in the real world.

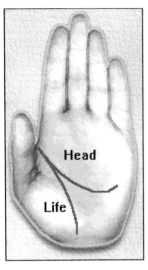 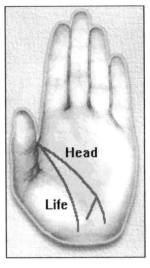 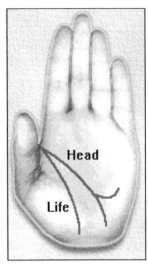

Hea-10   **Hea-11**   **Hea-12**

Hea-10. Your Head line is characterized by a termination occurring after upward movement.

You possess an ability to be realistic. You are very talented in business matters and are capable of managing your money, wealth being very important to you. An extremely materialistic person, you are interested only in filling your pockets and are also usually very tight-fisted. Such a tendency is even greater if you find your Head line to be touching your Heart line.

Hea-11. Your Head line is characterized by a termination in a fork, downward.

This indicates that you tend to hesitate before making important decisions. You dare not trust your own judgment, even though you are capable of quick comprehension. You rely greatly upon others to guide you.

Hea-12. Your Head line is characterized by a termination in a fork, upward.

This is also called the line of business - you have an extraordinary aptitude in managing business. In most cases, your chance of success in the business world is great, and consequently, your financial situation is very comfortable.

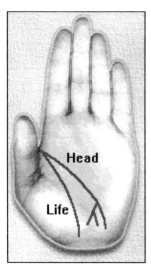
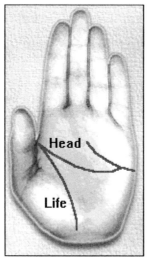
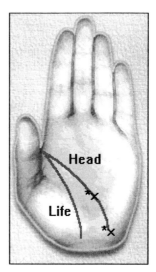

| Hea-13 | Hea-14 | Hea-15 |

Hea-13. Your Head line is characterized by a termination in many lines.

You have never had a fixed plan and you often change your direction. You hesitate before making important decisions and tend to abandon all your undertakings halfway through. You love fame but do not make enough effort to carry out your dreams.

Hea-14. Your Head line is characterized by an upward termination and by contact with the Heart line.

Money is very important to you, to the point that monetary wealth is the center and focus of your social relationships. A very materialistic person, you are interested only in filling your pockets and have no difficulty ignoring the rules of the game in order to achieve your goals, sometimes disregarding moral principles as well. Throughout your life, you will be ruled by money.

Hea-15. Your Head line is characterized by a star or a cross, found along or at the end of the line.

You may experience a physical ailment in the head, or a life plagued by mental disorder or nervous depression.

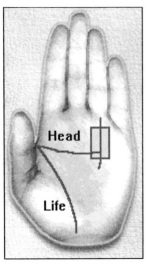 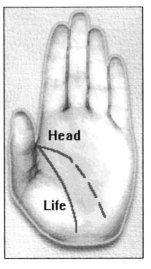 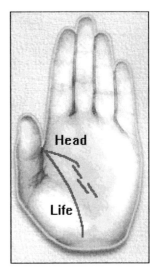

| **Hea-16** | **Hea-17** | **Hea-18** |

Hea-16. Your Head line enters the Mount of the Sun or touches the line of Success.

You are very creative and have great artistic abilities. You can become famous or rich in the world of art or literature.

Hea-17. Your Head line is characterized by intermittent breaks.

This is an indication of mental difficulties which may interfere in your chances for success. You are very nervous and pessimistic, your poor judgment responsible for many errors made. Consequently, failure is written in your hand. Serious mental problems or insanity are also a possibility, especially if your broken Head line ends in an island.

Hea-18. Your Head line is characterized by a ladder-like break.

You have much difficulty concentrating on a particular subject. Lack of patience and determination can mean great failure in your career. You count on other people to guide you in most important decisions.

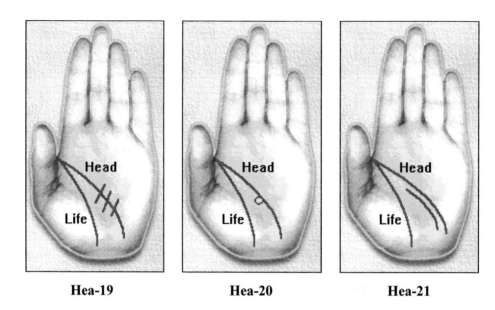

| Hea-19 | Hea-20 | Hea-21 |

Hea-19. Your Head line is characterized by a break in multi-line.

You are very sensitive and nervous. You are of a difficult and suspicious character. Therefore, your social relations are very poor.

Hea-20. Island on your Head line.

Very nervous and always anxious, you have some difficulty comprehending matters and also face mental problems.

Hea-21. A double Head line.

You are of superior intelligence and possess the ability to comprehend matters quickly. You have good judgment, allowing you to make important decisions. Success is made possible by your absolute confidence in your own abilities and your extraordinary courage. Wealth and glory will be yours. You also have a great imagination. It is as if a double personality exists beneath these lines.

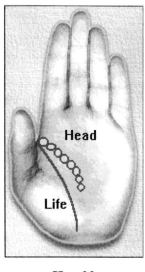

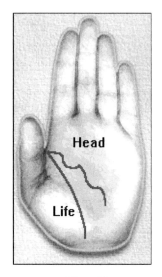

Hea-22   **Hea-23**

Hea-22. A chained Head line.

You are very nervous, your concentration and your spirit weak. You have a great desire to carry out tasks but your mental problems prevent you from doing so. You are very unstable and uncertain. Your decisions are usually based on bad judgments.

Hea-23. Your Head line is characterized by its wavy fluctuations.

Your ideas and plans are constantly changing, as is your direction. Your tendency to abandon projects will make achieving success in life difficult.

The Heart line

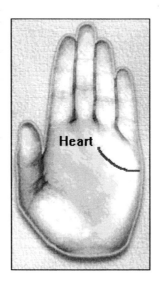

The Heart Line represents your love, your affection and happiness, it also indicates the humor and health of your heart. The starting point of the Heart line is located just under the fourth· finger, at 3/4 the length of your palm.

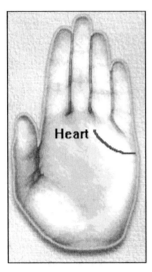 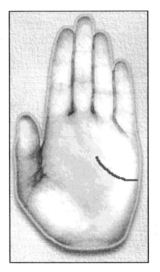 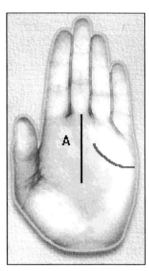

Her-1   **Her-2**   **Her-3**

Her-1. The starting point of your Heart line is higher.

You are only thinking of material pleasure and at the same time, quite selfish and tight-fisted. You spend money on yourself but never on others.

Her-2. The starting point of your Heart line is lower.

A lack of patience is revealed by your Heart line. You want great success but you do not want to make an effort. With a rebellious temperament, you have difficulty determining your goals and thus have little success in your career.

Her-3. Your Heart line stops before line A.

Your Heart line is short which indicates a lack of vitality and passion in your life. You have cold relationships, as you possess no affection for other people. Sympathy is not in your realm of feeling. A short Heart line may also indicate heart disease.

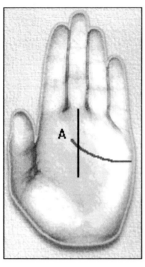 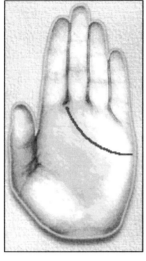 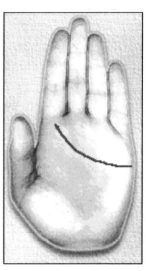

| **Her-4** | **Her-5** | **Her-6** |

Her-4. Your Heart line goes beyond line A.

Your Heart line is long, throughout life, you are guided and dominated by emotion, whether it is regarding business or social relationships. If the line is too long, this indicates that you are too possessive, you will have many problems in your love life.

Her-5. Your Heart line is characterized by a termination between the index and middle finger.

Your life, thoughts, and actions are guided by emotion. You feel special affection for the opposite sex, as well as sympathy for others, but you do feel hurt if you do not receive a similar response. Generally speaking, you have a very strong heart.

Her-6. Your Heart line is characterized by a termination below the index finger.

You are very sentimental, possessive and jealous. People attempt to trap you in your love promises and thus, love problems will plague you always. You are ready to die for pure and sincere loves but if your partner leaves you, you will have difficulty coping.

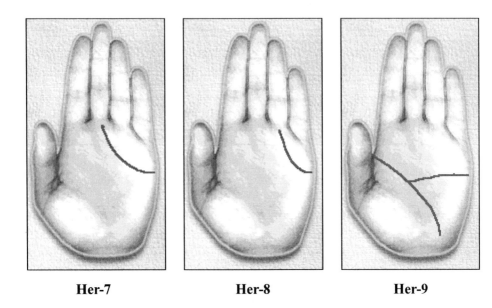

| Her-7 | Her-8 | Her-9 |

Her-7. Your Heart line is characterized by a termination below the middle finger.

You are not very expressive and often try to restrict your feelings. Very passionate and selfish, you may be blinded by love. You consider love and sex to be the same thing and seek physical pleasure above all other.

Her-8. Your Heart line is characterized by a termination below third finger.

You are quite cold in your love relationships, thinking only of yourself and your own sexual satisfaction. You never show feeling. Very ruthless, you can switch partners easily to find physical pleasure. For you, love is sex and sex is love.

Her-9. Your Heart line is characterized by a termination on the Head line.

You are looking for success in your career more than in love. Very pragmatic, you find personal satisfaction in your work rather than in love. You prioritize your career over love because your logic dominates your emotions.

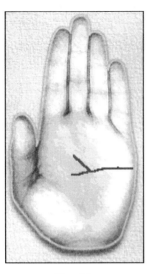 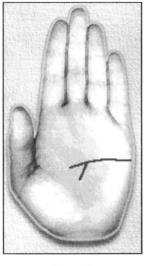 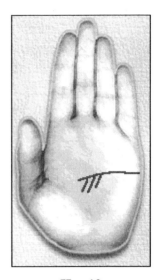

| **Her-10** | **Her-11** | **Her-12** |

Her-10. Your Heart line is characterized by a termination in a fork, upward.

Love is very important to you and you can sacrifice everything in order to realize love. You prefer a happy marriage over a successful career.

Her-11. Your Heart line is characterized by a termination in a fork, downward.

Your feelings vary between cold and hot. Very jealous by nature, you will have difficulty maintaining a healthy love relationship.

Her-12. Your Heart line is characterized by a termination in a downward multi-line.

Your heart is very fragile and people hurt and knock you down easily. You are very excited by the prospect of new love but often it leads nowhere and it is you who are left in pain. You are familiar with lovesickness.

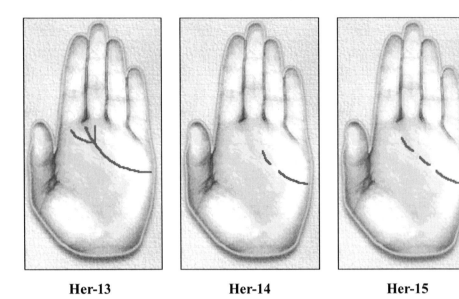

| Her-13 | Her-14 | Her-15 |

Her-13. Your Heart line terminates in three branches: one under the index finger, one between the index and middle finger, one under the middle finger.

You are a very well-balanced person in terms of emotions. Feelings do not dominate everything and you are capable of controlling your feeling with reason. You find love to be more important than sex, seeking more than just sexual pleasure in your love relationships. You rarely make promises of love because your heart is ruled by reason.

Her-14. A break on your Heart line.

Your emotions are very fragile and you are easily attracted by the promise of love. Sometimes you are stubbornly blinded by love. Quite selfish, you seek sexual pleasure more than others.

Her-15. An intermittent break on your Heart line.

You readily change partners in order to satisfy your sexual pleasure. You have a quick-changing temperament and this pushes your friends away from you. You lack honesty and therefore have difficulty maintaining a lasting relationship.

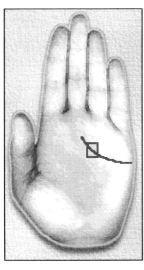
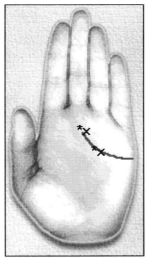
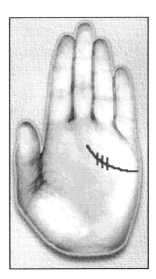

Her-16   **Her-17**   **Her-18**

Her-16. Your Heart line is characterized by a square.

You will be tormented by great love-sickness throughout your life. The search to find true love will be a constant source of anxiety.

Her-17. Your Heart line is characterized by the presence of a star or a cross.

You may experience minor heart problems or troubles in your love relationships. It is possible to recover from these wounds.

Her-18. Your Heart line is intersected by small lines.

You either have heart disease or problems in your love relationships.

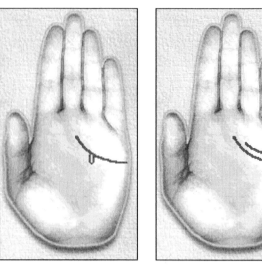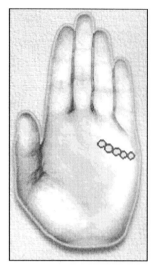

Her-19 **Her-20** **Her-21**

Her-19. Islands on your Heart line.

You are so uncertain that you can never maintain permanent love in your life. Your feelings of love change from morning to night and this can be said of your temperament in general.

Her-20. A double heart line.

Very open and optimistic, you are a champion in public relations and people love your company. Feelings are very important and you think of other people's interests before your own. You prefer giving to receiving.

Her-21. A chained heart line.

You are very emotionally unstable. By nature, you are melancholy and tend to create problems in your love life. You can be very excited and at the same time depressed when faced with making a decision. Monitor your heart.

The Fate line

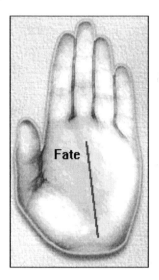

The Fate line is the line which normally begins at the wrist and continues up to the middle finger. It reveals your life destiny, as well as the good and bad luck of your career. It is quite important, as this line partially determines your social success.

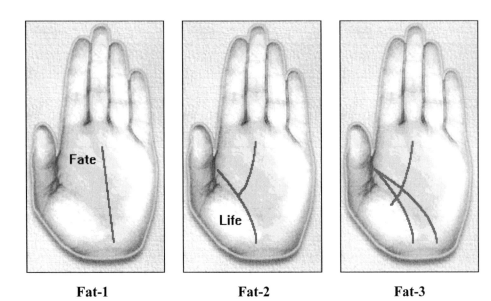

| Fat-1 | Fat-2 | Fat-3 |

Fat-1. Your Fate line begins at the wrist and nearly reaches the middle finger.

It is characterized by its length. Therefore, you experience much good luck as a young person. You may receive help and support from your parents, perhaps even surviving because of their fortunes. Later in life, luck remains at your side, helping you to achieve success in life. Financially and materially speaking, your life is always easy. If this line is not intersected by the Heart or Head line, your success will be greater, as it indicates an ability to triumph under any circumstances.

Fat-2. Your Fate line originates from the Life line.

Therefore, you must endure a difficult period before achieving success. This will prove a very valuable and necessary experience, helping you to reach the top. Opportunities will present themselves, requiring only minimal effort on your part. Do not worry - success will be yours. Your empire will be built almost single-handedly, thanks to your abilities and talents. Your success is your own doing and no other person may take credit. Although the beginning is difficult, your final reward will be great.

Fat-3. The starting point of your Fate line is inside the Life line.

You have many opportunities presented to you but you owe your success to yourself and to your own efforts, with help from your family and no one else.

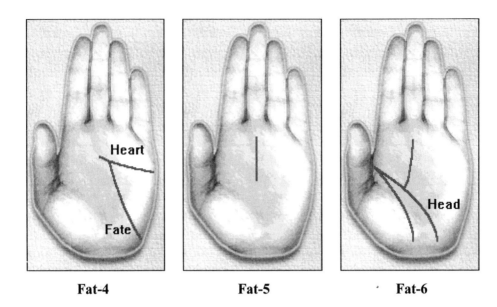

Fat-4　　　　　　**Fat-5**　　　　·　**Fat-6**

Fat-4. Your Fate line begins on the Mount of the Moon.

Therefore, you need help in finding luck. Your success cannot depend on your effort alone. Although this is important, you will have difficulty finding your way without the help of others. All your talents may prove useless and your efforts lost. You are best suited to a profession which allows you to interact with others, including journalism and other media-related careers, public relations, diplomacy. If your Fate line touches your Heart line, your success will be greatly dependent upon the help of your spouse or in-laws.

Fat-5, Fat-6. The starting point of your Fate line is in the middle of the palm or on the Head line.

The beginning is very difficult, even impossible. You have to build a solid foundation and make great effort to achieve this. Your chance will arrive at around the age of 40, when your base is solidly built. Your success is the fruit of your own labor, so do not count on anything else.

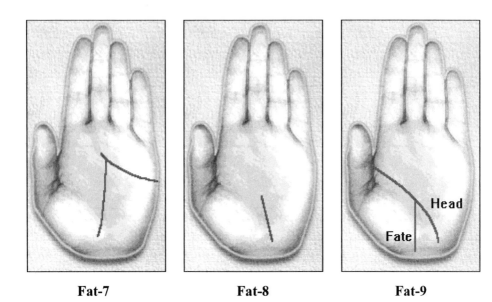

| Fat-7 | Fat-8 | Fat-9 |

Fat-7. Your Fate line is characterized by a termination on the Heart line.

Your sentiment impedes your success in life, dictating your thinking and actions. Your reasoning is influenced by your heart and not by your head. Thus, many problems in your love life will disrupt your career.

Fat-8. Your Fate line is characterized by a termination in the middle of the palm.

This indicates that the beginning of your life is quite easy and you will meet with much success during this period. But around the age of 40, you will encounter many obstacles. Your lack of determination will cause many problems.

Fat-9. Your Fate line is characterized by a termination on the Head line.

It runs smoothly while you are young but around the age of 40, judgment errors will result in many failures. You must make a great effort to bypass this blockage and achieve the final success.

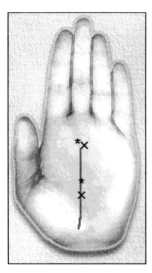 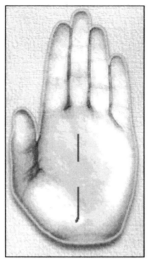 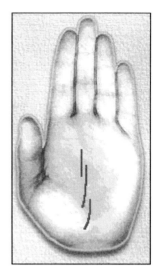

Fat-10   **Fat-11**   **Fat-12**

Fat-10. Your Fate line is characterized by a star or a cross, located either along it or at the end.

Therefore, you will experience a significant change, affecting either your financial situation or life in general.

Fat-11. Your Fate line is characterized by a break.

This indicates a decrease in luck around the age of 40. You will meet with fewer successes during this period. But a new life will recommence if the continuation line is clear.

Fat-12. Your Fate line is characterized by an overlapping break.

Your luck will end for a specific time, as you will encounter many difficulties in the middle of your career span. All should return to normal later and your vitality will return. New options will be revealed.

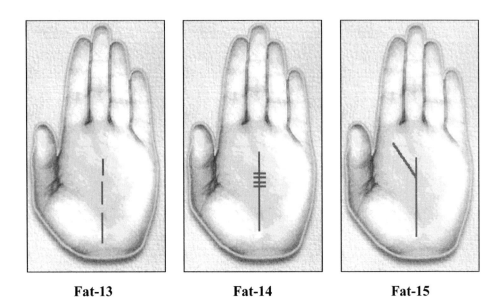

| Fat-13 | Fat-14 | Fat-15 |

Fat-13. Your Fate line is characterized by intermittent breaks.

The opportunities presented to you in life will cause great trouble. You will change jobs very oftcn and be discouraged by reoccurring difficulties. You may suffer numerous failures and, throughout life, your health will be poor.

Fat-14. Your Fate line is characterized by multiple breaks.

You will encounter many obstacles on the road to success and problems arise will repeatedly to trouble your career. Throughout your life, these difficulties will greatly affect your financial situation.

Fat-15. A split on your Fate line and one branch goes into index.

You are very aggressive in order to reach your success. To carry out your ambition, you dare to challenge your rivals who sometimes are stronger than you. You do not hesitate to make the necessary effort and you can always reach your goals.

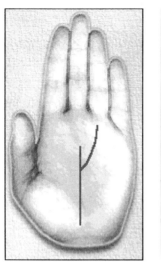
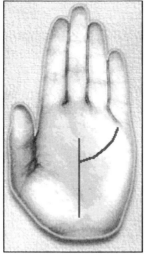
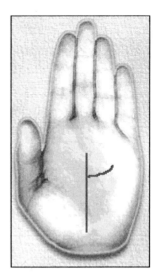

Fat-16   **Fat-17**   **Fat-18**

Fat-16. A split on your Fate line and one branch goes into the third finger.

This is the guide to glory. You will meet with great success in the world of art and business. Luck is just ahead to guide you.

Fat-17. A split on your Fate line and one branch goes into the fourth finger.

You have an extraordinary talent for business. The world of commerce is in your hand and the chance of finance cannot survive your attack. All conditions exist to create a royal life for you. Money, glory ... you have it all.

Fat-18. Fate line splits into two lines.

You will experience great change in your career, which may signify a turning point in your business. This may go from good to bad, or from bad to good.

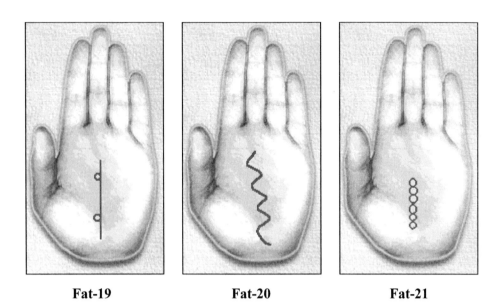

Fat-19   **Fat-20**   **Fat-21**

Fat-19. Islands on your Fate line.

This means that you will have many troubles with the opposite sex. Love is only a game for you and it can result in important financial losses and also diminish your chance. You may be also faced with a great failure in your career caused by lack of thought.

Fat-20. Your Fate line is wavy.

Your thought is very unstable. You often change jobs and direction because you are not sure of yourself. You lack passion in your work.

Fat-21. Yours is a chained line of Fate.

Therefore, while pursuing a career, you will repeatedly encounter many obstacles. The road to success is a very difficult one. Despite your numerous efforts, the end results will be disappointing. A difficult life awaits you.

The line of Success

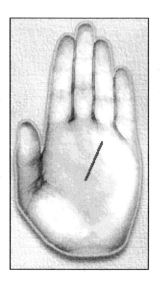

The line of Success has many starting points, usually beginning from the center of the hand, moving up the third finger. They reveal glory, accomplishment and the social (financial) status of your life.

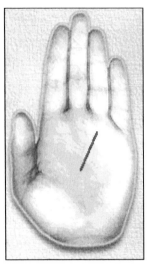 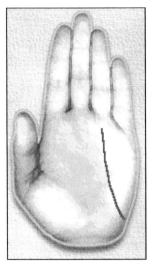 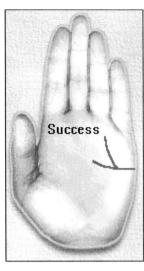

| Suc-1 | Suc-2 | Suc-3 |

Suc-1. The starting point of your line of Success is in the middle of the palm.

You had many difficulties when you were young and your social relationships seemed to be of little consolation - you seemed to be in the wrong world. But after the age of 40, luck starts to smile on you and provide some very interesting results, which will harvest the fruit of your labor.

Suc-2. Your line of Success begins on the Mount of the Moon.

You must rely upon your creativity and imagination to succeed in life. You will also need help from your family and others, to guide you on the path to success. Such a line is particularly suited to artists and writers.

Suc-3. The starting point of your line of Success is on the Heart line.

You had many difficulties when you were young, obstacles arising in all directions to challenge and teach you. Around the age of 40, all should take a positive turn and you will be very satisfied with your achievements.

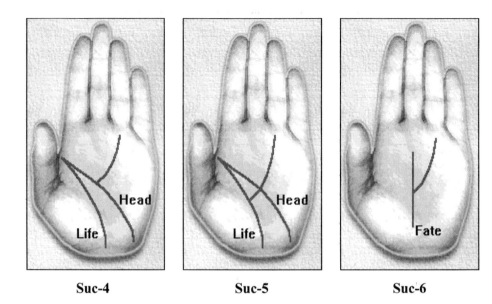

| Suc-4 | Suc-5 | Suc-6 |

Suc-4. The starting point of your line of Success is on the Head line.

This means you have a very sharp mind and extraordinary comprehension skills. You are capable of exploiting your social relationships to achieve your goals. Success is written in your hand, as you are very talented and eloquent but also very diligent.

Suc-5. The starting point of your line of Success is on the Life line.

You are very determined and your strength frightens your enemies. You want success and will do everything to achieve it. Your patience and effort will allow you to reach your goals without any help.

Suc-6. The starting point of your line of Success is on the Fate line.

This means you ignore the world around you and try everything within your power to create your own path. You want to go it alone, without help. Very often, you can realize your dreams and the results are better than what you had come to expect.

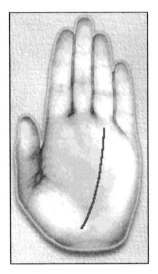 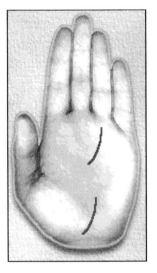 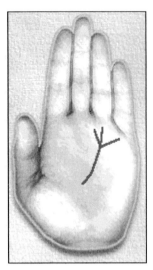

| **Suc-7** | **Suc-8** | **Suc-9** |

Suc-7. Your line of Success is characterized by its great length.

Your good luck and success began in your youth. You may owe this good fortune to your parents or family. With age, you continue to develop your talents and achieve success throughout your life.

Suc-8. Your line of Success is characterized by its short length.

Although you have had success in your youth, which you may owe to your parents or family, when you become older, this trend may not be as evident. Towards the end of your career, you will notice a decline in your achievements. Your financial situation will be affected.

Suc-9. Your line of Success ends in a division into three branches.

Your sympathy and honesty will assist you in life and your respectable reputation will help you to succeed in your career. Glory and celebrity are yours and you will have the chance to climb very high on the social ladder.

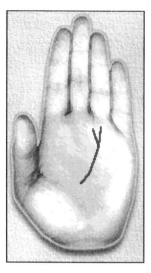 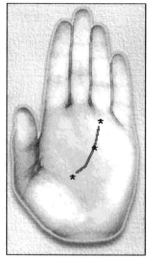 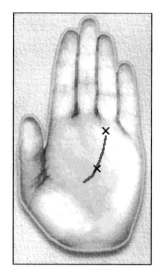

| Suc-10 | Suc-11 | Suc-12 |

Suc-10. Your line of Success ends in a division into two branches.

You will achieve half your expected success in life.

Suc-11. Your line of Success is characterized by the star located at the end.

You will be able to fully develop your talent, in order to succeed in life. Success is written in your stars. Happiness and glory await you at the end of the road. Your career will end in great success. A star on the line of Success is always positive, indicating great financial success.

Your line of Success is characterized by a star, located at the beginning and the end.

Success will be yours throughout life. No matter what you attempt, success is written in your stars.

Suc-12. Your line of Success is characterized by a cross.

A cross on the line of Success is always negative, regardless of where it is located. Therefore, you will encounter many obstacles on the road to success. Errors made on the journey will cause great trouble and affect your financial situation.

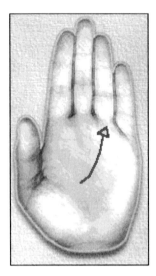 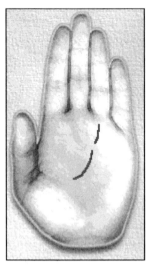 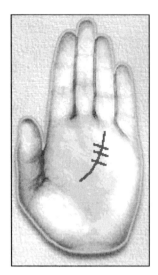

| Suc-13 | Suc-14 | Suc-15 |

Suc-13. Your line of Success is characterized by a triangle at the end, which is positive.

You will be greatly renowned near the end of your career.

Suc-14. A break on your line of Success.

Usually this indicates a short interruption on your road to success. Financial difficulties may arise during this period but everything should continue normally. If you have enough confidence and determination, it will not be difficult to move past your problems.

Suc-15. Your line of Success is characterized by multiple breaks.

You encounter many obstacles on your road to success. Your luck is not consistent. Your progress and finances are hindered by these incessant troubles.

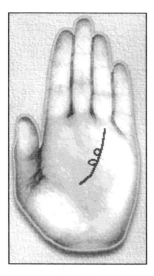 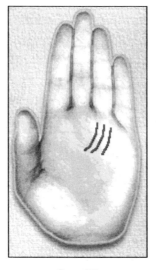 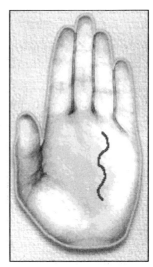

| Suc-16 | Suc-17 | Suc-18 |

Suc-16. Islands on your line of Success.

A very bad sign for your success: you are the scapegoat of all the problems in the world. Your social relationships will be very disturbed by some unthinkable errors, your reputation is falling down in the black hole.

Suc-17. You have small lines of Success.

You lack the confidence and patience for success. Even if you make a great effort, your success will be minimal.

Suc-18. Your line of Success is characterized by its waving fluctuations.

You will hesitate often on the road to success. In an effort to find the correct path, you will change your direction or career frequently. This will prevent you from achieving as expected.

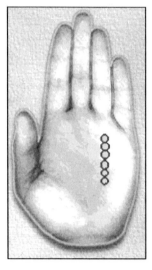
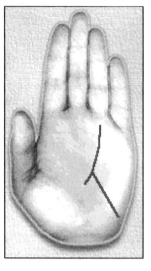
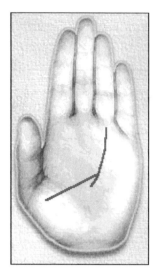

| Suc-19 | Suc-20 | Suc-21 |

Suc-19. Yours is a chained line of Success.

Your life will be filled only with imagined success. Despite your belief in your actions, nothing ever materializes out of your efforts to achieve.

Suc-20. A rising line from the Mount of the Moon cuts into your line of Success.

This indicates you will receive much help in your life, especially in business. Success is written in your hand and your career undergoes great development.

Suc-21. A rising line from the Mount of Venus cuts into your line of Success.

You have many talents in the world of art and literature. Thus, your success will be more brilliant in these particular areas.

Lines of Marriage

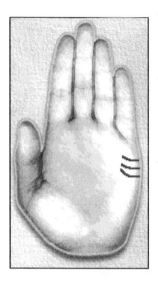

Lines of marriage are the small horizontal lines located on the Mount of Mercury (under the fourth finger) and are generally very short - take into account only the long ones. These lines reveal not only legal marriage, but also a union without legal formalities.

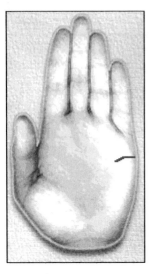 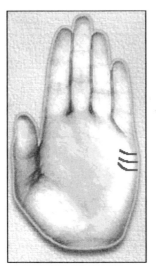 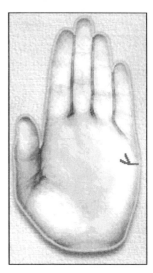

Mar-1	Mar-2	Mar-3

Mar-1. A descending line of Marriage.

This indicates that your union will encounter serious difficulties and that quarrels are very frequent in your married life. Fissures in your relationship are very evident and separation will not be long in coming.

Mar-2. A rising line of Marriage.

You prefer a solitary life, to live a single life does not scare you, and even that makes you happy, it seems that married life is not for you.

Mar-3. Line of Marriage in a fork.

The beginning of married life is very beautiful but the intervention of a third party will disrupt your union and separation will prove unavoidable.

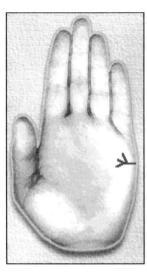 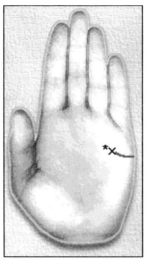 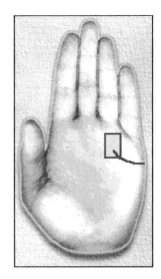

| **Mar-4** | **Mar-5** | **Mar-6** |

Mar-4. Line of Marriage in multi-line.

There is no positive emotion shared by you both and your union creates more pain than joy. You are too unstable and varying, and would rather dream of a new relationship.

Mar-5. Your line of Marriage terminates in a star or a cross.

Your union will terminate suddenly, due to unexpected separation or to the disappearance of your partner.

Mar-6. Your line of Marriage enters the Mount of the Sun.

Your union is a solid one. Your conjugal life is very beautiful and long-lasting.

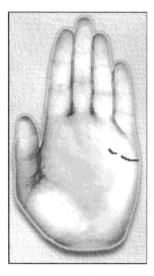

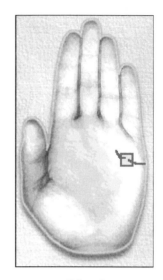

Mar-7   **Mar-8**

Mar-7. A break on your line of Marriage.

This means fissure in your relationship is evident. You live a married life but reality is quite different. You will stop this game sooner or later.

Mar-8. Your line of Marriage is characterized by a break, as well as the presence of a square.

You may experience a temporary break-up of your conjugal life but can reconcile at a later date.

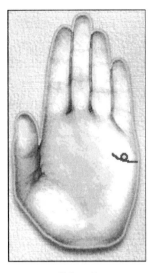

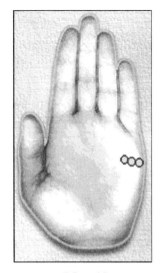

Mar-9   **Mar-10**

Mar-9. Islands on your line of Marriage.

This indicates difficulties in your relationship and you are not satisfied at all with your union. This lack of satisfaction could explode at any time and result in separation.

Mar-10. Yours is a chained line of Marriage.

If you are living in with a partner, it is not because of love. Rather, it is simply out of interest or to satisfy your sexual needs.

4. Sky Chart

The Chinese sky chart is a very important and complex branch of Chinese astrology. It is composed of 28 main stars (with a total of 115), which have a very important influence on our lives. According to one's date and time of birth, the position of these 28 stars in the 12 palaces of one's life can be established, and the future forecast accordingly.

The twenty-eight stars and the twelve palaces

The 12 palaces are as follows: palace of Life, Brothers, Spouse, Children, Finances, Health, Travels, Friends, Career, Property (or heritage), Happiness and Parents. Among the 28 stars, there are bad and good stars. According to their location, their positions can range from bad to average, good to excellent. Their influences are different, depending upon their positions.

For example, a good star in a bad position will have less leverage to exert a positive influence in your life. By contrast, if the star is in an excellent place, it can chase away the bad luck of other bad stars, as long as it is a powerful star. For the same reason, a bad star in a bad position will have a more ferocious influence but if its position is good, it cannot do much damage. The better the position, the better the influence.

If a good star and a bad star are located simultaneously in the same palace, luck will be mixed. The good luck will be overwhelmed by the bad. If the good star is more powerful or if there are more good stars than bad ones in the palace, your luck will be better. By the same token, if there are more bad stars in the palace, your luck will be worse.

Here is a list of the 28 principal stars and their characteristics:

- Star of the King: Good. The most powerful of all stars, its presence can chase away the bad luck of other bad stars; it reigns over Career.
- Opportunity of Heaven: Good. It reigns over Brothers.
- The Sun: Good and powerful. It reigns over Career.
- Warrior: Good or bad depending upon the palace and combination with other stars. It reigns over Finances.
- Equality: Good, quite powerful. It reigns over Happiness.
- Honesty: Good or bad depending upon the palace and combination with other stars. It reigns over Career.
- Palace of Heaven: Good and powerful. It reigns over Finances and Property.
- The Moon: Good. It reigns over Finances and Property.
- Voracious Wolf: Bad. It reigns over Happiness.
- Big Door: Bad. It reigns over Friends.
- Premier of Heaven: Good and powerful. It reigns over Career.
- Frame of Heaven: Good and powerful. It reigns over Life.
- Seven Killers: Bad.
- Defeated Army: Bad. It reigns over Spouse, Children and Friends.
- Preserved Office: Good. It reigns over Career.
- Horse of Heaven: Good. It reigns over Travels.
- Right and Left Aid: Good and very powerful.
- Twisted and Prosperous Literary: Good.

- Arm of Heaven: Good and powerful. It reigns over Career and Finances.
- Climbing Goat: Good or bad depending upon the palace and combination with other stars. It reigns over Health.
- Empty and Ruined Land: Bad. It reigns over Health, Finances and Career.
- Prosperity: Good. It reigns over Happiness and Finances.
- Power: Good and powerful. It reigns over Career.
- Exam: Good and powerful. It reigns over Career.
- Jealousy: Bad.

The five elements

The relationship between the five elements in Chinese astrology (metal, fire, wood, earth, and water) is important to the Chinese sky chart. This is due to the fact that these five elements may either be productive or destructive. Examples of productive relationships include water nourishing trees of wood; wood being used to feed fire; fire burning away to become ash, which in turn contributes to the creation of earth; earth producing metal; metal become liquid (water) when heated. Examples of destruction include wood sapping nutrition from the earth; earth absorbing water; water extinguishing fire; fire melting metal; metal cutting wood.

The element of one's year and the one of one's palace of Life, be it productive or destructive, has great influence on one's life. In addition, the body may be located in one of six different palaces: the palace of Life, of Spouse, of Finances, of Travels, of Career or of Happiness. Each of these will give various meanings to one's life.

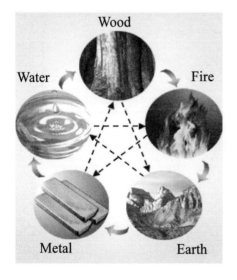

 Productive cycle

 Destructive cycle

Positioning of the stars and the palaces

To position the 28 stars and the 12 palaces, first draw a table with 12 squares like the one is shown below. These squares are numbered from 1 to 12 which correspond to the Chinese signs from rat to pig (the position of these signs in the squares are fixed). Then follow the following 10 steps.

6. Snake	7. Horse	8. Goat	9. Monkey
5. Dragon			10. Rooster
4. Rabbit			11. Dog
3. Tiger	2. Ox	1. Rat	12. Pig

(1) Find your Chinese month and day of birth.

Consult the "simplified table of Chinese years" to deduce your Chinese date of birth. The number of days in a Chinese month is either 29 or 30 days but never 31. In certain years, you will find there are some months in double such as in the year 2001 where you have 2 times April. This is because of the Chinese leap year.

To start, look in the table for a date which is the same or greater than your date of birth.

If you can find a date which is the same as your date of birth, the month and day which are next to it are your Chinese month and day of birth.

If you do not find the date which is the same as your date of birth, look for the next date which is greater than your date of birth, subtract your day of birth from the day of this date, then subtract the result from the Chinese day located next to it, you then obtain your Chinese day of birth.

Ex: If your date of birth is January 31st 2000, your Chinese month and day of birth are December 25th. If your date of birth is February 1st 2000, the next date which is greater than your date of birth is February 4th 2000. You must subtract your day of birth from the day of this date:

$$4 - 1 = 3$$

Next subtract this result from the Chinese day located next to it:

$$29 - 3 = 26$$

Therefore your Chinese day and month of birth are 26 December.

1900 Chinese mm/dd mm/dd	1901 Chinese mm/dd mm/dd	1902 Chinese mm/dd mm/dd	1903 Chinese mm/dd mm/dd	1904 Chinese mm/dd mm/dd
01/30 12/30	01/19 11/29	01/09 11/30	01/28 12/30	01/16 11/29
01/31 01/01	01/31 12/12	01/31 12/22	01/31 01/03	01/31 12/15
02/01 01/02	02/18 12/30	02/07 12/29	02/26 01/29	02/15 12/30
02/28 01/29	02/28 01/10	02/28 01/21	02/28 02/02	02/29 01/14
03/30 02/30	03/19 01/29	03/09 01/30	03/28 02/30	03/16 01/30
03/31 03/01	03/31 02/12	03/31 02/22	03/31 03/03	03/31 02/15
04/28 03/29	04/18 02/30	04/07 02/29	04/26 03/29	04/15 02/30
04/30 04/02	04/30 03/12	04/30 03/23	04/30 04/04	04/30 03/15
05/27 04/29	05/17 03/29	05/07 03/30	05/26 04/30	05/14 03/29
05/31 05/04	05/31 04/14	05/31 04/24	05/31 05/05	05/31 04/17
06/26 05/30	06/15 04/29	06/05 04/29	06/24 05/29	06/13 04/30
06/30 06/04	06/30 05/15	06/30 05/25	06/30 05/06	06/30 05/17
07/25 06/29	07/15 05/30	07/04 05/29	07/23 05/29	07/12 05/29
07/31 07/06	07/31 06/16	07/31 06/27	07/31 06/08	07/31 06/19
08/24 07/30	08/13 06/29	08/03 06/30	08/22 06/30	08/10 06/29
08/31 08/07	08/31 07/18	08/31 07/28	08/31 07/09	08/31 07/21
09/23 08/30	09/12 07/30	09/01 07/29	09/20 07/29	09/09 07/30
09/30 08/07	09/30 08/18	09/30 08/29	09/30 08/10	09/30 08/21
10/22 08/29	10/11 08/29	10/01 08/30	10/19 08/29	10/08 08/29
10/31 09/09	10/31 09/20	10/30 09/29	10/31 09/12	10/31 09/23
11/21 09/30	11/10 09/30	10/31 10/01	11/18 09/30	11/06 09/29
11/30 10/09	11/30 10/20	11/29 10/30	11/30 10/12	11/30 10/24
12/21 10/30	12/10 10/30	11/30 11/01	12/18 10/30	12/06 10/30
12/31 11/10	12/31 11/21	12/29 11/30	12/31 11/13	12/31 11/25
		12/31 12/02		

Simplified table of Chinese years

1905 Chinese mm/dd mm/dd	1906 Chinese mm/dd mm/dd	1907 Chinese mm/dd mm/dd	1908 Chinese mm/dd mm/dd	1909 Chinese mm/dd mm/dd
01/05 11/30	01/24 12/30	01/13 11/29	01/03 11/30	01/21 12/30
01/31 12/26	01/31 01/07	01/31 12/18	01/31 12/28	01/31 01/10
02/03 12/29	02/22 01/29	02/12 12/30	02/01 12/29	02/19 01/29
02/28 01/25	02/28 02/06	02/28 01/16	02/29 01/28	02/28 02/09
03/05 01/30	03/24 02/30	03/13 01/29	03/02 01/30	03/21 02/30
03/31 02/26	03/31 03/07	03/31 02/18	03/31 02/29	03/31 02/10
04/04 02/30	04/23 03/30	04/12 02/30	04/29 03/29	04/19 02/29
04/30 03/26	04/30 04/07	04/30 03/18	04/30 04/01	04/30 03/11
05/03 03/29	05/22 04/29	05/11 03/29	05/29 04/30	05/18 03/29
05/31 04/28	05/31 04/09	05/31 04/20	05/31 05/02	05/31 04/13
06/02 04/30	06/21 04/30	06/10 04/30	06/28 05/30	06/17 04/30
06/30 05/28	06/30 05/09	06/30 05/20	06/30 06/02	06/30 05/13
07/02 05/30	07/20 05/29	07/09 05/29	07/27 06/29	07/16 05/29
07/31 06/29	07/31 06/11	07/31 06/22	07/31 07/04	07/31 06/15
08/29 07/29	08/19 06/30	08/08 06/30	08/26 07/30	08/15 06/30
08/31 08/02	08/31 07/12	08/31 07/23	08/31 08/05	08/31 07/16
09/28 08/30	09/17 07/29	09/07 07/30	09/24 08/29	09/13 07/29
09/30 09/02	09/30 08/13	09/30 08/23	09/30 09/06	09/30 08/17
10/27 09/29	10/17 08/30	10/06 08/29	10/24 09/30	10/13 08/30
10/31 10/04	10/31 09/14	10/31 09/25	10/31 10/07	10/31 09/18
11/26 10/30	11/15 09/29	11/05 09/30	11/23 10/30	11/12 09/30
11/30 11/04	11/30 10/15	11/30 10/25	11/30 11/07	11/30 10/18
12/25 11/29	12/15 10/30	12/04 10/29	12/22 11/29	12/12 10/30
12/31 12/06	12/31 11/16	12/31 11/27	12/31 12/09	12/31 11/19

1910 Chinese mm/dd mm/dd	1911 Chinese mm/dd mm/dd	1912 Chinese mm/dd mm/dd	1913 Chinese mm/dd mm/dd	1914 Chinese mm/dd mm/dd
01/10 11/29	01/29 12/29	01/18 11/30	01/06 11/29	01/25 12/30
01/31 12/21	01/31 01/02	01/31 12/13	01/31 12/25	01/31 01/06
02/09 12/30	02/01 01/03	02/17 12/30	02/05 12/30	02/24 01/30
02/28 01/19	02/28 01/30	02/29 01/12	02/28 01/23	02/28 02/04
03/10 01/29	03/29 02/29	03/18 01/30	03/07 01/30	03/26 02/30
03/31 02/21	03/31 03/02	03/31 02/13	03/31 02/24	03/31 03/05
04/09 02/30	04/28 03/30	04/16 02/29	04/06 02/30	04/24 03/29
04/30 03/21	04/30 04/02	04/30 03/14	04/30 03/24	04/30 04/06
05/08 03/29	05/27 04/29	05/16 03/30	05/05 03/29	05/24 04/30
05/31 04/23	05/31 05/04	05/31 04/15	05/31 04/26	05/31 05/07
06/06 04/29	06/25 05/29	06/14 04/29	06/04 04/30	06/22 05/29
06/30 05/24	06/30 06/05	06/30 05/16	06/30 05/26	06/30 05/08
07/06 05/30	07/25 06/30	07/13 05/29	07/03 05/29	07/22 05/30
07/31 06/25	07/31 06/06	07/31 06/18	07/31 06/28	07/31 06/09
08/04 06/29	08/23 06/29	08/12 06/30	08/01 06/29	08/20 06/29
08/31 07/27	08/31 07/08	08/31 07/19	08/31 07/30	08/31 07/11
09/03 07/30	09/21 07/29	09/10 07/29	09/29 08/29	09/19 07/30
09/30 08/27	09/30 08/09	09/30 08/20	09/30 09/01	09/30 08/11
10/02 08/29	10/21 08/30	10/09 08/29	10/28 09/29	10/18 08/29
10/31 09/29	10/31 09/10	10/31 09/22	10/31 10/03	10/31 09/13
11/01 09/30	11/20 09/30	11/08 09/30	11/27 10/30	11/16 09/29
11/30 10/29	11/30 10/10	11/30 10/22	11/30 11/03	11/30 10/14
12/01 10/30	12/19 10/29	12/08 10/30	12/26 11/29	12/16 10/30
12/31 11/30	12/31 11/12	12/31 11/23	12/31 12/05	12/31 11/15

1915 Chinese		1916 Chinese		1917 Chinese		1918 Chinese		1919 Chinese	
mm/dd	mm/dd	mm/dd	mm/dd	mm/dd	mm/dd	mm/dd	mm/dd	mm/dd	mm/dd
01/14	11/29	01/04	11/29	01/22	12/29	01/12	12/30	01/01	11/30
01/31	12/17	01/31	12/27	01/31	01/09	01/31	12/19	01/31	12/30
02/13	12/30	02/02	12/29	02/21	01/30	02/10	12/29	02/01	01/01
02/28	01/15	02/29	01/27	02/28	02/07	02/28	01/18	02/28	01/28
03/15	01/30	03/03	01/30	03/22	02/29	03/12	01/30	03/01	01/29
03/31	02/16	03/31	02/28	03/31	03/09	03/31	02/19	03/31	02/30
04/13	02/29	04/02	02/30	04/20	03/29	04/10	02/29	04/29	03/29
04/30	03/17	04/30	03/28	04/30	04/10	04/30	03/20	04/30	04/01
05/13	03/30	05/01	03/29	05/20	04/30	05/09	03/29	05/28	04/29
05/31	04/18	05/31	04/30	05/31	05/11	05/31	04/22	05/31	05/03
06/12	04/30	06/29	05/29	06/18	05/29	06/08	04/30	06/27	05/30
06/30	05/18	06/30	06/01	06/30	06/12	06/30	05/22	06/30	06/03
07/11	05/29	07/29	06/30	07/18	06/30	07/07	05/29	07/26	06/29
07/31	06/20	07/31	07/02	07/31	07/13	07/31	06/24	07/31	07/05
08/10	06/30	08/28	07/30	08/17	07/30	08/06	06/30	08/24	07/29
08/31	07/21	08/31	08/03	08/31	08/14	08/31	07/25	08/31	07/07
09/08	07/29	09/26	08/29	09/15	08/29	09/04	07/29	09/23	07/30
09/30	08/22	09/30	09/04	09/30	09/15	09/30	08/26	09/30	08/07
10/08	08/30	10/26	09/30	10/15	09/30	10/04	08/30	10/23	08/30
10/31	09/23	10/31	10/05	10/31	10/16	10/31	09/27	10/31	09/08
11/06	09/29	11/24	10/29	11/14	10/30	11/03	09/30	11/21	09/29
11/30	10/24	11/30	11/06	11/30	11/16	11/30	10/27	11/30	10/09
12/06	10/30	12/24	11/30	12/13	11/29	12/02	10/29	12/21	10/30
12/31	11/25	12/31	12/07	12/31	12/18	12/31	11/29	12/31	11/10

1920 Chinese		1921 Chinese		1922 Chinese		1923 Chinese		1924 Chinese	
mm/dd	mm/dd	mm/dd	mm/dd	mm/dd	mm/dd	mm/dd	mm/dd	mm/dd	mm/dd
01/20	11/30	01/08	11/30	01/27	12/30	01/16	11/30	01/05	11/29
01/31	12/11	01/31	12/23	01/31	01/04	01/31	12/15	01/31	12/26
02/19	12/30	02/07	12/30	02/26	01/30	02/15	12/30	02/04	12/30
02/29	01/10	02/28	01/21	02/28	02/02	02/28	01/13	02/29	01/25
03/19	01/29	03/09	01/30	03/27	02/29	03/16	01/29	03/04	01/29
03/31	02/12	03/31	02/22	03/31	03/04	03/31	02/15	03/31	02/27
04/18	02/30	04/07	02/29	04/26	03/30	04/15	02/30	04/03	02/30
04/30	03/12	04/30	03/23	04/30	04/04	04/30	03/15	04/30	03/27
05/17	03/29	05/07	03/30	05/26	04/30	05/15	03/30	05/03	03/30
05/31	04/14	05/31	04/24	05/31	05/05	05/31	04/16	05/31	04/28
06/15	04/29	06/05	04/29	06/24	05/29	06/13	04/29	06/01	04/29
06/30	05/15	06/30	05/25	06/30	05/06	06/30	05/17	06/30	05/29
07/15	05/30	07/04	05/29	07/23	05/29	07/13	05/30	07/01	05/30
07/31	06/16	07/31	06/27	07/31	06/08	07/31	06/18	07/31	06/30
08/13	06/29	08/03	06/30	08/22	06/30	08/11	06/29	08/29	07/29
08/31	07/18	08/31	07/28	08/31	07/09	08/31	07/20	08/31	08/02
09/11	07/29	09/01	07/29	09/20	07/29	09/10	07/30	09/28	08/30
09/30	08/19	09/30	08/29	09/30	08/10	09/30	08/20	09/30	09/02
10/11	08/30	10/30	09/30	10/19	08/29	10/09	08/29	10/27	09/29
10/31	09/20	10/31	10/01	10/31	09/12	10/31	09/22	10/31	10/04
11/09	09/29	11/28	10/29	11/18	09/30	11/07	09/29	11/26	10/30
11/30	10/21	11/30	11/02	11/30	10/12	11/30	10/23	11/30	11/04
12/09	10/30	12/28	11/30	12/17	10/29	12/07	10/30	12/25	11/29
12/31	11/22	12/31	12/03	12/31	11/14	12/31	11/24	12/31	12/06

1925	Chinese	1926	Chinese	1927	Chinese	1928	Chinese	1929	Chinese
mm/dd	mm/dd	mm/dd	mm/dd	mm/dd	mm/dd	mm/dd	mm/dd	mm/dd	mm/dd
01/23	12/29	01/13	11/29	01/03	11/30	01/22	12/30	01/10	11/30
01/31	01/08	01/31	12/18	01/31	12/28	01/31	01/09	01/31	12/21
02/22	01/30	02/12	12/30	02/01	12/29	02/20	01/29	02/09	12/30
02/28	02/06	02/28	01/16	02/28	01/27	02/29	02/09	02/28	01/19
03/23	02/29	03/13	01/29	03/03	01/30	03/21	02/30	03/10	01/29
03/31	03/08	03/31	02/18	03/31	02/28	03/31	02/10	03/31	02/21
04/22	03/30	04/11	02/29	04/01	02/29	04/19	02/29	04/09	02/30
04/30	04/08	04/30	03/19	04/30	03/29	04/30	03/11	04/30	03/21
05/21	04/29	05/11	03/30	05/30	04/30	05/18	03/29	05/08	03/29
05/31	04/10	05/31	04/20	05/31	05/01	05/31	04/13	05/31	04/23
06/20	04/30	06/09	04/29	06/28	05/29	06/17	04/30	06/06	04/29
06/30	05/10	06/30	05/21	06/30	06/02	06/30	05/13	06/30	05/24
07/20	05/30	07/09	05/30	07/28	06/30	07/16	05/29	07/06	05/30
07/31	06/11	07/31	06/22	07/31	07/03	07/31	06/15	07/31	06/25
08/18	06/29	08/07	06/29	08/26	07/29	08/14	06/29	08/04	06/29
08/31	07/13	08/31	07/24	08/31	08/05	08/31	07/17	08/31	07/27
09/17	07/30	09/06	07/30	09/25	08/30	09/13	07/30	09/02	07/29
09/30	08/13	09/30	08/24	09/30	09/05	09/30	08/17	09/30	08/28
10/17	08/30	10/06	08/30	10/24	09/29	10/12	08/29	10/02	08/30
10/31	09/14	10/31	09/25	10/31	10/07	10/31	09/19	10/31	09/29
11/15	09/29	11/04	09/29	11/23	10/30	11/11	09/30	11/01	10/01
11/30	10/15	11/30	10/26	11/30	11/07	11/30	10/19	11/30	10/30
12/15	10/30	12/04	10/30	12/23	11/30	12/11	10/30	12/30	11/30
12/31	11/16	12/31	11/27	12/31	12/08	12/31	11/20	12/31	12/01

1930 Chinese mm/dd mm/dd	1931 Chinese mm/dd mm/dd	1932 Chinese mm/dd mm/dd	1933 Chinese mm/dd mm/dd	1934 Chinese mm/dd mm/dd
01/29 12/30	01/18 11/30	01/07 11/30	01/25 12/30	01/14 11/29
01/31 01/02	01/31 12/13	01/31 12/24	01/31 01/06	01/31 12/17
02/27 01/29	02/16 12/29	02/05 12/29	02/23 01/29	02/13 12/30
02/28 02/01	02/28 01/12	02/29 01/24	02/28 02/05	02/28 01/15
03/29 02/30	03/18 01/30	03/06 01/30	03/25 02/30	03/14 01/29
03/31 03/02	03/31 02/13	03/31 02/25	03/31 03/06	03/31 02/17
04/28 03/30	04/17 02/30	04/05 02/30	04/24 03/30	04/13 02/30
04/30 04/02	04/30 03/13	04/30 03/25	04/30 04/06	04/30 03/17
05/27 04/29	05/16 03/29	05/05 03/30	05/23 04/29	05/12 03/29
05/31 05/04	05/31 04/15	05/31 04/26	05/31 05/08	05/31 04/19
06/25 05/29	06/15 04/30	06/03 04/29	06/22 05/30	06/11 04/30
06/30 06/05	06/30 05/15	06/30 05/27	06/30 05/08	06/30 05/19
07/25 06/30	07/14 05/29	07/03 05/30	07/21 05/29	07/11 05/30
07/31 06/06	07/31 06/17	07/31 06/28	07/31 06/10	07/31 06/20
08/23 06/29	08/13 06/30	08/01 06/29	08/20 06/30	08/09 06/29
08/31 07/08	08/31 07/18	08/31 07/30	08/31 07/11	08/31 07/22
09/21 07/29	09/11 07/29	09/29 08/29	09/19 07/30	09/08 07/30
09/30 08/09	09/30 08/19	09/30 09/01	09/30 08/11	09/30 08/22
10/21 08/30	10/10 08/29	10/28 09/29	10/18 08/29	10/07 08/29
10/31 09/10	10/31 09/21	10/31 10/03	10/31 09/13	10/31 09/24
11/19 09/29	11/09 09/30	11/27 10/30	11/17 09/30	11/06 09/30
11/30 10/11	11/30 10/21	11/30 11/03	11/30 10/13	11/30 10/24
12/19 10/30	12/08 10/29	12/26 11/29	12/16 10/29	12/06 10/30
12/31 11/12	12/31 11/23	12/31 12/05	12/31 11/15	12/31 11/25

1935 mm/dd	Chinese mm/dd	1936 mm/dd	Chinese mm/dd	1937 mm/dd	Chinese mm/dd	1938 mm/dd	Chinese mm/dd	1939 mm/dd	Chinese mm/dd
01/04	11/29	01/23	12/29	01/12	11/30	01/01	11/30	01/19	11/29
01/31	12/27	01/31	01/08	01/31	12/19	01/30	12/29	01/31	12/12
02/03	12/30	02/22	01/30	02/10	12/29	01/31	01/01	02/18	12/30
02/28	01/25	02/29	02/07	02/28	01/18	02/01	01/02	02/28	01/10
03/04	01/29	03/22	02/29	03/12	01/30	02/28	01/29	03/20	01/30
03/31	02/27	03/31	03/09	03/31	02/19	03/01	01/30	03/31	02/11
04/02	02/29	04/20	03/29	04/10	02/29	03/31	02/30	04/19	02/30
04/30	03/28	04/30	03/10	04/30	03/20	04/29	03/29	04/30	03/11
05/02	03/30	05/20	03/30	05/09	03/29	04/30	04/01	05/18	03/29
05/31	04/29	05/31	04/11	05/31	04/22	05/28	04/29	05/31	04/13
06/01	05/01	06/18	04/29	06/08	04/30	05/31	05/03	06/16	04/29
06/30	05/30	06/30	05/12	06/30	05/22	06/27	05/30	06/30	05/14
07/29	06/29	07/17	05/29	07/07	05/29	06/30	06/03	07/16	05/30
07/31	07/02	07/31	06/14	07/31	06/24	07/26	06/29	07/31	06/15
08/28	07/30	08/16	06/30	08/05	06/29	07/31	07/05	08/14	06/29
08/31	08/03	08/31	07/15	08/31	07/26	08/24	07/29	08/31	07/17
09/27	08/30	09/15	07/30	09/04	07/30	08/31	07/07	09/12	07/29
09/30	09/03	09/30	08/15	09/30	08/26	09/23	07/30	09/30	08/18
10/26	09/29	10/14	08/29	10/03	08/29	09/30	08/07	10/12	08/30
10/31	10/05	10/31	09/17	10/31	09/28	10/22	08/29	10/31	09/19
11/25	10/30	11/13	09/30	11/02	09/30	10/31	09/09	11/10	09/29
11/30	11/05	11/30	10/17	11/30	10/28	11/21	09/30	11/30	10/20
12/25	11/30	12/13	10/30	12/02	10/30	11/30	10/09	12/10	10/30
12/31	12/06	12/31	11/18	12/31	11/29	12/21	10/30	12/31	11/21
						12/31	11/10		

1940 mm/dd	Chinese mm/dd	1941 mm/dd	Chinese mm/dd	1942 mm/dd	Chinese mm/dd	1943 mm/dd	Chinese mm/dd	1944 mm/dd	Chinese mm/dd
01/08	11/29	01/26	12/29	01/16	11/30	01/05	11/29	01/24	12/29
01/31	12/23	01/31	01/05	01/31	12/15	01/31	11/26	01/31	01/07
02/07	12/30	02/25	01/30	02/14	12/29	02/04	12/30	02/23	01/30
02/29	01/22	02/28	02/03	02/28	01/14	02/28	01/24	02/29	02/06
03/08	01/30	03/27	02/30	03/16	01/30	03/05	01/29	03/23	02/29
03/31	02/23	03/31	03/04	03/31	02/15	03/31	02/26	03/31	03/08
04/07	02/30	04/25	03/29	04/14	02/29	04/04	02/30	04/22	03/30
04/30	03/23	04/30	04/05	04/30	03/16	04/30	03/26	04/30	04/08
05/06	03/29	05/25	04/30	05/14	03/30	05/03	03/29	05/21	04/29
05/31	04/25	05/31	05/06	05/31	04/17	05/31	04/28	05/31	04/10
06/05	04/30	06/24	05/30	06/13	04/30	06/02	04/30	06/20	04/30
06/30	05/25	06/30	06/06	06/30	05/17	06/30	05/28	06/30	05/10
07/04	05/29	07/23	06/29	07/12	05/29	07/01	05/29	07/19	05/29
07/31	06/27	07/31	06/08	07/31	06/19	07/31	06/30	07/31	06/12
08/03	06/30	08/22	06/30	08/11	06/30	08/30	07/30	08/18	06/30
08/31	07/28	08/31	07/09	08/31	07/20	08/31	08/01	08/31	07/13
09/01	07/29	09/20	07/29	09/09	07/29	09/28	08/29	09/16	07/29
09/30	08/29	09/30	08/10	09/30	08/21	09/30	09/02	09/30	08/14
10/30	09/30	10/19	08/29	10/09	08/30	10/28	09/30	10/16	08/30
10/31	10/01	10/31	09/12	10/31	09/22	10/31	10/03	10/31	09/15
11/28	10/29	11/18	09/30	11/07	09/29	11/26	10/29	11/15	09/30
11/30	11/02	11/30	10/12	11/30	10/23	11/30	11/04	11/30	10/15
12/28	11/30	12/17	10/29	12/07	10/30	12/26	11/30	12/14	10/29
12/31	12/03	12/31	11/14	12/31	11/24	12/31	12/05	12/31	11/17

1945 Chinese mm/dd mm/dd		1946 Chinese mm/dd mm/dd		1947 Chinese mm/dd mm/dd		1948 Chinese mm/dd mm/dd		1949 Chinese mm/dd mm/dd	
01/13	11/30	01/02	11/29	01/21	12/30	01/10	11/30	01/28	12/30
01/31	12/18	01/31	12/29	01/31	01/10	01/31	12/21	01/31	01/03
02/12	12/30	02/01	12/30	02/20	01/30	02/09	12/30	02/27	01/30
02/28	01/16	02/28	01/27	02/28	02/08	02/29	01/20	02/28	02/01
03/13	01/29	03/03	01/30	03/22	02/30	03/10	01/30	03/28	02/29
03/31	02/18	03/31	02/28	03/31	02/09	03/31	02/21	03/31	03/03
04/11	02/29	04/01	02/29	04/20	02/29	04/08	02/29	04/27	03/30
04/30	03/19	04/30	03/29	04/30	03/10	04/30	03/22	04/30	04/03
05/11	03/30	05/30	04/30	05/19	03/29	05/08	03/30	05/27	04/30
05/31	04/20	05/31	05/01	05/31	04/12	05/31	04/23	05/31	05/04
06/09	04/29	06/28	05/29	06/18	04/30	06/06	04/29	06/25	05/29
06/30	05/21	06/30	06/02	06/30	05/12	06/30	05/24	06/30	06/05
07/08	05/29	07/27	06/29	07/17	05/29	07/06	05/30	07/25	06/30
07/31	06/23	07/31	07/04	07/31	06/14	07/31	06/25	07/31	07/06
08/07	06/30	08/26	07/30	08/15	06/29	08/04	06/29	08/23	07/29
08/31	07/24	08/31	08/05	08/31	07/16	08/31	07/27	08/31	07/08
09/05	07/29	09/24	08/29	09/14	07/30	09/02	07/29	09/21	07/29
09/30	08/25	09/30	09/06	09/30	08/16	09/30	08/28	09/30	08/09
10/05	08/30	10/24	09/30	10/13	08/29	10/02	08/30	10/21	08/30
10/31	09/26	10/31	10/07	10/31	09/18	10/31	09/29	10/31	09/10
11/04	09/30	11/23	10/30	11/12	09/30	11/01	10/01	11/19	09/29
11/30	10/26	11/30	11/07	11/30	10/18	11/30	10/30	11/30	10/11
12/04	10/30	12/22	11/29	12/11	10/29	12/29	11/29	12/19	10/30
12/31	11/27	12/31	12/09	12/31	11/20	12/31	12/02	12/31	11/12

1950 Chinese		1951 Chinese		1952 Chinese		1953 Chinese		1954 Chinese	
mm/dd	mm/dd	mm/dd	mm/dd	mm/dd	mm/dd	mm/dd	mm/dd	mm/dd	mm/dd
01/17	11/29	01/07	11/30	01/26	12/30	01/14	11/29	01/04	11/30
01/31	12/14	01/31	12/24	01/31	01/05	01/31	12/17	01/31	12/27
02/16	12/30	02/05	12/29	02/24	01/29	02/13	12/30	02/02	12/29
02/28	01/12	02/28	01/23	02/29	02/05	02/28	01/15	02/28	01/26
03/17	01/29	03/07	01/30	03/25	02/30	03/14	01/29	03/04	01/30
03/31	02/14	03/31	02/24	03/31	03/06	03/31	02/17	03/31	02/27
04/16	02/30	04/05	02/29	04/23	03/29	04/13	02/30	04/02	02/29
04/30	03/14	04/30	03/25	04/30	04/07	04/30	03/17	04/30	03/28
05/16	03/30	05/05	03/30	05/23	04/30	05/12	03/29	05/02	03/30
05/31	04/15	05/31	04/26	05/31	05/08	05/31	04/19	05/31	04/29
06/14	04/29	06/04	04/30	06/21	05/29	06/10	04/29	06/29	05/29
06/30	05/16	06/30	05/26	06/30	05/09	06/30	05/20	06/30	06/01
07/14	05/30	07/03	05/29	07/21	05/30	07/10	05/30	07/29	06/30
07/31	06/17	07/31	06/28	07/31	06/10	07/31	06/21	07/31	07/02
08/13	06/30	08/02	06/30	08/19	06/29	08/09	06/30	08/27	07/29
08/31	07/18	08/31	07/29	08/31	07/12	08/31	07/22	08/31	08/04
09/11	07/29	09/01	08/01	09/18	07/30	09/07	07/29	09/26	08/30
09/30	08/19	09/30	08/30	09/30	08/12	09/30	08/23	09/30	09/04
10/10	08/29	10/29	09/29	10/18	08/30	10/07	08/30	10/26	09/30
10/31	09/21	10/31	10/02	10/31	09/13	10/31	09/24	10/31	10/05
11/09	09/30	11/28	10/30	11/16	09/29	11/06	09/30	11/25	10/30
11/30	10/21	11/30	11/02	11/30	10/14	11/30	10/24	11/30	11/05
12/08	10/29	12/27	11/29	12/16	10/30	12/05	10/29	12/24	11/29
12/31	11/23	12/31	12/04	12/31	11/15	12/31	11/26	12/31	12/07

1955 Chinese mm/dd mm/dd		1956 Chinese mm/dd mm/dd		1957 Chinese mm/dd mm/dd		1958 Chinese mm/dd mm/dd		1959 Chinese mm/dd mm/dd	
01/23	12/30	01/12	11/30	01/30	12/30	01/19	11/30	01/08	11/29
01/31	01/08	01/31	12/19	01/31	01/01	01/31	12/12	01/31	12/23
02/21	01/29	02/11	12/30	02/01	01/02	02/17	12/29	02/07	12/30
02/28	02/07	02/29	01/18	02/28	01/29	02/28	01/11	02/28	01/21
03/23	02/30	03/11	01/29	03/01	01/30	03/19	01/30	03/08	01/29
03/31	03/08	03/31	02/20	03/30	02/29	03/31	02/12	03/31	02/23
04/21	03/29	04/10	02/30	03/31	03/01	04/18	02/30	04/07	02/30
04/30	03/09	04/30	03/20	04/29	03/30	04/30	03/12	04/30	03/23
05/21	03/30	05/09	03/29	04/30	04/01	05/18	03/30	05/07	03/30
05/31	04/10	05/31	04/22	05/28	04/29	05/31	04/13	05/31	04/24
06/19	04/29	06/08	04/30	05/31	05/03	06/16	04/29	06/05	04/29
06/30	05/11	06/30	05/22	06/27	05/30	06/30	05/14	06/30	05/25
07/18	05/29	07/07	05/29	06/30	06/03	07/16	05/30	07/05	05/30
07/31	06/13	07/31	06/24	07/26	06/29	07/31	06/15	07/31	06/26
08/17	06/30	08/05	06/29	07/31	07/05	08/14	06/29	08/03	06/29
08/31	07/14	08/31	07/26	08/24	07/29	08/31	07/17	08/31	07/28
09/15	07/29	09/04	07/30	08/31	08/07	09/12	07/29	09/02	07/30
09/30	08/15	09/30	08/26	09/23	08/30	09/30	08/18	09/30	08/28
10/15	08/30	10/03	08/29	09/30	08/07	10/12	08/30	10/01	08/29
10/31	09/16	10/31	09/28	10/22	08/29	10/31	09/19	10/31	09/30
11/13	09/29	11/02	09/30	10/31	09/09	11/10	09/29	11/29	10/29
11/30	10/17	11/30	10/28	11/21	09/30	11/30	10/20	11/30	11/01
12/13	10/30	12/02	10/30	11/30	10/09	12/10	10/30	12/29	11/30
12/31	11/18	12/31	11/29	12/20	10/29	12/31	11/21	12/31	12/02
				12/31	11/11				

1960 Chinese mm/dd mm/dd	1961 Chinese mm/dd mm/dd	1962 Chinese mm/dd mm/dd	1963 Chinese mm/dd mm/dd	1964 Chinese mm/dd mm/dd
01/27 12/29	01/16 11/30	01/05 11/29	01/24 12/29	01/14 11/30
01/31 01/04	01/31 12/15	01/31 12/26	01/31 01/07	01/31 12/17
02/26 01/30	02/14 12/29	02/04 12/30	02/23 01/30	02/12 12/29
02/29 02/03	02/28 01/14	02/28 01/24	02/28 02/05	02/29 01/17
03/26 02/29	03/16 01/30	03/05 01/29	03/24 02/29	03/13 01/30
03/31 03/05	03/31 02/15	03/31 02/26	03/31 03/07	03/31 02/18
04/25 03/30	04/14 02/29	04/04 02/30	04/23 03/30	04/11 02/29
04/30 04/05	04/30 03/16	04/30 03/26	04/30 04/07	04/30 03/19
05/24 04/29	05/14 03/30	05/03 03/29	05/22 04/29	05/11 03/30
05/31 05/07	05/31 04/17	05/31 04/28	05/31 04/09	05/31 04/20
06/23 05/30	06/12 04/29	06/01 04/29	06/20 04/29	06/09 04/29
06/30 06/07	06/30 05/18	06/30 05/29	06/30 05/10	06/30 05/21
07/23 06/30	07/12 05/30	07/01 05/30	07/20 05/30	07/08 05/29
07/31 06/08	07/31 06/19	07/30 06/29	07/31 06/11	07/31 06/23
08/21 06/29	08/10 06/29	07/31 07/01	08/18 06/29	08/07 06/30
08/31 07/10	08/31 07/21	08/29 07/30	08/31 07/13	08/31 07/24
09/20 07/30	09/09 07/30	08/31 08/02	09/17 07/30	09/05 07/29
09/30 08/10	09/30 08/21	09/28 08/30	09/30 08/13	09/30 08/25
10/19 08/29	10/09 08/30	09/30 09/02	10/16 08/29	10/05 08/30
10/31 09/12	10/31 09/22	10/27 09/29	10/31 09/15	10/31 09/26
11/18 09/30	11/07 09/29	10/31 10/04	11/15 09/30	11/03 09/29
11/30 10/12	11/30 10/23	11/26 10/30	11/30 10/15	11/30 10/27
12/17 10/29	12/07 10/30	11/30 11/04	12/15 10/30	12/03 10/30
12/31 11/14	12/31 11/24	12/26 11/30	12/31 11/16	12/31 11/28
		12/31 12/05		

1965 Chinese		1966 Chinese		1967 Chinese		1968 Chinese		1969 Chinese	
mm/dd	mm/dd	mm/dd	mm/dd	mm/dd	mm/dd	mm/dd	mm/dd	mm/dd	mm/dd
01/02	11/30	01/20	12/29	01/10	11/30	01/29	12/30	01/17	11/29
01/31	12/29	01/31	01/11	01/31	12/21	01/31	01/02	01/31	12/14
02/01	12/30	02/19	01/30	02/08	12/29	02/27	01/29	02/16	12/30
02/28	01/27	02/28	02/09	02/28	01/20	02/29	02/02	02/28	01/12
03/02	01/29	03/21	02/30	03/10	01/30	03/28	02/30	03/17	01/29
03/31	02/29	03/31	03/10	03/31	02/21	03/31	03/03	03/31	02/14
04/01	02/30	04/20	03/30	04/09	02/30	04/26	03/29	04/16	02/30
04/30	03/29	04/30	03/10	04/30	03/21	04/30	04/04	04/30	03/14
05/30	04/30	05/19	03/29	05/08	03/29	05/26	04/30	05/15	03/29
05/31	05/01	05/31	04/12	05/31	04/23	05/31	05/05	05/31	04/16
06/28	05/29	06/18	04/30	06/07	04/30	06/25	05/30	06/14	04/30
06/30	06/02	06/30	05/12	06/30	05/23	06/30	06/05	06/30	05/16
07/27	06/29	07/17	05/29	07/07	05/30	07/24	06/29	07/13	05/29
07/31	07/04	07/31	06/14	07/31	06/24	07/31	07/07	07/31	06/18
08/26	07/30	08/15	06/29	08/05	06/29	08/23	07/30	08/12	06/30
08/31	08/05	08/31	07/16	08/31	07/26	08/31	07/08	08/31	07/19
09/24	08/29	09/14	07/30	09/03	07/29	09/21	07/29	09/11	07/30
09/30	09/06	09/30	08/16	09/30	08/27	09/30	08/09	09/30	08/19
10/23	09/29	10/13	08/29	10/03	08/30	10/21	08/30	10/10	08/29
10/31	10/08	10/31	09/18	10/31	09/28	10/31	09/10	10/31	09/21
11/22	10/30	11/11	09/29	11/01	09/29	11/19	09/29	11/09	09/30
11/30	11/08	11/30	10/19	11/30	10/29	11/30	10/11	11/30	10/21
12/22	11/30	12/11	10/30	12/01	10/30	12/19	10/30	12/08	10/29
12/31	12/09	12/31	11/20	12/30	11/29	12/31	11/12	12/31	11/23
				12/31	12/01				

1970 Chinese mm/dd mm/dd	1971 Chinese mm/dd mm/dd	1972 Chinese mm/dd mm/dd	1973 Chinese mm/dd mm/dd	1974 Chinese mm/dd mm/dd
01/07 11/30	01/26 12/30	01/15 11/29	01/03 11/29	01/22 12/30
01/31 12/24	01/31 01/05	01/31 12/16	01/31 12/28	01/31 01/09
02/05 12/29	02/24 01/29	02/14 12/30	02/02 12/30	02/21 01/30
02/28 01/23	02/28 02/04	02/29 01/15	02/28 01/26	02/28 02/07
03/07 01/30	03/26 02/30	03/14 01/29	03/04 01/30	03/23 02/30
03/31 02/24	03/31 03/05	03/31 02/17	03/31 02/27	03/31 03/08
04/05 02/29	04/24 03/29	04/13 02/30	04/02 02/29	04/21 03/29
04/30 03/25	04/30 04/06	04/30 03/17	04/30 03/28	04/30 04/09
05/04 03/29	05/23 04/29	05/12 03/29	05/02 03/30	05/21 04/30
05/31 04/27	05/31 05/08	05/31 04/19	05/31 04/29	05/31 04/10
06/03 04/30	06/22 05/30	06/10 04/29	06/29 05/29	06/19 04/29
06/30 05/27	06/30 05/08	06/30 05/20	06/30 06/01	06/30 05/11
07/02 05/29	07/21 05/29	07/10 05/30	07/29 06/30	07/18 05/29
07/31 06/29	07/31 06/10	07/31 06/21	07/31 07/02	07/31 06/13
08/01 06/30	08/20 06/30	08/08 06/29	08/27 07/29	08/17 06/30
08/31 07/30	08/31 07/11	08/31 07/23	08/31 08/04	08/31 07/14
09/29 08/29	09/18 07/29	09/07 07/30	09/25 08/29	09/15 07/29
09/30 09/01	09/30 08/12	09/30 08/23	09/30 09/05	09/30 08/15
10/29 09/30	10/18 08/30	10/06 08/29	10/25 09/30	10/14 08/29
10/31 10/02	10/31 09/13	10/31 09/25	10/31 10/06	10/31 09/17
11/28 10/30	11/17 09/30	11/05 09/30	11/24 10/30	11/13 09/30
11/30 11/02	11/30 10/13	11/30 10/25	11/30 11/06	11/30 10/17
12/27 11/29	12/17 10/30	12/05 10/30	12/23 11/29	12/13 10/30
12/31 12/04	12/31 11/14	12/31 11/26	12/31 12/08	12/31 11/18

1975 Chinese		1976 Chinese		1977 Chinese		1978 Chinese		1979 Chinese	
mm/dd	mm/dd	mm/dd	mm/dd	mm/dd	mm/dd	mm/dd	mm/dd	mm/dd	mm/dd
01/11	11/29	01/30	12/30	01/18	11/29	01/08	11/29	01/27	12/29
01/31	12/20	01/31	01/01	01/31	12/13	01/31	12/23	01/31	01/04
02/10	12/30	02/01	01/02	02/17	12/30	02/06	12/29	02/26	01/30
02/28	01/18	02/29	01/30	02/28	01/11	02/28	01/22	02/28	02/02
03/12	01/30	03/30	02/30	03/19	01/30	03/08	01/30	03/27	02/29
03/31	02/19	03/31	03/01	03/31	02/12	03/31	02/23	03/31	03/04
04/11	02/30	04/28	03/29	04/17	02/29	04/06	02/29	04/25	03/29
04/30	03/19	04/30	04/02	04/30	03/13	04/30	03/24	04/30	04/05
05/10	03/29	05/28	04/30	05/17	03/30	05/06	03/30	05/25	04/30
05/31	04/21	05/31	05/03	05/31	04/14	05/31	04/25	05/31	05/06
06/09	04/30	06/26	05/29	06/16	04/30	06/05	04/30	06/23	05/29
06/30	05/21	06/30	06/04	06/30	05/14	06/30	05/25	06/30	06/07
07/08	05/29	07/26	06/30	07/15	05/29	07/04	05/29	07/23	06/30
07/31	06/23	07/31	07/05	07/31	06/16	07/31	06/27	07/31	06/08
08/06	06/29	08/24	07/29	08/14	06/30	08/03	06/30	08/22	06/30
08/31	07/25	08/31	08/07	08/31	07/17	08/31	07/28	08/31	07/09
09/05	07/30	09/23	08/30	09/12	07/29	09/01	07/29	09/20	07/29
09/30	08/25	09/30	08/07	09/30	08/18	09/30	08/29	09/30	08/10
10/04	08/29	10/22	08/29	10/12	08/30	10/01	08/30	10/20	08/30
10/31	09/27	10/31	09/09	10/31	09/19	10/31	09/30	10/31	09/11
11/02	09/29	11/20	09/29	11/10	09/29	11/29	10/29	11/19	09/30
11/30	10/28	11/30	10/10	11/30	10/20	11/30	11/01	11/30	10/11
12/02	10/30	12/20	10/30	12/10	10/30	12/29	11/30	12/18	10/29
12/31	11/29	12/31	11/11	12/31	11/21	12/31	12/02	12/31	11/13

1980 Chinese mm/dd mm/dd	1981 Chinese mm/dd mm/dd	1982 Chinese mm/dd mm/dd	1983 Chinese mm/dd mm/dd	1984 Chinese mm/dd mm/dd
01/17 11/30	01/05 11/30	01/24 12/30	01/13 11/30	01/02 11/30
01/31 12/14	01/31 12/26	01/31 01/07	01/31 12/18	01/31 12/29
02/15 12/29	02/04 12/30	02/23 01/30	02/12 12/30	02/01 12/30
02/29 01/14	02/28 01/24	02/28 02/05	02/28 01/16	02/29 01/28
03/16 01/30	03/05 01/29	03/24 02/29	03/14 01/30	03/02 01/30
03/31 02/15	03/31 02/26	03/31 03/07	03/31 02/17	03/31 02/29
04/14 02/29	04/04 02/30	04/23 03/30	04/12 02/29	04/01 03/01
04/30 03/16	04/30 03/26	04/30 04/07	04/30 03/18	04/30 03/30
05/13 03/29	05/03 03/29	05/22 04/29	05/12 03/30	05/30 04/30
05/31 04/18	05/31 04/28	05/31 04/09	05/31 04/19	05/31 05/01
06/12 04/30	06/01 04/29	06/20 04/29	06/10 04/29	06/28 05/29
06/30 05/18	06/30 05/29	06/30 05/10	06/30 05/20	06/30 06/02
07/11 05/29	07/01 05/30	07/20 05/30	07/09 05/29	07/27 06/29
07/31 06/20	07/30 06/29	07/31 06/11	07/31 06/22	07/31 07/04
08/10 06/30	07/31 07/01	08/18 06/29	08/08 06/30	08/26 07/30
08/31 07/21	08/28 07/29	08/31 07/13	08/31 07/23	08/31 08/05
09/08 07/29	08/31 08/03	09/16 07/29	09/06 07/29	09/24 08/29
09/30 08/22	09/27 08/30	09/30 08/14	09/30 08/24	09/30 09/06
10/08 08/30	09/30 09/03	10/16 08/30	10/05 08/29	10/23 09/29
10/31 09/23	10/27 09/30	10/31 09/15	10/31 09/26	10/31 10/08
11/07 09/30	10/31 10/04	11/14 09/29	11/04 09/30	11/22 10/30
11/30 10/23	11/25 10/29	11/30 10/16	11/30 10/26	11/30 10/08
12/06 10/29	11/30 11/05	12/14 10/30	12/03 10/29	12/21 10/29
12/31 11/25	12/25 11/30	12/31 11/17	12/31 11/28	12/31 11/10
	12/31 12/06			

| 1985 Chinese | | 1986 Chinese | | 1987 Chinese | | 1988 Chinese | | 1989 Chinese | |
mm/dd	mm/dd	mm/dd	mm/dd	mm/dd	mm/dd	mm/dd	mm/dd	mm/dd	mm/dd
01/20	11/30	01/09	11/29	01/28	12/29	01/18	11/29	01/07	11/30
01/31	12/11	01/31	12/22	01/31	01/03	01/31	12/13	01/31	12/24
02/19	12/30	02/08	12/30	02/27	01/30	02/16	12/29	02/05	12/29
02/28	01/09	02/28	01/20	02/28	02/01	02/29	01/13	02/28	01/23
03/20	01/29	03/09	01/29	03/28	02/29	03/17	01/30	03/07	01/30
03/31	02/11	03/31	02/22	03/31	03/03	03/31	02/14	03/31	02/24
04/19	02/30	04/08	02/30	04/27	03/30	04/15	02/29	04/05	02/29
04/30	03/11	04/30	03/22	04/30	04/03	04/30	03/15	04/30	03/25
05/19	03/30	05/08	03/30	05/26	04/29	05/15	03/30	05/04	03/29
05/31	04/12	05/31	04/23	05/31	05/05	05/31	04/16	05/31	04/27
06/17	04/29	06/06	04/29	06/25	05/30	06/13	04/29	06/03	04/30
06/30	05/13	06/30	05/24	06/30	06/05	06/30	05/17	06/30	05/27
07/17	05/30	07/06	05/30	07/25	06/30	07/13	05/30	07/02	05/29
07/31	06/14	07/31	06/25	07/31	06/06	07/31	06/18	07/31	06/29
08/15	06/29	08/05	06/30	08/23	06/29	08/11	06/29	08/01	06/30
08/31	07/16	08/31	07/26	08/31	07/08	08/31	07/20	08/30	07/29
09/14	07/30	09/03	07/29	09/22	07/30	09/10	07/30	08/31	08/01
09/30	08/16	09/30	08/27	09/30	08/08	09/30	08/20	09/29	08/30
10/13	08/29	10/03	08/30	10/22	08/30	10/10	08/30	09/30	09/01
10/31	09/18	10/31	09/28	10/31	09/09	10/31	09/21	10/28	09/29
11/11	09/29	11/01	09/29	11/20	09/29	11/08	09/29	10/31	10/03
11/30	10/19	11/30	10/29	11/30	10/10	11/30	10/22	11/27	10/30
12/11	10/30	12/01	10/30	12/20	10/30	12/08	10/30	11/30	11/03
12/31	11/20	12/30	11/29	12/31	11/11	12/31	11/23	12/27	11/30
		12/31	12/01					12/31	12/04

1990 mm/dd	Chinese mm/dd	1991 mm/dd	Chinese mm/dd	1992 mm/dd	Chinese mm/dd	1993 mm/dd	Chinese mm/dd	1994 mm/dd	Chinese mm/dd
01/26	12/30	01/15	11/30	01/04	11/30	01/22	12/30	01/11	11/30
01/31	01/05	01/31	12/16	01/31	12/27	01/31	01/09	01/31	12/20
02/24	01/29	02/14	12/30	02/03	12/30	02/20	01/29	02/09	12/29
02/28	02/04	02/28	01/14	02/29	01/26	02/28	02/08	02/28	01/19
03/26	02/30	03/15	01/29	03/03	01/29	03/22	02/30	03/11	01/30
03/31	03/05	03/31	02/16	03/31	02/28	03/31	03/09	03/31	02/20
04/24	03/29	04/14	02/30	04/02	02/30	04/21	03/30	04/10	02/30
04/30	04/06	04/30	03/16	04/30	03/28	04/30	03/09	04/30	03/20
05/23	04/29	05/13	03/29	05/02	03/30	05/20	03/29	05/10	03/30
05/31	05/08	05/31	04/18	05/31	04/29	05/31	04/11	05/31	04/21
06/22	05/30	06/11	04/29	06/29	05/29	06/19	04/30	06/08	04/29
06/30	05/08	06/30	05/19	06/30	06/01	06/30	05/11	06/30	05/22
07/21	05/29	07/11	05/30	07/29	06/30	07/18	05/29	07/08	05/30
07/31	06/10	07/31	06/20	07/31	07/02	07/31	06/13	07/31	06/23
08/19	06/29	08/09	06/29	08/27	07/29	08/17	06/30	08/06	06/29
08/31	07/12	08/31	07/22	08/31	08/04	08/31	07/14	08/31	07/25
09/18	07/30	09/07	07/29	09/25	08/29	09/15	07/29	09/05	07/30
09/30	08/12	09/30	08/23	09/30	09/05	09/30	08/15	09/30	08/25
10/17	08/29	10/07	08/30	10/25	09/30	10/14	08/29	10/04	08/29
10/31	09/14	10/31	09/24	10/31	10/06	10/31	09/17	10/31	09/27
11/16	09/30	11/05	09/29	11/23	10/29	11/13	09/30	11/02	09/29
11/30	10/14	11/30	10/25	11/30	11/07	11/30	10/17	11/30	10/28
12/16	10/30	12/05	10/30	12/23	11/30	12/12	10/29	12/02	10/30
12/31	11/15	12/31	11/26	12/31	12/08	12/31	11/19	12/31	11/29

| 1995 Chinese | | 1996 Chinese | | 1997 Chinese | | 1998 Chinese | | 1999 Chinese | |
mm/dd	mm/dd	mm/dd	mm/dd	mm/dd	mm/dd	mm/dd	mm/dd	mm/dd	mm/dd
01/30	12/30	01/19	11/29	01/08	11/29	01/27	12/29	01/16	11/29
01/31	01/01	01/31	12/12	01/31	12/23	01/31	01/04	01/31	12/15
02/01	01/02	02/18	12/30	02/06	12/29	02/26	01/30	02/15	12/30
02/28	01/29	02/29	01/11	02/28	01/22	02/28	02/02	02/28	01/13
03/30	02/30	03/18	01/29	03/08	01/30	03/27	02/29	03/17	01/30
03/31	03/01	03/31	02/13	03/31	02/23	03/31	03/04	03/31	02/14
04/29	03/30	04/17	02/30	04/06	02/29	04/25	03/29	04/15	02/29
04/30	04/01	04/30	03/13	04/30	03/24	04/30	04/05	04/30	03/15
05/28	04/29	05/16	03/29	05/06	03/30	05/25	04/30	05/14	03/29
05/31	05/03	05/31	04/15	05/31	04/25	05/31	05/06	05/31	04/17
06/27	05/30	06/15	04/30	06/04	04/29	06/23	05/29	06/13	04/30
06/30	06/03	06/30	05/15	06/30	05/26	06/30	05/07	06/30	05/17
07/26	06/29	07/14	05/29	07/04	05/30	07/22	05/29	07/12	05/29
07/31	07/05	07/31	06/17	07/31	06/27	07/31	06/09	07/31	06/19
08/25	07/30	08/13	06/30	08/02	06/29	08/21	06/30	08/10	06/29
08/31	08/06	08/31	07/18	08/31	07/29	08/31	07/10	08/31	07/21
09/24	08/30	09/11	07/29	09/01	07/30	09/20	07/30	09/09	07/30
09/30	08/06	09/30	08/19	09/30	08/29	09/30	08/10	09/30	08/21
10/23	08/29	10/11	08/30	10/01	08/30	10/19	08/29	10/08	08/29
10/31	09/08	10/31	09/20	10/30	09/29	10/31	09/12	10/31	09/23
11/21	09/29	11/10	09/30	10/31	10/01	11/18	09/30	11/07	09/30
11/30	10/09	11/30	10/20	11/29	10/30	11/30	10/12	11/30	10/23
12/21	10/30	12/10	10/30	11/30	11/01	12/18	10/30	12/07	10/30
12/31	11/10	12/31	11/21	12/29	11/30	12/31	11/13	12/31	11/24
				12/31	12/02				

2000 mm/dd	Chinese mm/dd	2001 mm/dd	Chinese mm/dd	2002 mm/dd	Chinese mm/dd	2003 mm/dd	Chinese mm/dd	2004 mm/dd	Chinese mm/dd
01/06	11/30	01/23	12/29	01/12	11/29	01/02	11/30	01/21	12/30
01/31	12/25	01/31	01/08	01/31	12/19	01/31	12/29	01/31	01/10
02/04	12/29	02/22	01/30	02/11	12/30	02/01	01/01	02/19	01/29
02/29	01/25	02/28	02/06	02/28	01/17	02/28	01/28	02/29	02/10
03/05	01/30	03/24	02/30	03/13	01/30	03/02	01/30	03/20	02/30
03/31	02/26	03/31	03/07	03/31	02/18	03/31	02/29	03/31	02/11
04/04	02/30	04/22	03/29	04/12	02/30	04/01	02/30	04/18	02/29
04/30	03/26	04/30	04/08	04/30	03/18	04/30	03/29	04/30	03/12
05/03	03/29	05/22	04/30	05/11	03/29	05/30	04/30	05/18	03/30
05/31	04/28	05/31	04/09	05/31	04/20	05/31	05/01	05/31	04/13
06/01	04/29	06/20	04/29	06/10	04/30	06/29	05/30	06/17	04/30
06/30	05/29	06/30	05/10	06/30	05/20	06/30	06/01	06/30	05/13
07/30	06/29	07/20	05/30	07/09	05/29	07/28	06/29	07/16	05/29
07/31	07/01	07/31	06/11	07/31	06/22	07/31	07/03	07/31	06/15
08/28	07/29	08/18	06/29	08/08	06/30	08/27	07/30	08/15	06/30
08/31	08/03	08/31	07/13	08/31	07/23	08/31	08/04	08/31	07/16
09/27	08/30	09/16	07/29	09/06	07/29	09/25	08/29	09/13	07/29
09/30	09/03	09/30	08/14	09/30	08/24	09/30	09/05	09/30	08/17
10/26	09/29	10/16	08/30	10/05	08/29	10/24	09/29	10/13	08/30
10/31	10/05	10/31	09/15	10/31	09/26	10/31	10/07	10/31	09/18
11/25	10/30	11/14	09/29	11/04	09/30	11/23	10/30	11/11	09/29
11/30	11/05	11/30	10/16	11/30	10/26	11/30	11/07	11/30	10/19
12/25	11/30	12/14	10/30	12/03	10/29	12/22	11/29	12/11	10/30
12/31	12/06	12/31	11/17	12/31	11/28	12/31	12/09	12/31	11/20

2005 Chinese mm/dd mm/dd	2006 Chinese mm/dd mm/dd	2007 Chinese mm/dd mm/dd	2008 Chinese mm/dd mm/dd	2009 Chinese mm/dd mm/dd
01/09 11/29	01/28 12/29	01/18 11/30	01/07 11/29	01/25 12/30
01/31 12/22	01/31 01/03	01/31 12/13	01/31 12/24	01/31 01/06
02/08 12/30	02/27 01/30	02/17 12/30	02/06 12/30	02/24 01/30
02/28 01/20	02/28 02/01	02/28 01/11	02/29 01/23	02/28 02/04
03/09 01/29	03/28 02/29	03/18 01/29	03/07 01/30	03/26 02/30
03/31 02/22	03/31 03/03	03/31 02/13	03/31 02/24	03/31 03/05
04/08 02/30	04/27 03/30	04/16 02/29	04/05 02/29	04/24 03/29
04/30 03/22	04/30 04/03	04/30 03/14	04/30 03/25	04/30 04/06
05/07 03/29	05/26 04/29	05/16 03/30	05/04 03/29	05/23 04/29
05/31 04/24	05/31 05/05	05/31 04/15	05/31 04/27	05/31 05/08
06/06 04/30	06/25 05/30	06/14 04/29	06/03 04/30	06/22 05/30
06/30 05/24	06/30 06/05	06/30 05/16	06/30 05/27	06/30 05/08
07/05 05/29	07/24 06/29	07/13 05/29	07/02 05/29	07/21 05/29
07/31 06/26	07/31 07/07	07/31 06/18	07/31 06/29	07/31 06/10
08/04 06/30	08/23 07/30	08/12 06/30	08/30 07/30	08/19 06/29
08/31 07/27	08/31 07/08	08/31 07/19	08/31 08/01	08/31 07/12
09/03 07/30	09/21 07/29	09/10 07/29	09/28 08/29	09/18 07/30
09/30 08/27	09/30 08/09	09/30 08/20	09/30 09/02	09/30 08/12
10/02 08/29	10/21 08/30	10/10 08/30	10/28 09/30	10/17 08/29
10/31 09/29	10/31 09/10	10/31 09/21	10/31 10/03	10/31 09/14
11/01 09/30	11/20 09/30	11/09 09/30	11/27 10/30	11/16 09/30
11/30 10/29	11/30 10/10	11/30 10/21	11/30 11/03	11/30 10/14
12/30 11/30	12/19 10/29	12/09 10/30	12/26 11/29	12/15 10/29
12/31 12/01	12/31 11/12	12/31 11/22	12/31 12/05	12/31 11/16

Simplified table of Chinese years

To illustrate the calculation that follows, we will take as an example the date of February 1st 2000 at 2 a.m. as your date and time of birth.

So write down your year, your Chinese month and day of birth as well as your time of birth in the middle square:

December 26th, 2000 at 2 a.m.

6. Snake	**7. Horse**	**8. Goat**	**9. Monkey**
5. Dragon			**10. Rooster**
4. Rabbit	Date, time of birth: Dec. 26, 2000 2 a.m.		**11. Dog**
3. Tiger	**2. Ox**	**1. Rat**	**12. Pig**

(2) Find your palace of Life and the other 11 palaces.

To find out the palace of Life, consult the following table by using your Chinese month of birth (the columns) and time of birth (the rows), the intersection of the two is the square where your palace of Life is located. Write it down in the corresponding square.

Depending on which square is your palace of Life, it is associated with an element.

- If it is in square 1 or 12, it is associated with the element of water.

- If it is in square 2 or 5 or 8 or 11, it is associated with the element of earth.

- If it is in square 3 or 4, it is associated with the element of wood.

- If it is in square 6 or 7, it is associated with the element of fire.

- If it is in square 9 or 10, it is associated with the element of metal.

Write it down in the middle square.

Month of birth → Time of birth ↓	1	2	3	4	5	6	7	8	9	10	11	12
23h - 1h	3	4	5	6	7	8	9	10	11	12	1	2
1h - 3h	2	3	4	5	6	7	8	9	10	11	12	1
3h - 5h	1	2	3	4	5	6	7	8	9	10	11	12
5h - 7h	12	1	2	3	4	5	6	7	8	9	10	11
7h - 9h	11	12	1	2	3	4	5	6	7	8	9	10
9h - 11h	10	11	12	1	2	3	4	5	6	7	8	9
11h - 13h	9	10	11	12	1	2	3	4	5	6	7	8
13h - 15h	8	9	10	11	12	1	2	3	4	5	6	7
15h - 17h	7	8	9	10	11	12	1	2	3	4	5	6
17h - 19h	6	7	8	9	10	11	12	1	2	3	4	5
19h - 21h	5	6	7	8	9	10	11	12	1	2	3	4
21h - 23h	4	5	6	7	8	9	10	11	12	1	2	3

Table to find the palace of Life

Once you have found your palace of Life, starting from this square and go clockwise, write down in order in the 11 remaining squares the following 11 palaces: Parents, Happiness, Property, Career, Friends, Travels, Health, Finances, Children, Spouse, Brothers.

Ex: In your case, it will be the intersection of column 12 (Chinese month of birth December) and row 1h - 3h (time of birth 2 a.m.), therefore your palace of Life is located in square 1.

Friends **6. Snake**	Travels **7. Horse**	Health **8. Goat**	Finances **9. Monkey**
Career **5. Dragon**	Element of the palace of Life: Water		Children **10. Rooster**
Property **4. Rabbit**	Date, time of birth: Dec. 26, 2000 2 a.m.		Spouse **11. Dog**
Happiness **3. Tiger**	Parents **2. Ox**	Life **1. Rat**	Brothers **12. Pig**

(3) Find the position of your Body.

Consult the following table by using your Chinese month of birth and time of birth. The intersection of the two is the square where your Body is located. Write it down in the corresponding square.

Month of birth → Time of birth ↓	1	2	3	4	5	6	7	8	9	10	11	12
23h - 1h	3	4	5	6	7	8	9	10	11	12	1	2
1h - 3h	4	5	6	7	8	9	10	11	12	1	2	3
3h - 5h	5	6	7	8	9	10	11	12	1	2	3	4
5h - 7h	6	7	8	9	10	11	12	1	2	3	4	5
7h - 9h	7	8	9	10	11	12	1	2	3	4	5	6
9h - 11h	8	9	10	11	12	1	2	3	4	5	6	7
11h - 13h	9	10	11	12	1	2	3	4	5	6	7	8
13h - 15h	10	11	12	1	2	3	4	5	6	7	8	9
15h - 17h	11	12	1	2	3	4	5	6	7	8	9	10
17h - 19h	12	1	2	3	4	5	6	7	8	9	10	11
19h - 21h	1	2	3	4	5	6	7	8	9	10	11	12
21h - 23h	2	3	4	5	6	7	8	9	10	11	12	1

Table to find the body

Ex: In your case, it will be the intersection of column 12 (Chinese month of birth December) and row 1h - 3h (time of birth 2 a.m.). Therefore your Body is located in square 3.

Friends **6. Snake**	Travels **7. Horse**	Health **8. Goat**	Finances **9. Monkey**
Career **5. Dragon**	Element of the palace of Life: Water Date, time of birth: Dec. 26, 2000 2 a.m.		Children **10. Rooster**
Property **4. Rabbit**			Spouse **11. Dog**
The body Happiness **3. Tiger**	Parents **2. Ox**	Life **1. Rat**	Brothers **12. Pig**

(4) Position the star of the King.

To position the star of the King, you must first find the element of your "situation". To do that, look in the "years table for sky chart" the alphabet letter which corresponds to your year of birth (Chinese years are composed of 10 Heavenly Stems from A to J and of 12 Earthly Branches from rat to pig), using this letter and the number of the square of your palace of Life which you have found in step 2, then consult the "situation" table. The intersection of the two is the element of your "situation".

Then using this element and your Chinese day of birth, find in the following star of the King table the location of the King - the intersection of the element and the day.

Write it down in the square. Write down in the middle square the alphabet letter and the element associated with your year according to the sky chart (in the "years table for sky chart"). You will need them later.

SIGN	STEM	SKY CHART ELEMENT	YEAR
Rat	G	Earth	1900/01/31 to 1901/02/18
Ox	H	Earth	1901/02/19 to 1902/02/07
Tiger	I	Metal	1902/02/08 to 1903/01/28
Rabbit	J	Metal	1903/01/29 to 1904/02/15
Dragon	A	Fire	1904/02/16 to 1905/02/03
Snake	B	Fire	1905/02/04 to 1906/01/24
Horse	C	Water	1906/01/25 to 1907/02/12
Goat	D	Water	1907/02/13 to 1908/02/01
Monkey	E	Earth	1908/02/02 to 1909/01/21
Rooster	F	Earth	1909/01/22 to 1910/02/09
Dog	G	Metal	1910/02/10 to 1911/01/29
Pig	H	Metal	1911/01/30 to 1912/02/17
Rat	I	Wood	1912/02/18 to 1913/02/05
Ox	J	Wood	1913/02/06 to 1914/01/25
Tiger	A	Water	1914/01/26 to 1915/02/13
Rabbit	B	Water	1915/02/14 to 1916/02/02
Dragon	C	Earth	1916/02/03 to 1917/01/22
Snake	D	Earth	1917/01/23 to 1918/02/10
Horse	E	Fire	1918/02/11 to 1919/01/31
Goat	F	Fire	1919/02/01 to 1920/02/19
Monkey	G	Wood	1920/02/20 to 1921/02/07
Rooster	H	Wood	1921/02/08 to 1922/01/27
Dog	I	Water	1922/01/28 to 1923/02/15
Pig	J	Water	1923/02/16 to 1924/02/04
Rat	A	Metal	1924/02/05 to 1925/01/23
Ox	B	Metal	1925/01/24 to 1926/02/12
Tiger	C	Fire	1926/02/13 to 1927/02/01

Rabbit	D	Fire	1927/02/02 to 1928/01/22
Dragon	E	Wood	1928/01/23 to 1929/02/09
Snake	F	Wood	1929/02/10 to 1930/01/29
Horse	G	Earth	1930/01/30 to 1931/02/16
Goat	H	Earth	1931/02/17 to 1932/02/05
Monkey	I	Metal	1932/02/06 to 1933/01/25
Rooster	J	Metal	1933/01/26 to 1934/02/13
Dog	A	Fire	1934/02/14 to 1935/02/03
Pig	B	Fire	1935/02/04 to 1936/01/23
Rat	C	Water	1936/01/24 to 1937/02/10
Ox	D	Water	1937/02/11 to 1938/01/30
Tiger	E	Earth	1938/01/31 to 1939/02/18
Rabbit	F	Earth	1939/02/19 to 1940/02/07
Dragon	G	Metal	1940/02/08 to 1941/01/26
Snake	H	Metal	1941/01/27 to 1942/02/14
Horse	I	Wood	1942/02/15 to 1943/02/04
Goat	J	Wood	1943/02/05 to 1944/01/24
Monkey	A	Water	1944/01/25 to 1945/02/12
Rooster	B	Water	1945/02/13 to 1946/02/01
Dog	C	Earth	1946/02/02 to 1947/01/21
Pig	D	Earth	1947/01/22 to 1948/02/09
Rat	E	Fire	1948/02/10 to 1949/01/28
Ox	F	Fire	1949/01/29 to 1950/02/16
Tiger	G	Wood	1950/02/17 to 1951/02/05
Rabbit	H	Wood	1951/02/06 to 1952/01/26
Dragon	I	Water	1952/01/27 to 1953/02/13
Snake	J	Water	1953/02/14 to 1954/02/02
Horse	A	Metal	1954/02/03 to 1955/01/23
Goat	B	Metal	1955/01/24 to 1956/02/11
Monkey	C	Fire	1956/02/12 to 1957/01/30
Rooster	D	Fire	1957/01/31 to 1958/02/17
Dog	E	Wood	1958/02/18 to 1959/02/07
Pig	F	Wood	1959/02/08 to 1960/01/27
Rat	G	Earth	1960/01/28 to 1961/02/14
Ox	H	Earth	1961/02/15 to 1962/02/04
Tiger	I	Metal	1962/02/05 to 1963/01/24
Rabbit	J	Metal	1963/01/25 to 1964/02/12
Dragon	A	Fire	1964/02/13 to 1965/02/01
Snake	B	Fire	1965/02/02 to 1966/01/20
Horse	C	Water	1966/01/21 to 1967/02/08
Goat	D	Water	1967/02/09 to 1968/01/29
Monkey	E	Earth	1968/01/30 to 1969/02/16
Rooster	F	Earth	1969/02/17 to 1970/02/05
Dog	G	Metal	1970/02/06 to 1971/01/26
Pig	H	Metal	1971/01/27 to 1972/02/14

Rat	I	Wood	1972/02/15 to 1973/02/02
Ox	J	Wood	1973/02/03 to 1974/01/22
Tiger	A	Water	1974/01/23 to 1975/02/10
Rabbit	B	Water	1975/02/11 to 1976/01/30
Dragon	C	Earth	1976/01/31 to 1977/02/17
Snake	D	Earth	1977/02/18 to 1978/02/06
Horse	E	Fire	1978/02/07 to 1979/01/27
Goat	F	Fire	1979/01/28 to 1980/02/15
Monkey	G	Wood	1980/02/16 to 1981/02/04
Rooster	H	Wood	1981/02/05 to 1982/01/24
Dog	I	Water	1982/01/25 to 1983/02/12
Pig	J	Water	1983/02/13 to 1984/02/01
Rat	A	Metal	1984/02/02 to 1985/02/19
Ox	B	Metal	1985/02/20 to 1986/02/08
Tiger	C	Fire	1986/02/09 to 1987/01/28
Rabbit	D	Fire	1987/01/29 to 1988/02/16
Dragon	E	Wood	1988/02/17 to 1989/02/05
Snake	F	Wood	1989/02/06 to 1990/01/26
Horse	G	Earth	1990/01/27 to 1991/02/14
Goat	H	Earth	1991/02/15 to 1992/02/03
Monkey	I	Metal	1992/02/04 to 1993/01/22
Rooster	J	Metal	1993/01/23 to 1994/02/09
Dog	A	Fire	1994/02/10 to 1995/01/30
Pig	B	Fire	1995/01/31 to 1996/02/18
Rat	C	Water	1996/02/19 to 1997/02/06
Ox	D	Water	1997/02/07 to 1998/01/27
Tiger	E	Earth	1998/01/28 to 1999/02/15
Rabbit	F	Earth	1999/02/16 to 2000/02/04
Dragon	G	Metal	2000/02/05 to 2001/01/23
Snake	H	Metal	2001/01/24 to 2002/02/11
Horse	I	Wood	2002/02/12 to 2003/01/31
Goat	J	Wood	2003/02/01 to 2004/01/21
Monkey	A	Water	2004/01/22 to 2005/02/08
Rooster	B	Water	2005/02/09 to 2006/01/28
Dog	C	Earth	2006/01/29 to 2007/02/17
Pig	D	Earth	2007/02/18 to 2008/02/06
Rat	E	Fire	2008/02/07 to 2009/01/25
Ox	F	Fire	2009/01/26 to 2010/02/13

Years table for sky chart

10 stems → Palace of Life ↓	A, F	B, G	C, H	D, I	E, J
Square 1, 2	Water	Fire	Earth	Wood	Metal
Square 3, 4	Fire	Earth	Wood	Metal	Water
Square 5, 6	Wood	Metal	Water	Water	Earth
Square 7, 8	Earth	Wood	Metal	Water	Fire
Square 9, 10	Metal	Fire	Fire	Earth	Wood
Square 11, 12	Fire	Earth	Wood	Metal	Fire

Table to find the element of "situation"

Element of situation → Day of birth ↓	Water	Wood	Metal	Earth	Fire
1	2	5	12	7	10
2	3	2	5	12	7
3	3	3	2	5	12
4	4	6	3	2	5
5	4	3	1	3	2
6	5	4	6	8	3
7	5	7	3	1	11
8	6	4	4	6	8
9	6	5	2	3	1
10	7	8	7	4	6
11	7	5	4	9	3
12	8	6	5	2	4
13	8	9	3	7	12
14	9	6	8	4	9
15	9	7	5	5	2
16	10	10	6	10	7
17	10	7	4	3	4
18	11	8	9	8	5
19	11	11	6	5	1
20	12	8	7	6	10
21	12	9	5	11	3
22	1	12	10	4	8
23	1	9	7	9	5
24	2	10	8	6	6
25	2	1	6	7	2
26	3	10	11	12	11
27	3	11	8	5	4
28	4	2	9	10	9
29	4	11	7	7	6
30	5	12	12	8	7

Table to find the location of the star of the King

Ex: In your case, your alphabet letter is F (date of birth Feb. 1st, 2000) and your palace of Life is located in square 1, which gives your "situation" the element of water. Then the intersection of element water and your Chinese day of birth (26) give the number 3; therefore the star of the King is in square 3. Write it down in the square.

Friends **6. Snake**	Travels **7. Horse**	Health **8. Goat**	Finances **9. Monkey**
Career **5. Dragon**			Children **10. Rooster**
	Element of the palace of Life: Water Element of the year: Earth Stem: F		
Property **4. Rabbit**	Date, time of birth: Dec. 26, 2000 2 a.m.		Spouse **11. Dog**
King The body Happiness **3. Tiger**	Parents **2. Ox**	Life **1. Rat**	Brothers **12. Pig**

(5) Place the 13 other stars.

Once you have placed the star of the King, consult the following table to place the other 13 stars in this order: Opportunity of Heaven, the Sun, Warrior, Equality, Honesty, Palace of Heaven, the Moon, Voracious Wolf, Big Door, Premier of Heaven, Frame of Heaven, Seven Killers, and Defeated Army.

Square & position of the King → / 13 other stars ↓	1.3	2.1	3.1	4.2	5.4	6.2	7.1	8.1	9.2	10.3	11.4	12.2
Opportunity heaven	12.3	1.1	2.4	3.2	4.2	5.1	6.3	7.1	8.4	9.3	10.2	11.1
The Sun	10.4	11.4	12.4	1.4	2.4	3.2	4.1	5.2	6.2	7.1	8.3	9.4
Warrior	9.3	10.2	11.1	12.3	1.2	2.1	3.4	4.4	5.1	6.3	7.2	8.1
Equality	8.4	9.2	10.3	11.3	12.1	1.2	2.4	3.4	4.1	5.3	6.1	7.4
Honesty	5.2	6.4	7.3	8.1	9.1	10.3	11.1	12.4	1.3	2.2	3.1	4.3
Palace of heaven	5.1	4.3	3.1	2.1	1.1	12.2	11.2	10.4	9.3	8.1	7.2	6.3
The Moon	6.4	5.4	4.4	3.4	2.1	1.1	12.1	11.2	10.2	9.3	8.3	7.4
Voracious wolf	7.2	6.4	5.1	4.2	3.3	2.1	1.2	12.4	11.1	10.3	9.3	8.1
Big door	8.4	7.2	6.3	5.3	4.1	3.1	2.2	1.2	12.2	11.2	10.1	9.1
Premier of heaven	9.1	8.4	7.2	6.3	5.2	4.4	3.1	2.1	1.1	12.3	11.4	10.4
Frame of heaven	10.2	9.4	8.2	7.1	6.4	5.2	4.1	3.1	2.2	1.1	12.4	11.2
Seven killers	11.1	10.4	9.1	8.2	7.2	6.3	5.2	4.4	3.1	2.1	1.2	12.3
Defeated army	3.4	2.2	1.1	12.3	11.2	10.4	9.4	8.1	7.1	6.4	5.2	4.2

Table to find the square and the position of the other 13 stars
compare to the star of the King

The number before the period is the number of the square where the star will be located, the number after the period means whether its position is excellent (1), good (2), average (3) or bad (4). For example, if the star of the King is in square 1, it is considered as in an average position (3); if it is in square 2, it is in an excellent position (1), and so on. Write down this position next to the star of the King.

Depending in which square the star of the King is located, the other 13 stars are located in the square where they intersect with the star of the King.

Ex: In your case, the star of the King is in square 3, therefore the star of the Opportunity of Heaven is in square 2 and the Sun is in square 12 and so on. Write down the other 13 star and their position in their respective square.

Big door 3 Friends **6. Snake**	Honesty 3 Premier Heaven 2 Travels **7. Horse**	Frame heaven 2 Health **8. Goat**	Seven killers 1 Finances **9. Monkey**
Voracious wolf 1 Career **5. Dragon**	1: Excellent 2: Good 3: Average 4: Bad		Equality 3 Children **10. Rooster**
Moon 4 Property **4. Rabbit**	Element of the palace of Life: Water Element of the year: Earth Stem: F Date, time of birth: Dec. 26, 2000 2 a.m.		Warrior 1 Spouse **11. Dog**
King 1 Palace heaven 1 The body Happiness **3. Tiger**	Oppor. heaven 4 Parents **2. Ox**	Defeated army 1 Life **1. Rat**	Sun 4 Brothers **12. Pig**

(6) Position the star of the Preserved Office, of the Climbing Goat and of the Arm of Heaven.

According to the alphabet letter that you have found in step (4), consult the following table to place these 3 stars in their correspondent square.

10 Stems → Stars ↓	A	B	C	D	E	F	G	H	I	J
Preserved office	3	4	6	7	6	7	9	10	12	1
Climbing goat	4	5	7	8	7	8	10	11	1	2
Arm of heaven	8	9	10	10	8	9	3	3	6	6

Big door　　　　3 Friends **6. Snake**	Honesty　　　　3 Premier Heaven 2 Preserved office Travels **7. Horse**	Frame heaven　2 Climbing goat Health **8. Goat**	Seven killers　　1 Arm of heaven Finances **9. Monkey**
Voracious wolf　1 Career **5. Dragon**	1: Excellent 2: Good 3: Average 4: Bad		Equality　　　　3 Children **10. Rooster**
Moon　　　　　4 Property **4. Rabbit**	Element of the palace of Life: Water Element of the year: Earth Stem: F Date, time of birth: Dec. 26, 2000 　　　　　　　　　2 a.m.		Warrior　　　　1 Spouse **11. Dog**
King　　　　　1 Palace heaven　1 The body Happiness **3. Tiger**	Oppor. heaven　4 Parents **2. Ox**	Defeated army　1 Life **1. Rat**	Sun　　　　　　4 Brothers **12. Pig**

(7) Position the star of the Right and Left Aid.

According to your Chinese month of birth, consult the following table to position these two stars.

Month of birth → Stars ↓	1	2	3	4	5	6	7	8	9	10	11	12
Left aid	5	6	7	8	9	10	11	12	1	2	3	4
Right aid	11	10	9	8	7	6	5	4	3	2	1	12

Big door 3 Friends **6. Snake**	Honesty 3 Premier Heaven 2 Preserved office Travels **7. Horse**	Frame heaven 2 Climbing goat Health **8. Goat**	Seven killers 1 Arm of heaven Finances **9. Monkey**
Voracious wolf 1 Career **5. Dragon**	1: Excellent 2: Good 3: Average 4: Bad		Equality 3 Children **10. Rooster**
Moon 4 Left aid Property **4. Rabbit**	Element of the palace of Life: Water Element of the year: Earth Stem: F Date, time of birth: Dec. 26, 2000 2 a.m.		Warrior 1 Spouse **11. Dog**
King 1 Palace heaven 1 The body Happiness **3. Tiger**	Oppor. heaven 4 Parents **2. Ox**	Defeated army 1 Life **1. Rat**	Sun 4 Right aid Brothers **12. Pig**

(8) Position the stars of the Twisted and Prosperous Literary, and of the Empty and Ruined Land.

According to your time of birth, consult the following table to place these four stars.

Time of birth → Stars ↓	23 - 1h	1 - 3h	3 - 5h	5 - 7h	7 - 9h	9 - 11h	11 - 13h	13 - 15h	15 - 17h	17 - 19h	19 - 21h	21 - 23h
Prosperous literary	11	10	9	8	7	6	5	4	3	2	1	12
Twisted literary	5	6	7	8	9	10	11	12	1	2	3	4
Ruined land	12	1	2	3	4	5	6	7	8	9	10	11
Empty land	12	11	10	9	8	7	6	5	4	3	2	1

Big door　　　　3 Twisted literary Friends **6. Snake**	Honesty　　　　3 Premier Heaven 2 Preserved office Travels **7. Horse**	Frame heaven　2 Climbing goat Health **8. Goat**	Seven killers　1 Arm of heaven Finances **9. Monkey**
Voracious wolf　1 Career **5. Dragon**	1: Excellent 2: Good 3: Average 4: Bad		Equality　　　　3 Prosp. literary Children **10. Rooster**
Moon　　　　　4 Left aid Property **4. Rabbit**	Element of the palace of Life: Water Element of the year: Earth Stem: F Date, time of birth: Dec. 26, 2000 　　　　　　　　　2 a.m.		Warrior　　　　1 Empty land Spouse **11. Dog**
King　　　　　1 Palace heaven　1 The body Happiness **3. Tiger**	Oppor. heaven　4 Parents **2. Ox**	Defeated army　1 Ruined land Life **1. Rat**	Sun　　　　　4 Right aid Brothers **12. Pig**

(9) Position the star of the Horse of Heaven.

According to your Chinese sign (you can find it in the "year table for sky chart" in step 4), consult the following table and place the star of the Horse of Heaven in the corresponding square.

Chinese sign → Star ↓	Rat, Dragon, Monkey	Ox, Snake, Rooster	Tiger, Horse, Dog	Rabbit, Goat, Pig
Horse of heaven	3	12	9	6

Big door 3 Twisted literary Horse heaven Friends **6. Snake**	Honesty 3 Premier Heaven 2 Preserved office Travels **7. Horse**	Frame heaven 2 Climbing goat Health **8. Goat**	Seven killers 1 Arm of heaven Finances **9. Monkey**
Voracious wolf 1 Career **5. Dragon**	1: Excellent 2: Good 3: Average 4: Bad		Equality 3 Prosp. literary Children **10. Rooster**
Moon 4 Left aid Property **4. Rabbit**	Element of the palace of Life: Water Element of the year: Earth Stem: F Date, time of birth: Dec. 26, 2000 2 a.m.		Warrior 1 Empty land Spouse **11. Dog**
King 1 Palace heaven 1 The body Happiness **3. Tiger**	Oppor. heaven 4 Parents **2. Ox**	Defeated army 1 Ruined land Life **1. Rat**	Sun 4 Right aid Brothers **12. Pig**

(10) Position the star of Prosperity, of Power, of the Exam and of Jealousy.

According to the alphabet letter that you have obtained in step 4, place these four stars in the same square as the one which is found in the intersection.

Stars → / Stem ↓	Prosperity	Power	Exam	Jealousy
A	honesty	defeated army	warrior	sun
B	opportunity of heaven	frame of heaven	king	moon
C	equality	opportunity of heaven	prosperous literary	honesty
D	moon	equality	opportunity of heaven	big door
E	voracious wolf	moon	right aid	opportunity of heaven
F	warrior	voracious wolf	frame of heaven	twisted literary
G	sun	warrior	equality	moon
H	big door	sun	twisted literary	prosperous literary
I	frame of heaven	king	left aid	Warrior
J	defeated army	big door	moon	voracious wolf

Ex: In your case, your alphabet letter is F, therefore you position the star of Prosperity in the same square as the star of the Warrior, then place the star of Power in the same square as the star of the Voracious Wolf and so on.

Big door 3 Twisted literary Horse heaven Jealousy Friends **6. Snake**	Honesty 3 Premier Heaven 2 Preserved office Travels **7. Horse**	Frame heaven 2 Climbing goat Exam Health **8. Goat**	Seven killers 1 Arm of heaven Finances **9. Monkey**
Voracious wolf 1 Power Career **5. Dragon**	1: Excellent 2: Good 3: Average 4: Bad		Equality 3 Prosp. literary Children **10. Rooster**
Moon 4 Left aid Property **4. Rabbit**	Element of the palace of Life: Water Element of the year: Earth Stem: F Date, time of birth: Dec. 26, 2000 2 a.m.		Warrior 1 Empty land Prosperity Spouse **11. Dog**
King 1 Palace heaven 1 The body Happiness **3. Tiger**	Oppor. heaven 4 Parents **2. Ox**	Defeated army 1 Ruined land Life **1. Rat**	Sun 4 Right aid Brothers **12. Pig**

This finishes the exercise of determining the location and position of the stars and palaces. If after this you still find some palaces which are empty, it means that there is no star located in that palace, then you need to borrow the stars from another palace. This means to place the same stars of this palace in the empty one. Apply the following rules for this process:

If the palace of Life is empty, borrow the stars of the palace of Travels and vice versa.

If the palace of Brothers is empty, borrow the stars of the palace of Friends and vice versa.

If the palace of Spouse is empty, borrow the stars of the palace of Career and vice versa.

If the palace of Children is empty, borrow the stars of the palace of Property and vice versa.

If the palace of Finances is empty, borrow the stars of the palace of Happiness and vice versa.

If the palace of Health is empty, borrow the stars of the palace of Parents and vice versa.

Interpretation of the elements

1. The element of your palace of Life and the element of your year are the same. This means you will have a very easy life. You tend to adapt and integrate yourself very easily to your environment. Whether you are poor or rich, you live according to your means. Your environment provides you with all that is necessary for living, creating conditions which will allow you to live free of any major concerns. You take whatever is given to you and try to avoid making too many demands.

   You try to discover the road of your life by yourself and, in general, are capable of managing without asking anyone for help. In short, you have the ability to adapt to your environment, allowing you to live happily and easily in this world. Life is also made easier for you by the constant presence of luck.

2. The element of your palace of Life produces the element of your year. This means you will have an easy life in this world. Your environment provides all that is necessary without your having to make any requests. All essential and favorable conditions are created, ensuring your happiness and lack of trouble.

   Throughout your life, no effort is required in order to obtain what you desire. Everything is given to you, which may create a feeling of being spoiled. You will benefit from all the good things on this earth and never become tired. In short, you have great luck in life and know how to enjoy living.

3. The element of your year produces the element of your palace of Life. This [*EARTH PRODUCES METAL*] means your life is full of creativity and innovation. If your environment does not always provide you with what is necessary to live, you make every attempt to create conditions favorable to living the easiest life possible.

   You contribute a great deal to society and to life in general. You sometimes attempt to alter your environment and introduce new elements to your life in order to create as accurately as possible the surroundings you desire. This sometimes takes the form of sacrifice. In short, you will give more than you will receive throughout your life. Your contributions to society surpass those given to you in return. In life, it is you who is the creator and sculptor.

4. The element of your palace of Life destroys the element of your year. This means you will have a very difficult life in this world. Your environment presents you with many obstacles and with unfavorable conditions, preventing you from progressing and developing. Reaching your goals

requires great effort and you may have to endure much failure before achieving the ultimate victory.

Throughout your life, you may exert yourself greatly with minimal results. You may be forced to work very hard to achieve what you desire, causing you to become tough and resilient, a person who accepts the necessity of making more effort than others. In short, luck is never on your side. In order to succeed, you are obliged to make great effort and to endure many failures. Life is not easy.

5. The element of your year destroys the element of your palace of Life. This reveals your dislike for your environment and your life. You are unsatisfied with society and what it has to offer you. You desire change and make all efforts necessary for realizing your dreams.

   You are very ambitious but sometimes overestimate your own abilities. Your tendency to revolt pits you against society. Throughout life, you will become tired frequently, as you constantly make a great effort, without attaining desired results. In conclusion, your life is full of obstacles and you always feel yourself to be in opposition to the environment and society. You wish to make changes and go to great lengths to realize this ambition, but at times are forced to endure failure as a result of being overly ambitious. Your frequent fatigue will not always be greatly rewarded, results sometimes being much smaller than expected.

Interpretation of the body

1. Your body is found in your palace of Life. This means you are egocentric and self-centered. A return to the source is characteristic of your life. Once a goal is set, you go to any lengths to succeed. Thus your chance for success is great. Determined to realize your ambitions and possessing determination in general, you are capable of easily reaching your goals due to power of concentration. This will help you resolve any difficulty you may encounter on your way. You will do whatever is necessary to arrive at your destination. In your life, success is usual.

2. Your body is found in your palace of Career. This means the center of your life is your career. You are a relentless worker, making great effort to advance your professional life. Throughout life, you do everything to succeed in society. This may even bring you to ignore your family and anything unessential to your career. You seek glory above all else. Your determination and concentration at work may assure you brilliant success in your career. You will achieve respectable status in society.

3. Your body is found in your palace of Travels. This means your life is centered outside the home. This is where you go to meet people, as your strength lies in social relationships. Even your career will be built around such relationships, as the professions which best suit you are diplomacy, public relations, media, interpersonal relations, sales, etc. Throughout life, you enjoy traveling and do so frequently. You enjoy exchanging ideas with others and tend to leave a familiar environment to explore new territories and discover new ideas.

4. Your body is found in your palace of Finances. This means your life centers around money - it is essential to you and is your only motivation. You seek financial success above all else, even glory. To you, money decides social status. Professions which best suit you should be sought in the fields of business and commerce. In short, all your activities and social relations center around money. Whether it be on a familial or intimate level, financial success is essential to your life.

5. Your body is found in your palace of Spouse. This means your life centers around love, emotions, and relationships with the opposite sex. Success in life even depends greatly on success in love. In turn, difficulties in love may affect other aspects of life.

   Throughout life, you place a great emphasis on relations with the opposite sex and pursue activities in line with these. Your professional life is influenced in large part by your love life, the success of which can determine success in general. Sometimes, you must rely upon your spouse or partner in love to achieve success in life.

6. Your body is found in the palace of Happiness. This means your life centers around your family and its happiness. Whatever you do in life, your family remains the most important thing to you. You seek happiness for the members of your family above all else and would even abandon your professional career to preserve your family's happiness.

Throughout life, your family is the focus of your activities. Family carries more weight than money or glory and its tradition is very important to you. You will do whatever is necessary to ensure happiness for your family.

Interpretation of the twelve palaces

Palace of Life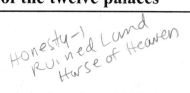

- The star of the King is in the palace of Life, in a position ranging from good to excellent. Therefore you are assured wealth and glory and you can be seen as a kind of King of the world. You will experience much good luck in life and high society will await you, despite any bad stars which may shine in other palaces. The star of the King can influence these palaces and chase away the bad luck, as it is the most powerful of all stars. All earthly wealth is yours and you are protected throughout your life.

- The star of the King is in the palace of Life, in an average position. Although you can not become the King of the world, this means you will be better off than the average person and in spite of its average position, this star can still protect you and bring you some earthly wealth. You will have a rich and glorious life and luck is often present. Your life will be very easy and you will have absolutely nothing to worry about.

- The star of the King is in the palace of Life and even though it is in a bad position, it can still exert some good influence. This is because the star of the King is the loftiest and most respectable of all the stars. Despite its bad position and the fact that it does not reign over the palace of life, you can still have an average life. Good luck will not be yours often but will visit from time to time. You will not have a very easy life nor will great earthly wealth be yours, but a tolerable life is still attainable.

- The star of the Opportunity of Heaven is in the palace of Life, in a position ranging from good to excellent. Thus, you will be presented with many opportunities which will bring you glory and wealth. You will have a greater chance to take advantage of them if you are capable of using these resources from Heaven. You may not amass a big fortune but will still lead a rich life. The better the position, the more of such wealth you will receive. Your profession will bring you great reward.

- The star of the Opportunity of Heaven is in the palace of Life and, in addition, the Moon is in the same palace. This means better luck in a faraway country or somewhere far from your birthplace. It is better to act as early as possible because the opportunities available can bring increased glory and wealth. If you are female, you will certainly be going far in order to pursue an adventure of love.

- The star of the Opportunity of Heaven is in the palace of Life and, in addition, the star of the Big Door is in the same palace. This means you will find your luck and fortune on your own and not with the help of your family. The big door is open and it is you who must make the move to find your own way. Do not count on others, as you need everything to be left in your own hands. You will create your own prosperity, although the Opportunity of Heaven will help you somewhat.

- The star of the Opportunity of Heaven is in the palace of Life, in an average position. This means you may not have a chance to amass great wealth but will encounter some good opportunities sent to you by Heaven. These will allow you to have an easy life. The luck of heaven will help you through some difficult situations.

- The star of the Opportunity of Heaven is in the palace of Life and it is in a bad position. This means good luck will not come often and you will have difficulty finding it. Therefore, your life will only be tolerable because of this bad position. Not much can be done for you and the star's influence on your life is very minor. Do not expect good winds to bring you luck, as this can only happen occasionally.

- The Sun is in the palace of Life, in a position ranging from average to excellent. This means you will have a glorious life and the Sun will provide light to allow you to find good luck on your way. It will provide the necessary resources to gain wealth and if the star of the Right or Left Aid or the Moon is in the same palace, the chances are even greater. These stars will increase the power of the light from the Sun, bringing you better opportunities on the road of life.

- The Sun is in the palace of Life and it is in a bad position. This means you will have a less than glorious life but this is still superior to the average, as the Sun is a very powerful star. Even if it is in a bad position, its radiance will always protect you on your journey and you will have a very easy life, free of worries. Everything is ready to bring you success in life.

- The Sun is in the palace of Life and is in the sign of the Horse (corresponding to lunar time from 11h to 13h). This means your luck is like the Sun at noon and the weather will be extremely pleasant. You will have wealth and also happiness and glory. The radiance of the Sun protects you throughout life and you will have great success in life, both socially and financially speaking.

- The Sun is in the palace of Life and is in the sign of the Rooster (corresponding to lunar time from 17h to 19h). This means your luck will be much less clear because the Sun will soon disappear and its radiance can not bring great influence. You will have a comfortable life with few worries but that is all. Your luck is not very solid, either socially or financially speaking.

- The Sun is in the palace of Life and is in the sign of the Dog or the Pig (corresponding to lunar time from 19h to 23h). This means your luck will be very disturbed, as the sun has lost all its power and light. Throughout your life, you become tired frequently and run in all directions. The harvest is very small and you will face many difficulties in your social and financial life. The power of the Sun can not give you much help.

- The star of the Warrior is in the palace of Life, in a position ranging from good to excellent. This means a very solid and defined life, with wealth and glory, as your warrior spirit helps you to conquer the world. The power you gain will allow you to amass great wealth and the star of the Warrior will also grant longevity.

- The star of the Warrior is in the palace of Life and the star of Literary (twisted or prosperous) is also in the same palace. This means you will have success no matter what, and big success at that. Whether you are in the private sector or public service, you will have great responsibilities, as the star of the Warrior and Literary form a unity to ensure a life of great success. As is the case in a company, you accumulate technical (warrior) and management (literary) skills at the same time, allowing you to reach high management.

- The star of the Warrior is in the palace of Life, as is the star of the Horse of Heaven or the Preserved Office. This means you will find fortune and glory in a faraway country because the Horse of Heaven leads you great distances in order to discover opportunity. This will bring you to the entrance, at which point you take the necessary steps to find your fortune. The Preserved Office is a very good star for your career, as it can chase away bad stars and bring you great success in life.

- The star of the Warrior is in the palace of Life, as is the star of the Voracious Wolf. This means you have an unfavorable life when you are young but you must fight a great deal. You try to succeed at any cost but whatever you do, it benefits others and not you. People devour the fruits of your labor and leave you nothing. You will have a better chance later in life.

- The star of the Warrior is in the palace of Life and is in a bad position. This means you will have difficulty conquering the world. You will have trouble exerting your force and there nothing you can do if the star of the Defeated Army is also in the same palace. Life will give you many difficulties and you are simply a defeated warrior. Do not expect good luck to save you, as you are in a very bad position.

- The star of the Warrior is in the palace of Life and is in an average position. This means you will have quite a stable life. You will be without great success, as you lack a determined warrior spirit necessary for conquering the world. You will have success in some battles but this will not bring you great wealth, rather just enough for a bearable life.

- The star of Equality or Honesty is in the palace of Life, in a position ranging from good to excellent. This means you will have a wealthy and glorious life, with happiness knocking at your door. Even though you may encounter bad stars, you are protected by good luck. The better the position, the better your luck, and you have nothing to worry about.

- The star of Equality or Honesty is in the palace of Life, in a bad position. This means you will have quite a difficult life. You will not have great success in life because the position of the stars is bad. Their influence can cause great trouble on the journey of life and you will have difficulty finding an alternative route by which to reach your goals.

- The star of Equality or Honesty is in the palace of Life, in an average position. This means you may not have great success but at least the situation will be tolerable. You will be able to find a way to achieve your goals and although everything is not rosy in your life, it is better than average.

- The star of the Palace of Heaven is in the palace of Life and is in a position ranging from good to excellent. This means you will have a rich and glorious life because you are in the Palace of Heaven and whether you want it or not, you are protected by its power. No bad stars can attack you and life will bring great success.

- The star of the Palace of Heaven is in the palace of Life and is in a bad position. This means that although you are protected by the Palace of Heaven, your life will not be as glorious and rich as you may imagine. You have a tolerable life without great success and you are not afraid of other bad stars. You do not have great success because the star of the Palace of Heaven is in a bad position, and has lost some of its power, so its influence will not be strong enough to protect you.

- The Moon is in the palace of Life, in a position ranging from good to excellent. This means that life will be quite rich. And even though the light of the Moon is less powerful than the light of the Sun, you will still have a very comfortable life. Good luck will visit you often and you will have many successes.

- The Moon is in the palace of Life, in a position ranging from average to bad. This means you will have a very difficult life. The Moon will not have enough light to bring a positive influence to your life, especially if you are born during the night. Throughout your life, luck will be very disturbed, so avoid dreaming of great success, as it will come only occasionally.

- The star of the Voracious Wolf is in the palace of Life, in a position ranging from good to excellent. This means you will have quite a stable life, without many worries. The star of the Voracious Wolf is bad but fortunately is in a good position. Therefore, its influence is less powerful and although your life will not be very rich, you will encounter enough good luck to give you a comfortable life.

- The star of the Voracious Wolf is in the palace of Life, in a position ranging from average to bad. This means you will have a very difficult life filled with danger. All the vice in this world will be present to destroy you and you will be subjected to some very harmful circumstances. The star of the Voracious Wolf is the worst star and is also in a bad position, which means its influence will be more ferocious. It will bring you great troubles and only the star of the King can have a positive influence on it.

- The star of the Big Door is in the palace of Life, in a position ranging from good to excellent. This means you will have a tolerable life without much success. The Big Door is a bad star and its influence is quite harmful to your life. Fortunately it is in a good position which will still bring you some good. Do not dream of wealth, as it will come rarely.

- The star of the Big Door is in the palace of Life, in a position ranging from average to bad. This means you will have a difficult life ahead. The influence of this star will pursue you all your life and will give you much trouble. Luck is very disturbed and you try to escape this by all means but can do nothing because of the bad position of this star. It can only bring you bad things.

- The star of the Premier of Heaven is in the palace of Life, in a position ranging from average to excellent. This means your life will be filled with much wealth and glory. In general, life will bring much good luck and success will be yours throughout life. The star of the Premier of Heaven is very lucky and you will receive its positive influence throughout your life. The better its position, the better your chance for a successful life.

- The star of the Premier of Heaven is in the palace of Life and is in a bad position. This means you still have a very easy life. With lots of good luck, the influence of this powerful star can bring much good luck, even if it is in a bad position. You will have a very comfortable life filled with success.

- The star of the Frame of Heaven is in the palace of Life, in a position ranging from average to excellent. This means you will have a life of good determination. You may not have wealth but you will have glory. Your chances will be better if the star of the Opportunity of Heaven is in the same palace and you will encounter much good luck, which will make your frame solid enough to support your life.

- The star of the Frame of Heaven is in the palace of Life and is in a bad position. This means life holds many bad things in store for you. You will not have much success in life because the star of the Frame of Heaven should not be found in a bad position and even worse, it reigns over the palace of life. Like the frame of a house which is not correctly built, the house will collapse sooner or later. Therefore you will have a quite difficult life and no great success, even if you make a great effort, for everything will collapse like a castle of sand by the end.

- The star of the Seven Killers is in the palace of Life. This star is a very bad star, even if it is in a good position, its influence will bring much trouble and you will therefore have great difficulty in life. You will have to go through some very hard times, unless other good stars are located in the same palace to save you, such as the star of the King or the Sun. Otherwise a life of difficulty awaits you.

- The star of the Defeated Army is in the palace of Life, in a position ranging from good to excellent. This means you will not have an easy life, unless the star of the King or the Sun is in the same palace to chase away this bad star. You will make a great effort for only a minute harvest, as good luck is not with you. The star of the Defeated Army is bad and even if it is in a good position, it will still bring some bad surprises.

- The star of the Defeated Army is in the palace of Life, in a position ranging from average to bad. This means you will have a life filled with difficulties, as this bad star is located in a bad position. Its influence will be more ferocious and you will be fighting for nothing, making a great effort and using the necessary means but always being the loser.

- The star of the Preserved Office is in the palace of Life. This means you will have great happiness in life, as the star of the Preserved Office is a very good star. Even though you may encounter some bad stars in this palace, you will have wealth and glory, as the star of the Preserved Office will protect you from bad influence. Happiness pursues you everywhere and your life will be better than most.

- The star of the Climbing Goat is in the palace of Life. This means you will receive great power, which will bring you glory and influence. You will climb higher and higher on the social ladder and wherever you go, devastation will lie in your wake. You will have great success in your career and a very glorious road is yours to travel.

- The star of the Arm of Heaven is in the palace of life. This means you will have a rich and glorious life, as this star is a very good one. Even if you face difficulty, you will have the necessary weapons to overcome it and to lead a royal life. If you do not have the top position, you will be able to attain the second one. Thus, your life will be an easy one.

- The star of the Right or Left Aid is in the palace of Life. This means you will obtain much help allowing you to find good luck. These stars are those of the Aide of the King and therefore you will not only have wealth but also power. You can always find the necessary resources to allow you a royal life, especially if the star of the King or the Sun is also present in the same palace. Then, you are like the king of the world and the position of the King or the Sun will be more solid strong.

- The star of the Twisted or Prosperous Literary is in the palace of Life. This means you will have a very successful life in the literary world. Your luck in this area is particularly good, especially if the two stars are located in the same palace. You are born to lead a life with a direct link to these talents, such as politics, law, etc.

- The star of the Empty Land or Ruined Land is in the palace of Life. This means you will have a difficult life, as these are bad stars and star of bad luck. You will have many difficulties throughout the journey of life, with failure more often than success. You will have big trouble accumulating profit and your hands are always empty.

- The star of the Horse of Heaven is in the palace of Life. This means you will have a life with much profit, big profit, as the Horse of Heaven will bring you to the places where good luck awaits you. You will be able to amass great wealth and luck will follow you everywhere. If other good stars (The King, the Sun, the Moon, etc.) are in the same palace, the influence of these stars will increase your luck.

- The star of Prosperity is in the palace of Life. This means you will have an extremely wealthy life, as the star of Prosperity is the star of finances. Thus, you will have particularly good luck in this area, especially if the star of the

Preserved Office is in this palace of Life at the same time. Then you will not only have an outstanding financial situation, but also have great power.

• The star of Power is in the palace of Life. This means you will have great power and even though you may not have great fortune, this power of heaven will bring you a very easy life full of success. This is especially true if you have the star of the Warrior in the same palace, as you then will be able attain a high military career.

• The star of the Exam is in the palace of Life. This means you will have a life of fame. Even though you may not have great fortune, this renown will bring you a very easy life full of success. Although you may encounter some bad stars, the influence of the star of the Exam will easily chase them away and you will have a much better chance if the star of Power or Prosperity is also located in the same palace. If so, the power of the Exam will increase to give you a more glorious life.

• The star of Jealousy is in the palace of Life. This means you will have quite a disrupted life. Although you may have success, it will not last long, as the star of Jealousy is the star of quarrel. Everything you have, whether it is wealth or fame, will last only for a very short time and will disappear very quickly. This is because people are jealous of your success and will try by all means to take all you have.

Palace of Brothers

• The star of the King, of the Warrior, of Honesty, of the Palace of Heaven or of the Premier of Heaven is in the palace of Brothers. This means you have at least two or three brothers and sisters, as well as a very comfortable financial situation. Your relations with your brothers and sisters are good, and harmony prevails in the family.

• The star of the Opportunity of Heaven, of Equality, or of the Frame of Heaven is in the palace of Brothers. This means that you have at least two or three brothers and sisters, all of you enjoying a very comfortable financial situation and your relations with the others are very good.

• The Sun and the Moon are simultaneously located in the palace of Brothers. This means you have many brothers and sisters. In spite of enviable financial situations, relationships are not very good in the family and quarrels are quite frequent.

- The Sun is in the palace of Brothers. This means you have many brothers and sisters - more brothers than sisters. You all enjoy very good financial situations and the relationships are very good in the family.

- The Moon is in the palace of Brothers. This means you have many brothers and sisters - more sisters than brothers. You all enjoy very good financial situations and the relationships are very good in the family.

- The star of the Voracious Wolf, of the Climbing Goat, of the Seven Killers, of the Big Door or of the Defeated Army is located in the palace of Brothers. This means that the relationships between brothers and sisters are not very good, quarrels are quite frequent and you may end up living far from each other.

- The star of the Preserved Office, of the Arm of Heaven, of the Right or Left Aid, of the Twisted or Prosperous Literary, of Prosperity, of Power or of the Exam is located in the palace of Brothers. This means if other good stars are in this palace, the power of these good stars will increase and the number of your brothers and sisters will also increase. You will also have a better chance for good relationships with each other. On the other hand, if bad stars are in this palace, the number of brothers and sisters will be fewer and your relations will be worse.

- The star of the Horse of Heaven or of Jealousy is in the palace of Brothers. This means that you do not get along with your brothers and sisters. You are very jealous of the success of your brothers and sisters and the favors that they obtain. You will end up living far from each other.

Palace of Spouse

- The star of the King, of the Opportunity of Heaven, or the Sun is located in the palace of Spouse. This means you will have a very good relationship with your spouse. Even if these stars are located in a bad position, the influence which they have is very good, as these are very powerful stars. Therefore you will have a very successful and long-lasting conjugal life, and these powerful stars will chase any bad ones to give you an absolutely successful love life.

- The star of the Warrior is in the palace of Spouse and is in a good position. This means you should marry late, as you will have a better relationship with your spouse. The better the position, the greater your chance for obtaining your spouse's inheritance. It is better if you are almost the same age, as this will make your relationship last longer.

- The star of Honesty, of the Voracious Wolf, of the Big Door, of the Seven Killers, of Jealousy or of the Defeated Army is in the palace of Spouse. This means you will have a very difficult relationship with your partner. You may have to marry several times before finding true happiness. If these stars are located in a good position, you will have a better chance to get around. Otherwise, separation awaits you, especially if the star of the Defeated Army is in this palace; your situation will be worse because this star reigns over the palace of Spouse.

- The star of Equality, of the Palace of Heaven, or the Moon is in the palace of Spouse, in a position ranging from average to excellent. This means you will have a very good relationship with your partner and it will last a long time. Perhaps you will marry quite late. You will have a very successful union and everything will be very nice for you. The better the position, the better your relationship.

- The star of the Premier of Heaven or of the Frame of Heaven is in the palace of Spouse, in a position ranging from average to excellent. This means you will have a very good relationship with your partner and it will last a long time. You will have a very successful union.

- The star of the Preserved Office, of the Climbing Goat, of the Arm of Heaven, of the Aid or Literary is in the palace of Spouse. This means that you will have a very good relationship with your partner. It can last for a long time and you will have a very successful union, especially if the two stars of the Aid are located in this palace at the same time. Then you will have the best relationship in the world and you will help each other, creating a perfect union.

- The star of the Warrior (in an average or bad position), of Equality, of the Palace of Heaven, The Moon, of the Premier of Heaven or of the Frame of Heaven is in the palace of Spouse and is located in a bad position. Therefore, you will suffer from the bad influence of these stars. You will have a difficult relationship with your partner and may have to marry several times, still having difficulty finding happiness. If good and powerful stars are located in a good position in this palace, these negative influences will be less ferocious. Otherwise do not be surprised if you end in separation. Also, your union will not last very long unless you marry late.

Palace of Children

- The star of the King, of the Opportunity of Heaven, of Equality, of Honesty, of the Palace of Heaven, of the Premier of Heaven, of the Frame of Heaven or of the Preserved Office is in the palace of Children. This means you will have at least two or three children and they will all have very good financial situations. The relationships amongst you are very good and may even help you to succeed in your career or family enterprise. If these stars are located in a bad position, your luck will somehow suffer from their negative influence.

- The Sun is in the palace of Children. This means that you will have at least three children, more boys than girls. Financially, they will enjoy very comfortable situations and the family relationships will be very good.

- The Moon is in the palace of Children. This means that you will have at least three children, more girls than boys. Financially, they will enjoy very comfortable situations and the family relationships will be very good.

- The star of the Voracious Wolf, of the Big Door, of the Seven Killers or of the Defeated Army is in the palace of Children. This means that you will have very few children and they will be quite difficult. Your relationships with them will not be very good, especially if the star of the Defeated Army is present, as it reigns over the palace of Children and you may encounter great troubles when you are older.

- The star of the Warrior is in the palace of Children. This means that you will have two children at most. In general, they are quite difficult and your relationships with them are not very good, unless the star of the Palace of Heaven or of the Premier of Heaven are located in the same palace, as they may bring you better luck.

- The star of the Climbing Goat, of the Ruined or Empty Land is in the palace of Children. This means that you will not have good relationships with your children. For the most part, they will live far from you and their financial situations may be quite difficult.

- The star of the Arm of Heaven, of the Right or Left Aid, of the Twisted or Prosperous Literary is in the palace of Children. This means that if good stars are already present in this palace, they can increase the number of children you have and improve your relationships with them. On the other hand, if bad stars are already present in this palace, this will reduce the number of children and worsen your relationships.

- The star of Prosperity, of Power, or of the Exam is in the palace of Children. This means that you will have children who wield great power in society.

- The star of the Horse of Heaven or of Jealousy is in the palace of Children. This means you do not have good relationships with your children and will live far from each other in an attempt to avoid conflict.

Palace of Finances

(handwritten: King of Heaven-2 / Premier of Power)

- The star of the King or of the Palace of Heaven is in the palace of Finances. This means that you will have very good luck in finance, as these two stars are very powerful. This is especially true of the star of the Palace of Heaven, because it reigns over finance. These stars bring great wealth to you, and you will be extremely rich. Big fortune will be yours and you have absolutely nothing to worry about. Even if the stars are located in a bad position, you will still have better than the average.

- The star of the Opportunity of Heaven, of the Warrior, the Sun or the Moon is in the palace of Finances, in addition, it is in a position from average to excellent. This means that you will have a big fortune. You may have to make some effort, but you will have great wealth, especially if other good stars are located in the same palace. You will have a better luck for your money matters - the better the position, the bigger your success, especially for the star of the Warrior or the Moon, which reigns over finance.

- The star of Equality is in the palace of Finances, in a position ranging from average to excellent. This means you will have a big fortune but not right away. You will be able to build everything with your bare hands and the more the time passes, the richer you become. If other good stars are in the same palace, the older you get, the more fortune you will amass.

- The star of Honesty, of the Big Door or of the Seven Killers is in the palace of Finances, in a position ranging from average to excellent. This means you will be tired frequently before finding wealth. The beginning will be quite difficult but by the end, all becomes easy for you. You can become richer if other good stars are located in the same palace, as they neutralize the negative influence of the bad stars.

- The star of the Voracious Wolf is in the palace of Finances, in a position ranging from average to excellent. This means you will amass your fortune by collecting the money which falls from the sky but not from your own effort. Even if you do not have a big fortune, you will have enough to support your needs.

- The star of the Premier, of the Arm of Heaven, of the Frame of Heaven, of the Climbing Goat, of the Preserved Office, of the Defeated Army, of the Horse of Heaven, of Power, of the Exam, of the Aid or the Literary is in the palace of Finances, in a position ranging from average to excellent. This means you will be quite rich and although you may not have a great fortune, you will be among the rich people. You will need to work hard for your fortune and although these stars will help you a bit, the large part of the work is up to you. If you have the Horse of Heaven in this palace, you will find your fortune in a faraway country.

- The star of the Empty Land or Ruined Land is in the palace of Finances. This means you will have great difficulty gathering your wealth. Even if other good stars are in the same palace, the bad luck of these two stars will chase money away. If you already have your fortune, you risk losing it and if you do not have your fortune already, do not expect too much. Luck will not come and you will always have empty hands because a very bad star is in your palace of finance. Thus, your chance is nil.

- The star of the Arm of Heaven or Prosperity is in the palace of Finances. This means you will be very rich. These are good stars which reign over finance. People will provide the necessary weapons for you to collect great fortune, you may not even need to make an effort and prosperity is already at your door. Good luck is written in this palace, awarding you an easy life.

Palace of Health

- The star of the King or of the Palace of Heaven is in the palace of Health. This means you will have very good health throughout your life. Sickness will have difficulty attacking you, as you are protected by these two very powerful stars. Your health problems, if any, will be minor. Even if these stars are in a bad position, they can exert a positive influence.

- The star of Honesty, of the Horse of Heaven, of Jealousy, of the Big Door, of the Seven Killers, of the Defeated Army, of the Preserved Office, of the Climbing Goat, of the Empty or Ruined Land is in the palace of Health. This means you will have many health problems throughout your life. These are the bad stars located in your palace and especially the star of the Climbing Goat, the Empty or Ruined Land which reign over the palace of health. Sickness may attack easily and the worse the position, the more difficult it will be for you to fight sickness, especially when you get older. At this time, you will be faced with all sorts of health problems and need a longer time to heal.

- The star of the Opportunity of Heaven, of The Sun, of the Warrior, of Equality, of The Moon, of the Voracious Wolf, of the Premier of Heaven, of the Frame of Heaven, of the Arm of Heaven, of Power, of Prosperity, of the Exam, of the Preserved Office, of the Aid or the Literary is in your palace of Health, in a position ranging from average to excellent. This means you will face very minor health problems. Sickness will have difficulty attacking you, as you are protected by these good stars. You may experience some small problems but will not last and you will not have a chronic disease.

- The star of the Opportunity of Heaven, of The Sun, of the Warrior, of Equality, of The Moon, of the Voracious Wolf, of the Premier of Heaven or of the Frame of Heaven is in your palace of Health, in a bad position. This means you will have much trouble with your health. Unless you are protected by other good stars in a good position, sickness can attack you easily and chronic diseases will be frequent, something you will have difficulty fighting.

Palace of Travels

- The star of the King or of the Palace of Heaven is located in your palace of Travels. This means you will have much good luck when you travel or are outside your usual residence. You will receive much help in the realization of your goals and the success of your travel. You are protected against all accidents and your harvest will be very bountiful.

- The star of the Horse of Heaven is in your palace of Travels. This means that you will have good luck when you are traveling or are outside your usual residence. This star reigns over traveling, therefore you will have no difficulty achieving your goals and will have success during your travels, as people will help you along the way. The Horse of Heaven will bring you to where the profit is and will not stop there, as you will have an abundant harvest.

- The star of the Opportunity of Heaven, of the Sun, of the Moon, of the Preserved Office, of Equality, of the Premier, of the Frame of Heaven, of Prosperity, of Power, of the Exam, of the Climbing Goat, of the Arm of Heaven, of the Aid or Literary is in your palace of Travels and in a position ranging from average to excellent. This means you will have good luck when you travel or are outside your usual residence. You will receive much help, allowing you to achieve your goals and have success in life. The better the position, the more abundant your harvest. You may have some incidents but they will not have any serious consequences.

- The star of the Warrior, of Honesty, of the Voracious Wolf, of the Big Door, of the Seven Killers or of the Defeated Army is in your palace of Travels, in a position ranging from average to excellent. This means you will have less luck when you are traveling or are outside your usual residence. You will have some help achieving your goals but numerous incidents interrupt your travel or create harmful consequences.

- If other stars located in your palace of Travels are in a bad position or are bad stars. This means you will suffer the bad influence of these stars. You will not have much luck when you travel or when you are outside your usual residence. You will have difficulty achieving your goals or having any success as you travel. Many incidents interrupt your travel and you search in all directions for your destinations but cannot find them. As your stars are located in a bad position, they can only create trouble for you. Unless you have other good stars in this palace, located in a good position, these negative influences will be ferocious.

Palace of Friends

- The stars of the King, of the Opportunity of Heaven, of Equality, of the Palace of Heaven, of the Big Door, of the Frame of Heaven, the Moon or the Sun is in the palace of Friends and it is located in a position ranging from good to excellent. This means you have many friends and your relationships with them are very good.

- The stars of the King, of the Opportunity of Heaven, of Equality, of the Palace of Heaven, of the Big Door, of the Frame of Heaven, the Moon or the Sun is in the palace of Friends and it is located in a position ranging from average to bad. This means you have very few friends and your relationships with them are not good.

- The star of the Warrior, of Honesty, of the Voracious Wolf, of the Premier of Heaven, of the Seven Killers or of the Defeated Army is in the palace of Friends, located in a position ranging from average to bad. This means your friends can not help you and may even erect obstacles in your way.

- The star of the Warrior, of Honesty, of the Voracious Wolf, of the Premier of Heaven, of the Seven Killers or of the Defeated Army is in the palace of Friends, located in a position ranging from good to excellent. This means your friends can give you great assistance in career matters.

- The star of the Arm of Heaven, of the Right or Left Aid, of the Twisted or Prosperous Literary is in the palace of Friends. This means that you will receive much help from your friends, which will provide you with weapons necessary for overcoming obstacles arising throughout your career.

- The star of the Preserved Office, of the Horse of Heaven, of the Climbing Goat or of the Ruined or Empty Land is in the palace of Friends. This means you have very few friends, all of whom can not help you and who consume all your profits.

- The star of Prosperity, of Power or of the Exam is in the palace of Friends. This means that you have friends with great power or wealth and who are capable of helping you significantly.

- The star of Jealousy is in the palace of Friends. This means that your friends are very jealous of your success and will try to take all that you have. They will attack you from behind and erect obstacles on the pathway of your profession.

Palace of Career

- The star of the King or of the Palace of Heaven is in the palace of Career. This means you will have very good luck during your career. These two stars are very powerful - especially the star of the King, which is the star of career. They bring you great power, whether you are in the private sector or public services. You will be given great responsibilities and a comfortable financial situation. You will have a very successful career.

- The star of the Opportunity of Heaven, of the Premier of Heaven, of the Frame of Heaven, of Equality, of Prosperity, of Power, of the Exam, the Moon or the Sun is in the palace of Career, in a position ranging from average to excellent. This means you will have very good luck during your career and great power, whether you are in the private sector or public service. Your career will be very successful and all will run very smoothly for you. The better the position, the better chance you have of being granted great responsibility, especially concerning the star of the Premier, the Sun, Power or Exam which govern the palace of Career.

- The star of the Preserved Office, of the Climbing Goat, of the Arm of Heaven, of the Horse of Heaven, of the Aid or Literary is in the palace of career, in a position ranging from average to excellent. This means you will have very good luck throughout your career. Some obstacles may arise in your professional path but they exist to show your competency. You may not have great power but will have more than the average. If you have the star of the Arm of Heaven or the Preserved Office, then the full power will be yours, as all the necessary weapons will be yours and this will facilitate your success.

- The star of the Warrior, of Honesty, of the Voracious Wolf, of the Big Door, of the Seven Killers or of the Defeated Army is in the palace of Career, in a position ranging from average to excellent. This means that you will have very good luck throughout your career and have great powers, especially if you are in the public service or the military. The star of the Warrior, of the Defeated Army or of the Seven Killers influence your power directly. The better the position, the bigger your power. You may not have a great fortune but you will have fame.

- If the other stars in the palace of Career are in a bad position or are bad stars. This means you will be under some bad influence from these stars. You will experience some failures and the road will be more difficult. You may not have great power but if you have more good stars located in a good position in this palace, these bad influences will cause less damage and your chances will improve.

Palace of Property

- The star of the King, of the Warrior, of Honesty, of the Palace of Heaven, of the Premier of Heaven, of the Frame of Heaven or the Sun is in the palace of Property. This means you will receive a valuable inheritance. These are good and powerful stars, especially the star of the Palace of Heaven which reigns over Property. They will bring you great success and even if they are located in a bad position, you will still enjoy an enviable inheritance.

- The star of the Opportunity of Heaven, of Equality, of the Moon, of the Preserved Office or of the Arm of Heaven is in the palace of Property. This means you will be capable of building your empire with your own hands, as well as amassing a great fortune. These stars will supply you with the necessary opportunities and weapons to seize your fortune. They will bring you success and even if they are located in a bad position, you will still obtain very interesting property.

- The star of the Voracious Wolf, of the Big Door, of the Seven Killers, of the Defeated Army, of the Climbing Goat, of Jealousy, of the Ruined or Empty Land is in the palace of Property. These are bad stars. Therefore, you will have difficulty entering into any kind of business. You attempt by all means to make a fortune, but luck is not with you, especially if the star of the Seven Killers, of the Defeated Army, of the Voracious Wolf or of the Big Door is located in a bad position in this palace. You will suffer under bad influence, gradually destroying your property. If these stars are located in a good position, their influence will be less ferocious.

- The star of Prosperity, of Power, of the Exam or of the Horse of Heaven is in the palace of Property. These are good stars, so you will have great success in your life. You will be able to build your empire and amass a very interesting property. Prosperity is written into your destiny.

- The star of the Right or Left Aid, of the Twisted or Prosperous Literary is in the palace of Property. This means if you have other good stars in this palace, your luck will increase and you will be able to accumulate and maintain property longer. On the other hand, if you have other bad stars in this palace, your luck will decrease and if you are unaware of the proper management procedures, you risk losing your property.

Palace of Happiness

- The star of the King, of the Opportunity of Heaven, of the Sun, of the Warrior, of Equality, of Honesty, of the Palace of Heaven, of the Moon, of the Premier of Heaven or of the Frame of Heaven is in the palace of Happiness. These are good stars, so this means you will encounter much happiness. The stars will bring you good luck even if they are in a bad position. The star of Equality is especially good and reigns over happiness. You may not have a large fortune but you will enjoy much happiness.

- The star of the Voracious Wolf, of the Big Door, of the Seven Killers or of the Defeated Army is in the palace of Happiness. This means you will experience a life of partial happiness and suffer from the negative influences of these bad stars, especially the star of the Voracious Wolf which reigns over happiness. Sometimes happiness arrives, remains temporarily and then disappears. You are constantly chasing after happiness but if these stars are located in a good position, you eventually know true happiness.

- The star of the Preserved Office, of the Climbing Goat, of the Arm of Heaven, of Prosperity, of Power or of the Exam is in the palace of Happiness. This means you will have a life full of happiness. You may be tired at first and the obstacles numerous. All doors seem to be closed but all will be easier by the end. You will experience a life of happiness, especially if the star of Prosperity is in this palace, as it is a good star which reigns over happiness. If there are other good stars in this palace, their power will increase and bring you a life full of joy. They can even ensure a long life.

- The star of the Ruined or Empty Land, of the Horse of Heaven or of Jealousy is in the palace of Happiness. This means you will have fewer opportunities for happiness in your life, as these stars exert a negative influence. Sometimes you will believe you have found true happiness and wish to hold on forever. The next day, however, it vanishes and you must begin again. The star of the Horse of Heaven may provide you with the opportunity to encounter happiness in a faraway country.

- The star of the Right or Left Aid, of the Twisted or Prosperous Literary is in the palace of Happiness. This means if other good stars are present in this palace, your chances of achieving happiness will increase. On the other hand, if other bad stars are located in this palace, your chances will be reduced.

Palace of Parents

- The star of the King, of the Opportunity of Heaven, of the Warrior, of Equality, of Honesty, of the Palace of Heaven, of the Premier of Heaven or of the Frame of Heaven is in the palace of Parents. This means your parents enjoy a very comfortable financial situation and you have a chance of receiving a valuable inheritance. The relationship between your parents is very good.

- The Sun or the Moon is in the palace of Parents. This means your parents enjoy a good financial situation and the relationship between your parents is very good.

- The Sun and the Moon located at the same time in the palace of Parents. This means your parents enjoy a good financial situation but do not get along with each other and will eventually separate.

- The star of the Voracious Wolf, of the Big Door, of the Seven Killers, of the Climbing Goat or of the Defeated Army is in the palace of Parents. This means the relationship between your parents is not very good and even if they are rich, you will not receive an inheritance from them. Thus, it is better for you to live far away from them.

- The star of the Arm of Heaven, of the Preserved Office, of the Right or Left Aid, of the Twisted or Prosperous Literary is in the palace of Parents. This means that your relationship with your parents is good and they will help you greatly in your career and your life in general.

- The star of the Ruined or Empty Land is in the palace of Parent. This means your parents make a great effort to amass a fortune but are always left with nothing. They will get tired frequently, without gaining a thing for their work.

- The star of the Horse of Heaven or of Jealousy is in the palace of Parents. This means disputes are frequent in the relationship between your parents and it is better to live far from them, as this will give you a better chance of receiving the inheritance.

- The star of Prosperity, of Power or of the Exam is in the palace of Parents. This means your parents either have power, great fortune or fame.

5. Feng Shui

Feng Shui, which literally means "wind and water", is the art of arranging and designing one's environment in order to create an ideal place to live and to prosper. This ancient Chinese practice is based on the concept of "chi", the energy force. Chinese people believed that this invisible energy force permeates our universe and our bodies, helping to make certain places and people healthier and more prosperous than others. Feng Shui reflects the respect of the Heaven (where the wind is located) and the Earth (where the water is located), which the Chinese have for thousands of years.

Feng Shui is not the answer to all of your problems, but following its guidance may help to strengthen family relationships, maintain good health and increase family wealth. Feng Shui can be applied to both your house and your place of business. Although in the following discussion I refer only to the house, remember that all of the same advice can be used for your business place as well.

Benefits of good Feng Shui

- Better health, sounder sleep
- Improves financial situation
- Enhances career possibilities
- Cultivates business opportunities
- Ameliorates family relationships
- Increases chance of pregnancy

---

* Common sense is needed in applying Feng Shui principles. The author and publisher can not be held responsible for any accident or injury to person or building.

The principles of Feng Shui

Chi

The principle of chi is of fundamental importance to Chinese culture. Chi governs everything from Chinese astrology and home building to Chinese medicine, in which acupuncture is used to unblock the chi in certain areas of one's body to allow healing. It even underlies Chinese martial arts such as Tai Chi, which is focused on controlling the flow of one's body chi. Chi travels constantly in and out of the body as it is inhaled and exhaled, and enters and exits a building through its doors and windows. How the chi flows within the building is determined by the positioning of certain furniture and its surroundings. The chi, whether positive or negative, will have an influence on your health, your prosperity and your overall well-being.

The chi of Feng Shui is based on the principles of yin and yang, the five elements of Chinese astrology and the Pagua of I Ching. To apply a Feng Shui remedy to your house, Feng Shui masters would look at how the chi flows around the house, its position relative to neighboring houses and the land, the placement of different furniture in the house as well as the shape of the furniture itself and the location of different rooms within the house.

These factors would all be considered when balancing the yin and yang, the five elements and the Pagua, in order to develop a solution for your problems.

There are different kinds of chi:

• Good Feng Shui chi flows smoothly and continuously into the house.

• Dust and clutter will create stagnant chi. This will slow down the flow of chi, which in turn blocks progress in your personal life. Therefore house cleaning is important in maintaining good Feng Shui.

• Long corridors or hallways create fast-moving chi which may cause you to miss opportunities in your life. The chi can be slowed down by hanging a crystal or wind chimes, or placing a heavy object such as statue in the middle of the corridor.

• Road traffic moving directly toward a house or building, such as at a T junction or the end of a cul-de-sac, will create fast-moving negative chi which is considered bad Feng Shui in Chinese culture. Planting a tree in front of the house will deflect the negative chi.

• Furniture and buildings with sharp corners create cutting chi which is very harmful to your personal chi and the chi of your house. Planting a tree outside the house will deflect the negative chi from other buildings, while hiding the sharp corners of furniture with soft material will eliminate their cutting chi.

Sharp corner of desk points to the bed is very harmful to your personal chi.

Yin and Yang

According to Chinese culture, everything in this universe has yin (negative) and yang (positive) qualities. Yin and yang are opposite and complementary at the same time, and they attract each other.

Yin	Yang
Dark	Bright
Moon	Sun
Water	Fire
Blue	Red
Female	Male
Negative	Positive
Passive	Active
Quiet	Noisy

The balance of yin and yang is very important in Feng Shui, because it helps to create a more harmonious place in which to live and to prosper. For example, a room which doesn't receive much light and is painted blue will be too yin; therefore you should add bright lighting to make it more yang, stimulating the chi.

The five elements

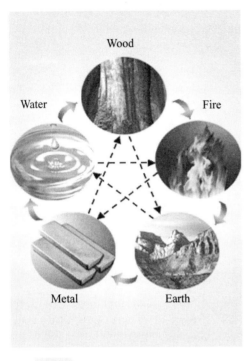

The relationships between the five elements in Chinese astrology (metal, fire, wood, earth, and water) may be either productive or destructive and are important to Feng Shui. For example, productive relationships include water nourishing trees of wood; wood being used to feed fire; fire burning away to become ash, which in turn contributes to the creation of earth; earth producing metal; metal becoming liquid (water) when heated. Examples of destruction include wood sapping nutrition from the earth; earth absorbing water; water extinguishing fire; fire melting metal; metal cutting wood. Also, each element is associated with a direction, a color and a shape.

   Productive cycle

   Destructive cycle

Element	Direction	Color	Shape
Wood	East	Green	Tall
Fire	South	Red	Pointed
Metal	West	White	Round
Water	North	Black	Wavy
Earth	Center	Yellow	Square

In addition to balancing the yin and yang principles, balancing the five elements is integral to creating a harmonious environment. For example, having the kitchen face the bathroom is not a good Feng Shui arrangement, because the fire element of the kitchen is not compatible with the water element of the bathroom. This may create health problem as well as conflicts for the occupants of the house.

As another example, consider a tall apartment building next door to a dome-shaped building. The tall building is associated with wood, while the dome is associated with metal. Since metal cuts wood this is a destructive relationship, thus the apartments in the tall building will have bad Feng Shui. However, if you lived in an apartment in the tall building, you could place a vase of flowers or a fish tank in the room nearest the dome in order to disperse the negative chi, since metal nourishes water.

Pagua

The Pagua of I Ching governs the eight different aspects of our life (Pa means eight in Chinese), while the central domain is represented by the Tai Chi symbol of yin and yang. Therefore there are nine sections in the Feng Shui Pagua, each with its own characteristics. When referring to only one section of the Pagua, we use the term Gua or corner.

1. Career: Represents your professional career, your job.

2. Knowledge: Represents your capability to learn and understand, covers all aspects of your intellectual development.

3. Family: Represents your relationships with close relatives.

4. Wealth: Represents all aspects of your finances and prosperity; this is where the money chi is located.

5. Fame: Represents personal achievement and public recognition, includes all aspects of your ability to obtain a respected social status.

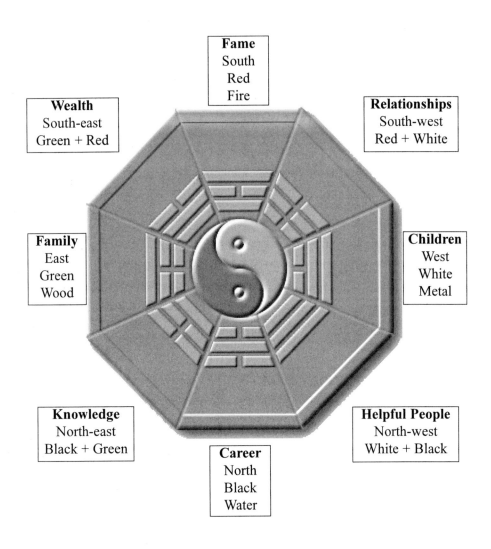

Fame
South
Red
Fire

Wealth
South-east
Green + Red

Relationships
South-west
Red + White

Family
East
Green
Wood

Children
West
White
Metal

Knowledge
North-east
Black + Green

Helpful People
North-west
White + Black

Career
North
Black
Water

Feng Shui Pagua

6. Relationships: Represents the ability to achieve mutual understanding with friends or lovers.

7. Children: Represents your descendants as well as your fertility.

8. Helpful People: Represents opportunities that people bring to you and help that you receive from other people.

9. Center: The Center of the Pagua is connected to all of the other eight areas. It is represented by the yin-yang symbol and by the element of earth, because the earth contains the necessary resources to support all our needs, whether family, wealth or fame. The Center represents all issues which are related to, but not included in, the other eight areas of Pagua. For instance, the issue of health: without a good Knowledge of health care, you will not have good health; without Wealth, it is difficult to obtain good health care; Helpful People may be pivotal in solving your health problems. Thus you can enhance the chi of your health by making adjustments in the Center area.

In the ancient Chinese house, the central room in the front of the house is called Ming Tang. This is where the host of the house would receive guests. It also serves as the entrance hall and is connected with all other rooms of the house.

Placing the Pagua over your home or room

The Pagua is used to determine the chi of your house (or any other room or building), which in turn affects corresponding aspects of your personal life. The orientation of the Pagua is always determined relative to the location of the main entrance and the center of the house, room or space in question - the entrance is aligned with one of the lower three Guas (namely Knowledge, Career and Helpful People) and the center of the house or room defines the center of the Pagua. Thus, the Pagua divides the house or room into 9 sections, not necessarily all the same size.

Here are some examples of how the orientation of Pagua is used to locate the different types of chi in your house or room.

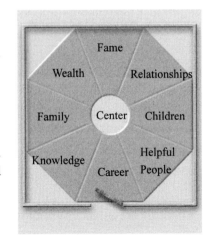

In this example, the entrance in located in the Career Gua which is correctly placed.

The entrance can stretch over 2 or 3 Guas. As the previous figure showed, it crosses over 3 Guas: Knowledge, Career and Helpful People.

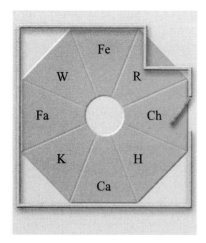

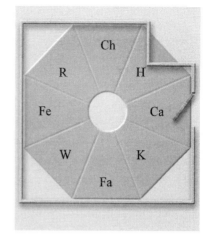

Figure 1   Figure 2

Figure 1 is an incorrectly placed Pagua. As mentioned earlier, the entrance has to be aligned with the lower three Guas (Knowledge, Career and Helpful People). In this case, the entrance is located in the Children Gua which is incorrect.

Figure 2 is an correctly placed Pagua, because the entrance is in the Career Gua.

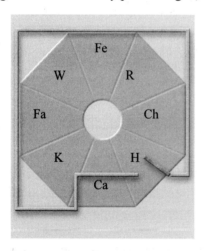

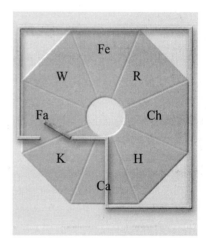

Figure 3   Figure 4

In figure 3, we have irregular Career and Helpful People Guas, and the entrance is in the Helpful People Gua. We consider in this case to have a protruding Knowledge Gua.

In figure 4, the entrance is in the missing Knowledge Gua, even though it seems to be in the Family Gua. Therefore the Pagua is considered correctly placed.

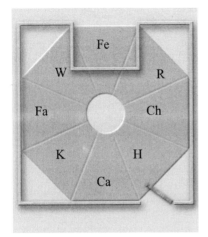

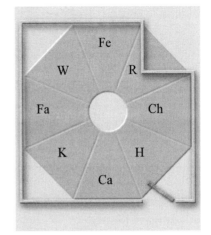

| Figure 5 | Figure 6 |

Figure 5 has a missing Fame Gua and the entrance is in the Helpful People Gua. Figure 6 has a half missing Relationships Gua.

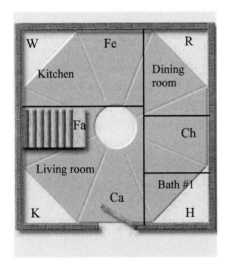

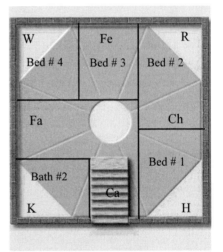

| First floor | Second floor |

Where there is more than one floor in the house, always place the Pagua based on the "entrance" of each floor. A stairway coming from the first floor is considered as the entrance to the second floor, therefore the Pagua has to be placed as shown here for the second floor

The dining room on the first floor and bedroom #4 on the second floor are in the same position in the floor plan, but in different Gua. The dining room is in the Relationships Gua and bedroom #4 is in the Wealth Gua.

Feng Shui remedies

There are many important items that Feng Shui masters use to adjust or remedy the chi of a home or business property. They are interchangeable.

1. A fish tank with goldfish can stimulate chi. It is also used to boost the chi of wealth because gold and water signify money. Also, in Chinese, the word "fish" phonetically means "surplus".

2. Bamboo flutes, usually tied with a red ribbon, can be hung from overhead beams or a sloping ceiling in accordance with the form of the Pagua to suppress negative chi. They should always be hung with the mouthpieces pointed downwards.

3. A crystal hung on a red string is used to stimulate positive chi and deflect negative chi, or to slow down chi when it travels too fast in a long corridor.

4. A mirror is used to stimulate positive chi or deflect negative chi. It is also used to draw in external chi, expand narrow spaces or enhance a missing corner or Gua.

5. Heavy objects such as statues, sculptures, rocks and plants are used to slow down fast-moving chi.

6. Light, whether natural sunlight or artificial lighting, is used to draw in and stimulate chi. This is especially useful when you need to expand the chi of a dark area or missing corner.

7. Wind chimes, sounds and music are used to activate stagnant chi, to disperse negative chi or to slow down chi when it travels too fast in a long corridor.

8. Water (fountain, pond, fish tank, etc.) is used to attract chi and wealth. It is also useful to stimulate chi and keep it circulating in and around the house.

9. Dividers, such as curtains, bookshelves and plants, can be used to separate rooms or work places, or to hide bad Feng Shui design.

10. Color has an important effect to the chi of your body as well as your house. It influences the flow of chi in two ways: first, it can be used to calm down fast-moving chi; and second, to stimulate the missing chi (or Gua) in a room. If you wish use a color as a remedy, you do not need to paint the room with that color, but can simply place colored objects in the room.

Pagua and its associated color

Element	Direction	Gua	Color
Wood	East	Family	Green
	South-east	Wealth	Green + red
Fire	South	Fame	Red
	South-west	Relationships	Red + white
Metal	West	Children	White
	North-west	Helpful people	White + black
Water	North	Career	Black
	North-east	Knowledge	Black + green
Earth	Center	Center	Yellow

The use of color can alleviate many problems in Feng Shui. For instance, if you have a long corridor facing the entrance, the fast-moving chi in the corridor will create problems for the chi of your house. The chi can be slowed down by painting the corridor with a yin color like green or blue.

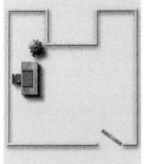

If your home office is missing the Fame Gua, this does not mean that it is necessary to paint the missing area in red; simply placing a red vase with some red roses there will stimulate the chi of the Fame Gua. Similarly, not many people like to paint a wall black, so if your want to activate your career chi, you can place a black desk at the Career corner instead.

Ideal location for a house

Chinese people believe that the ideal house to live in would be placed on the middle of a hillside, facing the rising sun, with a river passing across the front. The hill serves as a protective barrier for the back of house, the sun provides chi in the morning which will last for the entire day, and the water in front of the house will nourish the money chi of its occupant. These principles also apply to the ideal grave site.

Of course, not everyone will be able to build a house on a hillside, or have a river flow through the front yard. A substitute for the protective hill would be a tree or bush in the garden behind the house, while a pond or fountain in front of the house would simulate the money chi of the river.

General advice for good Feng Shui in a house

• According to Feng Shui, it is generally better to have less furniture and more room, as this allows the chi to flow freely bringing luck and fortune to your life.

• When placing furniture in the house, whether it is a bed, desk, chair or stove, always position it such that a person using it faces the door, without being directly in line with it. Turning one's back to the door will create negative chi, while facing the door directly is undesirable because the chi entering through the door is very strong.

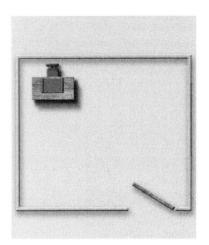 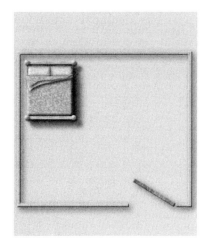

• According to Feng Shui, a sharp edge pointing towards you is like a knife which cuts your chi. Sharp edges occur in structural columns, the corners of a desk, tables, armoires, dressing tables and so on. A sharp edge can have a very negative impact on the chi of the person who sits, lies down or stands in a direct line with it. If it is not possible to move the offending furniture, hang wind chimes or a crystal between the sharp corner and the person, cover the sharp corner with a soft material, or place a plant so as to hide the sharp corner.

1. Internal doors

The front door of a house is considered to be the "mouth of the chi" - this is where the energy of the outside world enters. Internal doors (doors between rooms) allow the external chi to circulate through each room and throughout the house.

Doors must be properly aligned and they must swing freely open and shut without blockage. Otherwise the chi will become obstructed and stagnate within the room.

Doors should all be the same size; if some rooms in the house have smaller doors than others they will receive less chi, leading to an unbalance in your overall chi. To remedy this problem you can hang a mirror on the outside of the smaller door to expand the image of the door, or add brighter lighting to the room behind the smaller door to bring more chi into it.

2. Windows

Windows act like the eyes of your house. They provide a view of the outside world to those inside the house, and serve as entrances for outside chi and sunlight. Windows should be kept clean and should open and close freely without obstruction.

It is best to position a window to the east or south-east in order to bring in more sunlight, because sunlight gives energy. A window should not face a door directly, as this will allow the chi coming from the door to move too fast and quickly escape through the window. In such a case, the current created by the two openings will make the chi flow constantly. To slow down the chi and force it to stay a while before escaping, hang a crystal or wind chimes between the door and the window.

3. Stairs

Stairs carry chi from one floor to another. Therefore, it is important that they are well lit, wide and unobstructed. Dark, narrow stairs will hamper the flow of chi traveling up them, resulting in a deficiency of chi and a corresponding negative effect on the inhabitants of the upper floor. To remedy the situation, add brighter lighting on the staircase to expand the chi.

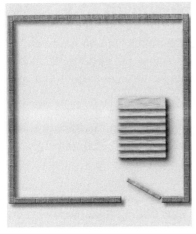

It is best for the staircase to be located at the side of the house with a change in direction midway. This design will allow the chi to go halfway up, take a break, then continue its route, preventing it from moving too fast. This is particularly important when the staircase faces the entrance - otherwise the chi coming through the entrance will move directly to the upper floor without first circulating through the rooms of the lower floor. To counteract the speeding chi, hang wind chimes or a crystal between the entrance and the stair, or place a heavy object (such as a sculpture or statue) at the base of the stair.

Spiral staircase: A spiral staircase will impart a spiral motion to chi, creating a whirlwind. The swirling chi will flow quickly and turbulently into the upper floor, disrupting the chi of its occupants. This can be alleviated by hanging wind chimes or a crystal halfway up the staircase to slow down the chi and make it flow more smoothly.

4. Structural columns

For good Feng Shui, structural columns must be spaced widely enough for the chi to flow freely between them. This will support and enhance the chi, just as the columns support the building. Round columns are preferable because they will smooth the flow of chi. Square columns have pointed edges, which are considered bad Feng Shui: sharp edges act like knives, generating cutting chi, which has a very negative impact on the chi of person sitting, standing or lying down in line with the edge. One remedy is to cover the edge with a soft material or use a plant to hide the edge.

5. Protruding corner or missing corner

If the part that juts out is less that 50% of the width of the house or room, it is a protruding corner. If it is more than 50%, then it is a missing corner.

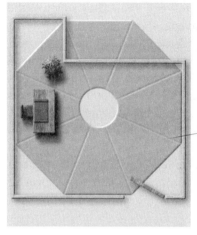

A protruding corner will increase the potency of the Gua for that corner. For example, a protruding Wealth corner will bring you more money chi. However, a protruding corner will also create cutting chi, so it would be important not to place a desk in line with it. If desired, you could place a potted plant at the corner to hide its cutting chi. If the house has a protruding corner outside (i.e., it is L-shaped), plant a tree or install a lamp at the opposite corner to balance it.

A missing corner indicates that part of a Gua is missing. Hence, you would not receive the full blessing of that Gua, or that part of your chi will be weakened. For example, if your house or room were missing the Wealth corner, you might encounter financial problems. To counter this you would need to make adjustments to raise the chi of the corner. This could include hanging wind chimes or crystals near it, putting a lamp at the missing corner to stimulate the weakened chi, or hanging a mirror to hide the missing corner and enhance the chi there. Furthermore, the sharp edge of a missing corner will create cutting chi. To avoid this move your desk, table, stove or bed out of line with the sharp edge, or cover the corner with soft material to hide the negative chi. If the house has a missing corner outside, try to plant a tree or install a lamp at the corner to stimulate the chi.

6. Overhead beams

Overhead beams are bad structures according to Feng Shui. They suppress the chi of anyone standing, sitting or lying directly underneath. If you have your bed, desk or stove underneath an overhead beam, it can create a negative impact on your wealth, your health and your finances as well as your relationships. To remedy the situation, move the furniture out from under the beam; if this is impossible, then hang two bamboo flutes from a red ribbon under the beam to disperse the negative chi.

7. Shadows

If your house lies partially in the shadow of another building, those corners which are shadowed will not receive their full input of energy and as a result the chi of those corners will be negatively affected. Try planting flowers, adding brighter lighting or hanging a crystal in the rooms of the shady corners to stimulate the chi.

Your home

Entrance

The entrance is considered by Chinese to be the "mouth of the chi". This is the place which connects your private space to the outside world, through which the external chi enters your house and travels to the different rooms inside.

The size of the entrance should be proportional to the size of your house. An entrance which is too large will allow the chi to escape from your house, while an entrance which is too small will prevent the external chi from entering easily.

The entrance should be well lit, clean and uncluttered. If the front door area does not receive any sun, add bright lighting to stimulate the chi.

1. According to Feng Shui, the door should open inward to bring the chi inside. If the door opens outward, it will allow the chi to escape from the house, which could wipe out your health and your fortunes. Try to rehang the door so that it opens inward. If this is not possible, hang a wind chime over the threshold to stimulate the entrance of chi.

2. A door which is too narrow will not let the chi enter easily. This will affect the Feng Shui of your entire house, as none of the rooms will get enough chi. This can have a grave impact on your health, your finances and your well-being in general. One remedy is to add lighting and mirrors to virtually enlarge the space and enhance the chi.

3. A door which is too large will cause the chi coming in to move too fast. It can also make the chi escape too easily from the house, thus producing an unbalance of chi. This can be remedied by placing a heavy object (a statue or large potted plant) next to the door to slow down the chi and to keep the chi from escaping from the house.

4. The front door should not be directly opposite the back door, because this will allow the chi coming into your house to escape quickly out the back without circulating through the other part of the house first. One remedy is to hang crystals, wind-chimes or a pair of bamboo flutes between the back door and the front door to prevent the chi from escaping too soon.

5. Having three or more doors aligned in a row is considered bad Feng Shui, because it will allow the chi to flow too fast between them, creating turbulence in the house. To smooth out the flow of chi hang a crystal or wind-chime over the middle door.

6. An entrance which faces a wall is also considered bad Feng Shui. With this arrangement, chi entering from outside will be obstructed by the wall and will not circulate freely. The resulting blocked chi will interfere your health, your finances and career - you will find that the opportunity for you to move up in your life becomes very limited. To remedy this situation, hang a mirror on the wall to disperse the chi to other parts of the house, add bright lighting in the entrance area to expand and free the obstructed chi.

Bedroom

The bedroom is one of the most important rooms in the house. Because we spend one third of our lives sleeping, the location of the bedroom and the position of the bed within it have profound influences in many aspects of our lives, including our relationships, sex life and health. Even our wealth is influenced by the bedroom, because without sleeping well it is difficult to maintain good health, and without good health it is difficult to accumulate wealth.

In the bedroom we sleep, rest and recharge our energy. Therefore it should be a quiet place to allow sound sleep, yet be a place filled with energy upon waking. The bedroom should be away from sources of noise, such as busy streets. A window facing east, north-east or south-east is highly desirable so that light from the rising sun in the morning will give you energy to face each new day.

The bedroom should be used only for sleeping, resting and making love. Avoid having a television set or computer in the room as these electronic devices will create electromagnetic energy which is incompatible with human chi. This will create problems for your relationship as well as your health.

Location of Bedroom

1. The bedroom should not be located in the center of the house. The center of the house is associated with the element of earth; because a large part of our body is made up of water (and earth absorbs water), this would create an unbalance in your personal chi. If you cannot move the bedroom elsewhere, hang a wind chime in the room to deflect the negative chi.

2. Avoid making the bedroom the first room you see when you enter the house. This is not a good Feng Shui location, because the bedroom is a very private place and should be kept out of sight from visitors. If you cannot move the bedroom, keep the door closed at all times. If there is no door, place a divider such as bookshelves to hide the bedroom.

3. A bedroom located adjacent to the bathroom or kitchen is also considered bad Feng Shui. This will create health problems, since the water energy in the bathroom and the fire energy of the kitchen will interfere with your chi during sleep. The problem will be most pronounced if you sleep with your head pointing toward the wall connecting the two rooms; a large part of your body is water, which would be extinguished by the fire element of the kitchen, or combined with the water element of the bathroom to create an overflow. To remedy these deleterious relationships, move the bed to another location in the room. If the bedroom is facing the bathroom or the kitchen, hang wind chimes or crystals between the two rooms to calm down the negative chi. If the bathroom is en suite to the bedroom, try to keep the door of the bathroom closed at all times and hang a crystal from the top of the doorframe.

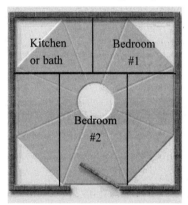

Bedroom #1 is in a good position if it is not next to or facing the kitchen or bathroom.

Bedroom #2 is not in a good position. Not only it is located in the center of the house, it is the first room you see when you enter the house.

4. The Relationship corner of your house is a very good location for the master bedroom. This will bring you increased luck in the search for a new relationship, or improve a current relationship. If, after considering all other Feng Shui aspects of the bed, you can place it at the Relationship corner of the bedroom, it will be better still, providing a very positive arrangement. This will give you a thriving relationship chi, which you should maintain by keeping the corner as clean and beautiful as possible, adding bright lighting or hanging paintings to further enhance the chi.

A bedroom with a missing or irregular Relationship corner will negatively affect the chi of your current or forthcoming relationship. To remedy the situation, hang a mirror at the corner to stimulate the chi.

5. A bedroom with a sloping ceiling is also considered bad Feng Shui because the sloping ceiling will suppress your chi, especially if you place your bed under the slope. This can create an array of problems concerning your health, career, wealth and relationship. Move the bed from underneath the slope if you can. Otherwise hang a mirror at the corner of the slope to enhance the chi.

Position of the bed

The bed should always face the entrance of the bedroom without being directly in line with it. The space under the bed should be kept empty and clean so that chi will not stagnate there. Stagnant chi in the bedroom can create problems for your health and relationships. Your head should be against a solid wall or a firm headboard.

These positions are the optimal, because they give you a better view of the doorway.

Neither good nor bad, as you face the entrance but you have a poor view of it. This can be improved by placing a mirror to give a better view of the entrance.

Bad positions, because they do not allow you to face the entrance. If you cannot move the bed to another position, place a mirror so that you can see the entrance.

All of these positions are very bad, because you are directly in line with the entrance. The energy flowing through the mouth of the chi is very powerful and will certainly disrupt your sleep, creating problems not only in your relationship chi but also in your life in general (health, wealth, etc.)

This is the worst position because your feet point directly towards the door. This is very bad Feng Shui, because it mimics the position in which a dead person is laid out and carried out of a room. Try to move the bed to other location, or place a divider between the bed and the door. You can also hang a crystal or wind chimes between the divider and the door to disperse the negative chi.

The sharp edges of wardrobes, columns, dressing tables, desks, etc. should not point to the bed, because they generate cutting chi which will cause problem for your health and relationships. If you can not move the furniture or the bed, place a plant to hide the sharp corner and hang a crystal between your bed and the sharp corner.

The bed should not be placed near the window, especially the head of the bed. This is important in order to protect your head from the chi flowing around the bed. Chi coming in through the door and going out the window will create turbulence in your relationship and your health, unless you leave some space between the bed and the window so that the chi can circulate without disturbing you.

If you have a dressing table with a mirror attached, the mirror should not face the bed. This is bad Feng Shui because your chi will get a shock if it sees its own reflection during the night.

If you plan to have children, it is a good idea to place your bed in the corner of the Children Gua. You can also hang a crystal at this corner to stimulate the chi.

Children's room

For the children's room, apply the same Feng Shui principles as you would use in an adult's room. It is best if the children's room occupies the Children Gua of the house, as this will help the chi of the child to grow. The bed should be positioned so that it faces the doorway without being directly in line with it. Also, it is better to place the bed against the wall, as this will put the child in a more secure position. The child's head should be against a headboard or wall which is not connected with the wall of the kitchen or bathroom, since the fire and water elements of these two rooms will stir up the chi of the child, making him or her more unstable.

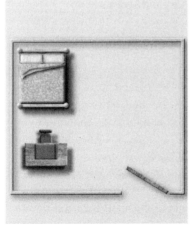

If you put a desk in the children's room, make sure that it is positioned so that when the child sits he or she faces the door, but is not in direct line with it. The desk should be positioned in the Knowledge Gua. To stimulate the chi of this area you can also hang wind chimes to enhance the chi.

Kitchen

According to Chinese culture, the kitchen is one of the most important rooms in the house. Since food represents wealth and personal finances, the place where food is prepared takes on great importance. In light of this, wealthy families always have plenty of food in the house. The kitchen also represents the element of fire, which creates energy (chi).

The Chinese place so much importance on the kitchen that traditionally each house is said to have its own "kitchen god". At the end of every year, the kitchen god will report to the Jade Emperor in heaven about the general well-being of the house.

In Chinese medicine the balance of yin food and yang food has a very important impact on the maintenance of healthy chi in the body. Therefore, the balance of yin and yang in the kitchen - mainly between water, from the refrigerator and sink, and fire, from the stove - is crucial to good health and good fortune.

• The kitchen should be well lit, clean and uncluttered.

• The cupboards and storage areas must be neat, well organized and uncluttered to avoid stagnation of chi.

• If the kitchen is very small, hang mirrors to expand and stimulate the chi, which in turn will increase the chi of your finances.

• The kitchen table should not be placed in line with the door.

Location of kitchen

1. The kitchen should not be located in the center of the house. The center of the house is represented by the element of earth, and since fire burns to produce ash (which becomes earth), this would invite the destruction of your finances. If you can not move the kitchen to another room, hang wind chimes over the area of the stove to counteract the negative chi.

2. The kitchen should not be the first room encountered when entering the house. This is not considered a good Feng Shui location because if the first thing that people see is your wealth, you will attract theft and find difficulty accumulating wealth. Your finances are a private matter. In addition, this arrangement will place the kitchen too close to the front door, so that the energy passing through it will be very strong; strong wind extinguishes fire, so the chi of your finances will be swept away. If you cannot move the kitchen to another

room, keep the kitchen door closed at all times and hang wind chimes in front of the door.

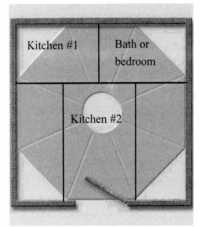

Kitchen #1 is a very good location if it is not next to or facing the bathroom or bedroom, because it is in the Wealth corner of the house, it will bring in the money chi.

Kitchen #2 is in a bad location because it is in the center of the house.

3. Relationship to bathroom and bedroom. The kitchen should not be beside, or opposite, the bathroom or bedroom. This is considered bad Feng Shui for the kitchen, because the fire element of the kitchen and the water element of the bathroom and bedroom (remember that a large part of the human body is water) are incompatible. Such an arrangement may create all kinds of health and financial problems for the occupants of the house. To remedy the situation, hang a crystal or wind chimes between the two rooms to deflect the negative chi.

4. Sloped ceiling. The kitchen should not have a sloped ceiling. This is bad Feng Shui because the sloped ceiling will suppress your financial chi, limiting your earning potential, especially if your stove is placed underneath the slope. This can create many problems for your finances. Move the stove from under the slope if you can, or hang a mirror at the edge of the slope to enhance the chi and hang two bamboo flutes under the sloped ceiling in the form of Pagua.

Position of the stove

According to Chinese culture, the positioning of the stove has great importance for your overall finances. It affects your financial situation more than any other appliance or piece of furniture in your home.

• The stove should not be placed directly in line with the door, or underneath the window. Chi flows in and out through the door, generating a strong flow of chi in its vicinity. If the wind gets into the kitchen from the door it can help ignite fire, or extinguish fire if it is too strong; similarly, the strong flow of chi will interfere with the fire of the stove, putting your finances on a bumpy road. As a result, you would sometimes accumulate great wealth rapidly, but other times your wealth would be gone with the wind. The chi can also escape from the door or window, meaning that your wealth will slip away faster. To counter these effects, move the stove to another location if possible. Otherwise, place a divider between the door and the stove, or place a heavy object (e.g., a pot of flowers, or a statue) next to the stove to calm the strong flow of chi.

 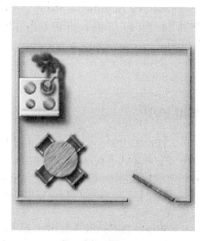

Bad position	Good position
In line with door, underneath window	Stove in the Wealth corner of kitchen

• The stove should be placed so that the cook can clearly see the door while cooking without being directly in line with it. If the cook's back is to the door, he or she may be surprised by someone coming from the door, affecting the food which is being cooked and affecting, in turn, your finances. To remedy the situation, move the stove so that the cook will face the doorway when cooking. If you cannot move the stove, hang a mirror near the stove area so that the cook can clearly see the door. The mirror will also serve to expand and stimulate your money chi.

• Placing the stove underneath overhead beams is considered bad Feng Shui. Your chi will be suppressed by the beams when you cook which, in turn, limits your earning power. Try to move the stove from under the beams, or if this isn't possible, hang two bamboo flutes under the beams in the form of Pagua to disperse the negative chi.

• The Wealth corner of your kitchen is a powerful spot. If you can place your stove at this corner while still meeting all of the other Feng Shui criteria, it will be very auspicious for the chi of your wealth. If, however, you don't place the stove in the Wealth corner, be sure to keep it clean and uncluttered.

• The refrigerator, sink or dish washer are associated with the water element and therefore should not be placed next to or facing the stove; since water destroys fire, the stove will be negatively affected by the chi of water, thereby affecting your finances. If you can not move the furniture, try to add a divider or hang a mirror at the stove area to deflect the chi.

• In order to keep the chi flowing in a balanced manner, all the burners of your stove should be in good working condition. You should use all of them regularly so that the chi of your wealth will not stagnate. This will increase your financial potential.

Bathroom

The bathroom is associated with the element of water which nourishes your body and also represents money and wealth. The chi of water accumulated in this room comes from many sources (the sink, bathtub, toilet, etc.) so it is very strong. Its constant flow will greatly affect your finances.

While both the kitchen and the bathroom have a great impact on your finances, they act differently. In the kitchen it is the stove which attracts your money chi, while in the bathroom it is the water which contains the money.

• Keep the door of the bathroom closed at all times so that your money chi will not escape and is not visible by other people.

• A clean, dry bathroom is good for your money chi. You should always be sure to keep this room (as well as the rest of the house) free of leaks, otherwise you may encounter financial problems.

• The bathroom should be well lit in order to stimulate the chi. Add a mirror to enhance the money chi.

Location of bathroom

1. The bathroom should not be the first room encountered when entering the house. This is considered bad Feng Shui, because if the first thing that people see when entering your house is your wealth, you will have difficulty accumulating wealth. Your finances are a private matter. In addition, this arrangement will place the bathroom too close to the front door, so that the energy coming through it will be too strong and will blow away the chi of your finances. If you cannot move the bathroom to another room, keep the door shut at all times and hang wind chimes in front of it.

2. The bathroom should not be located at the Wealth corner of the house. Although the water energy in your bathroom contains money chi, the water always goes down the drains of the bathtub, sink or toilet. It follows that your money chi would be washed out along with the water, causing great difficulty in accumulating wealth - even though you would gain wealth briefly, it would be flushed out sooner or later. If your bathroom happens to be at this corner, hang a crystal in the bathroom and put a mirror outside the door to calm down the negative chi.

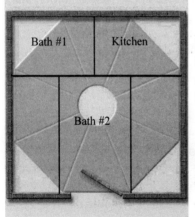

Bath #1 is in a bad location, because it is in the Wealth corner of the house and it is facing or next to the kitchen, it will destroy your money chi.

Bath #2 is also in a bad location because it is in the center of the house.

3. The bathroom should not be next to or facing the kitchen. The water element of the bathroom and the fire element of the kitchen are not compatible - this arrangement will create conflicting chi in your house. Because the money chi of water will destroy the money chi of fire, this is a disastrous combination for your

finances which will leave you with nothing in the end. To moderate the negative effects, close the bathroom door at all times and hang a crystal or wind chimes between the two rooms.

4. The bathroom should not be next to, facing or inside of the bedroom. This is bad Feng Shui because we spend one third of our time in the bedroom; since the human body is mostly made up of water, the water chi of the bedroom will combine with the water chi of the bathroom to create an overflow of water. This will result in multifarious health problems for the person who sleeps in the room. To remedy the situation, keep the bathroom door closed at all times and hang a crystal or wind chimes between the two rooms.

5. The bathroom should not be in the center of the house. The center of the house is represented by the element earth, and since earth absorbs water, your bathroom's money chi will be absorbed if it is located there. This will make it difficult to accumulate wealth - as soon as you get money, it will disappear. If you can not move the bathroom to another room, hang a crystal in the center of the bathroom to suppress the negative chi.

Location of toilet

Try not to place the toilet at the Wealth corner of the bathroom, because its powerful flushing action will wash away your money chi even more than the drain of your bathtub or sink. If your toilet is located at the Wealth corner, hang wind chimes over the toilet to disperse the negative chi and close the lid when flushing. Try not to install the toilet immediately beside the bathroom door; if this is unavoidable, keep the bathroom door closed at all times.

Dining room

The dining room is where you eat your meals and from time to time receive guests, therefore it should be a space which allows chi to flow freely. The location of the dining room is quite flexible, as long as it is not next to the bathroom. If the dining room is part of the kitchen, then it should be considered according to the Feng Shui principles of the kitchen.

The dinning table should be round, oval, or rectangular with round corners, surrounded by an even number of chairs. The table and chairs should be comfortable with well balanced legs, to ensure that the chi of the dining room is not agitated.

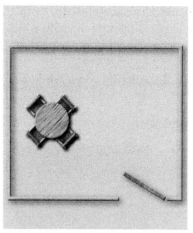

• The table and chairs should not be placed directly in line with the door, as this will allow the chi flowing in through the door to stir up your meal. If you cannot move the table, hang a crystal or wind chime between the door and the table to calm down the chi.

• The table should not have sharp edges, because this creates cutting chi, especially for those sitting at the corners. One remedy is to cover the sharp corners with soft material.

The living room

The living room is where the family gets together to relax, and where you receive visitors. Ideally the living room should be the first room encountered when entering the house. Also, it should be located at the center of the house where the earth element, containing the resources to nourish people's needs, will enhance the chi of you and your visitors.

• You should try to allow sunlight into the living room. If this is not possible, add brighter lighting to stimulate the chi. The flow of chi is vital in the living room, especially when you have visitors.

• You should nurture a relaxed and entertaining chi in the living room. This is not compatible with the chi of a working environment, so the living room should not be used for any work-related activity. Doing so will send a confused message to the chi of the living room, creating an unbalance in your own body's chi.

• The furniture should not have any sharp edges or corners, as these will emit cutting chi detrimental to you and your guests. It is better to have a round, oval or octagonal table. Any rectangular or square table should have rounded corners and edges to avoid producing cutting chi.

• Placing too many pieces of furniture in the living room will cause the chi to stagnate. A steady flow of chi is very important in the living room, where you will often receive visitors.

• Place all furniture, including sofas, couches and chairs, against the wall if possible. You should be especially carefully not to place them in the path which the chi follows, as this will create fluctuations in your chi.

• A fish tank with goldfish will enhance the chi of the living room while also attracting wealth to your house.

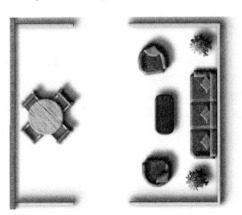

Business or office

The location of your business depends on what kind of business it is. For example, a boutique should be located on a busy street or at an intersection, while an accountant's office is best located at a quieter place.

Home office

You should separate your home office from the other rooms of your house if possible. The chi of the work-related room is not compatible with the chi of the other rooms in the house. If you do not separate the home office it will create an unbalance in the house's chi, affecting your overall well-being. If you cannot put it in a separate room, use a divider, such as bookshelves, a curtain or a plant, to provide virtual separation.

• Working in your bedroom will adversely affect your relationship chi, and should be avoided. If you must work there, use a divider to separate your bed from the work area.

• Your home office should be located at one of the following corners of your house: Wealth, Fame, Helping People or Career.

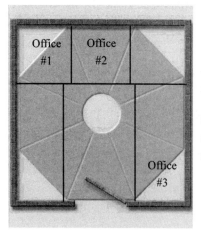

Office #1 (Wealth corner), office #2 (Fame corner) and office #3 (Helpful People corner) are all good locations.

• Your desk should face the door but not be directly in line with it. If your desk blocks your view of the entrance, move it to a better position or hang a mirror so that you can see the entrance. Your back should be against a solid wall, not under the window, because the chi coming in through the window can be disruptive. Also, it is not desirable to receive sunlight from behind.

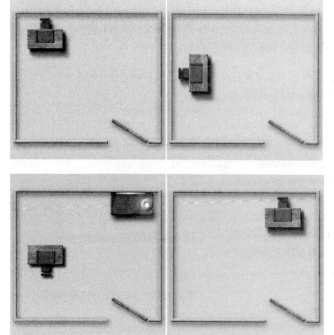

Good desk positions

Bad desk positions. In line with the door or not facing the door.

• The best Guas at which to place your desk are Wealth and Fame. It is a good idea to hang wind chimes or crystals at the corners of Helpful People and Career, as this will enhance your chi in these areas. The desk should not have sharp corners, because they create harmful cutting chi. If it does, you can negate the cutting chi by covering the sharp edges with soft material.

• Two desks in an office should not face each other directly. This would create conflict in the office. Rearrange the desks or, if this is impossible, hang a crystal between the two desks to disperse the negative chi.

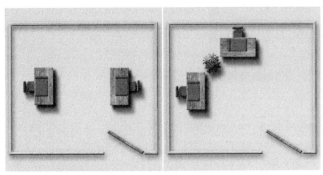

Bad desk positions   Good desk positions

• It is not advisable to place two offices opposite each other across a long corridor. The fast-moving chi in the corridor will create conflict between the two offices. If you have this kind of arrangement, keep both office doors closed at all times and hang crystals between the offices.

• A fish tank with goldfish is good Feng Shui for a business, whether it is a boutique or an office. Water and gold both signify money, so a goldfish tank will greatly stimulate your money chi and help to attract clients.

• A business or office should not be located at the end of an L-shaped building. This is known as the "elephant head and mouse tail" location, indicating that all of the money chi will go to the elephant, leaving the mouse with nothing. If you cannot move the office to a better location, add bright lighting and hang crystals or wind-chimes at the entrance to attract money chi.

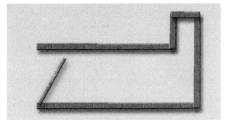

6. Face Reading

Face reading is the Chinese art of predicting a person's fortunes by analyzing the different elements of his or her face. It takes into account the shape of the following features of your face: ears, forehead, eyebrows, eyes, cheek, nose, mouth and chin. It can help to predict your future and guide you along the road of success.

The Chinese technique of face reading starts with the ears. The left ear tells your fate from birth until the age of seven, while the right ear corresponds to the ages of age 8 to 14. Next, the face is divided into 3 sections. The upper section includes the forehead, which determines your fate from age 15 to 30 and is called the celestial region. As the name suggests, your life during this period is dependent more on heaven than on your own efforts, and you are more or less protected by your parents and ancestors. The middle section, called the human region, runs from the eyebrows to the nose and dictates your destiny from 31 to 50. During this period, your success or your fortunes will rely mostly on your own efforts. Finally, the lower section, called the earthy region, includes the bottom of the nose to the chin and concerns your fate after the age of 50. This is a period in which your achievements on the earth are already well-established.

If the three regions are equally proportioned you will have a balanced life throughout your existence without any drastic changes, good or bad. If any of the three sections is larger or smaller than the other two, it means your fate will be better or worse during the corresponding time.

Ears

The ears determine your fortunes from birth until the age of 14 - the left ear from birth to 7 and the right ear from 8 to 14. Large and well-developed ears represent good luck during your childhood. Large and thick earlobes are a sign of intelligence, and are often associated with wealth and a long life.

Ears flat against sides of head

If your ears are aligned closely to your head, such that they can hardly be seen from directly in front, you will have very good luck. You will tend to lead a very wealthy and respected life thanks to success in business or politics. You are usually intelligent and eloquent which help you to maintain a leadership position in whatever path you follow. These ears are also associated with longevity. Generally speaking, your life will be filled with fortune and good luck.

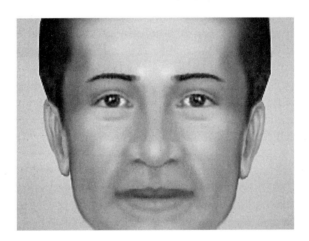

Thin ears and earlobes

This indicates that you have a difficult childhood. During your youth, you don't receive enough support from your parents and family, and good fortunes are always out of reach. However, take heart - the difficulties you encounter during this period can be very good training which will lead to success in later years.

Ears stick out

A highly intelligent person, you are gifted as a scholar or researcher, tending to excel in intellectual work. Your shrewdness makes you a very good strategist in any organization, whether it is in politics or business. You know when you can advance and when you should step backward without any hesitation. In general, you will have a very successful life.

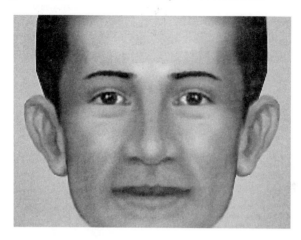

Ears high above eyebrows with large, thick earlobes

Clever and intelligent, you are a hard-working person who usually obtains good social status. Generally you will be good at accumulating wealth. If your earlobes are pendulous, you will have a very wealthy and glorious life, encountering success wherever you go - life tends to be effortless for you. Pendulous earlobes are also linked to longevity.

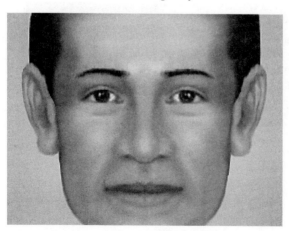

Large, thick ears

You are very fortunate in life, usually obtaining a high level of social status, whether in business or in politics. You always tend to be the one who takes the leadership position. Generally you are able to accumulate great wealth during your life. These ears are also associated with longevity.

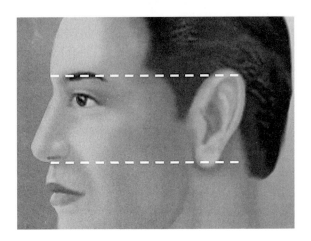

Small ears

Usually you will have difficulty succeeding in life. You will have to work hard in order to fulfill your dreams. Help is rarely available for you, and sometimes your ambitions are out of reach. You try hard to succeed but what you obtain is usually less than you expected.

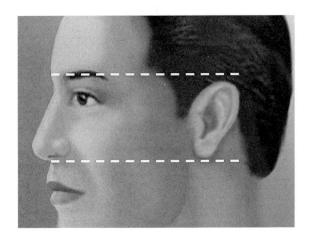

Pointed ears

You are very astute and hard-working. You do not mind working more than expected in order to succeed, even though you usually get less than you want. Thanks to this quality, you may sometimes achieve significant wealth, but you will tend to live a solitary life.

Ears large at the top with small earlobes

You have good luck while young, but starting around the middle of life, everything will become much more difficult for you. You will become quickly wearied while achieving only minimal results. Although you may find success from time to time, it will be short lived, and all will disappear in the end.

Forehead

The forehead is associated with a person's fate from age 15 to 30, and is called the celestial region. As its name indicates, your life during this period is determined by heaven rather than by your own efforts. You are more or less protected by your parents and your ancestors.

The forehead is comprised of three equal sections: the first section reflects your intelligence and your reasoning power, the second section concerns your memory and the last one represents your intuition.

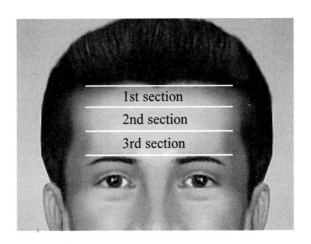

Narrow and low forehead

This is not considered a good omen for your youth. You will have a difficult childhood, lacking the support of heaven. This may also mean that you won't get enough protection from your parents and ancestors. Nonetheless, the difficulties that you will overcome during this period may provide a good training ground for your later years; they will strengthen your sense of determination that can lead to later success in life.

On the other hand, a narrow forehead is also a sign of narrow-mindedness and less-developed intelligence. Thus, you may make unfavorable judgments during your youth, and due to frequent errors you may lose confidence in your own ability to solve problems.

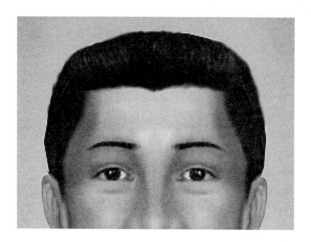

Broad, smooth forehead

A broad, high, smooth and well-developed forehead is highly desirable. This shows that you will have a favorable destiny in your early life, protected by parents and family. A broad forehead also indicates a high degree of intelligence and a good capacity for logical thought. You will be open to new ideas and are very generous in your dealings with others. A smooth forehead means that you will have a healthy, easy childhood life - everything will be given to you by heaven to support your early existence.

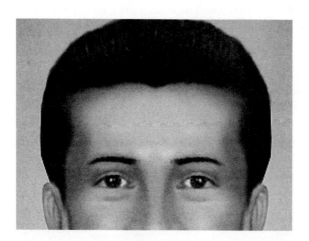

High forehead

A high forehead signifies high intelligence. It is most often found among scientists, researchers and other thinkers. You tend to be quite egocentric and emotional. Life is generally easy for you during your early age, because you get plenty of support from your parents and your surroundings.

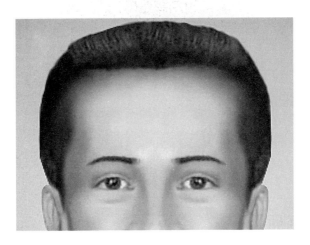

Concave forehead

A concave forehead generally means that during your childhood or adolescence, life will not be easy for you. This may mean that you may have an unhealthy childhood and that you have difficulty getting along with others. Generally speaking you receive little support from your parents and you have a less-developed intelligence. This will lead you to an unsuccessful early career development.

Full, rounded forehead

This is one of the best shapes for a forehead. It shows that you are highly intelligent and capable of logical thinking. A good memory is written on your forehead. Your early life will be strongly supported by your parents and you will have a healthy childhood. Everything will seem easy for you during this period - you will receive many gifts from heaven to nourish your growth and the start of your career.

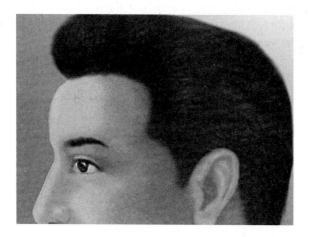

Eyebrows

The eyebrows can reveal one's destiny at the start of the middle years. The space between them is particularly important. In general, long, thick eyebrows are considered good, and the wider the space between the eyebrows, the better.

Upward-sloping eyebrows, with triangular outside ends

You are very intelligent, you are used to making clear-cut decisions and you dare to challenge authority. You dislike playing second fiddle, preferring to take charge. Generally speaking you have a more favorable destiny during the early and middle years of your life.

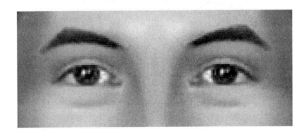

Upward sloping eyebrows

You are highly intelligent and very straight-forward in relating to others. Generally speaking, you tend to be very successful in life. You may obtain great riches and considerable power in your middle years.

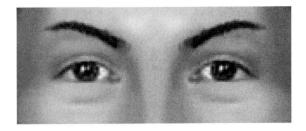

Downward sloping eyebrows

Usually this is an indication of limited success in your early years. You don't tend to be very ambitious and have a hard time focusing on your career goal. You could be intelligent but you encounter great difficulties in your early life.

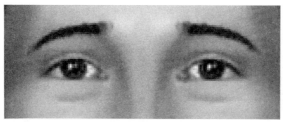

Half-moon eyebrows

The shape of these eyebrows shows that you are easy-going and you tend to be very generous in dealings with others. Generally speaking you will have a very comfortable financial situation during the middle years of your life.

Short eyebrows

You are very smart. Whatever you want to do, you do it without hesitation. You may need to work hard to become successful in life, but generally you will get what you want.

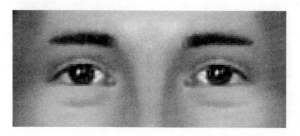

Long, straight eyebrows

Generally you have a very solid financial situation. If you are not wealthy, you could gain in a position of power. Either way, you have no reason to worry about financial need. Long eyebrows are also associated with a long life and abundant vitality.

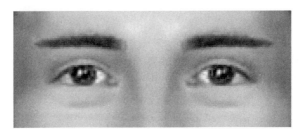

Long, thin eyebrows

You rarely challenge any orders coming from authority. You will always follow rules and regulations. You tend to be very disciplinary which may sometimes lead to a successful career in your middle age. Sexually speaking, you are very attractive to the opposite sex, whether male or female.

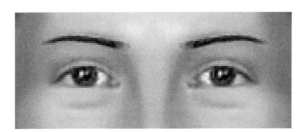

Thick eyebrows

You always want to rush in order to finish up what you're working at. You can be very generous towards others. You are quite adventurous and often dare to try new ideas which others would balk at. Generally you are very successful in life because of your interest in breaking new ground.

Close-set eyebrows, or eyebrows that meet

This type of eyebrows is not considered favorable in Chinese culture. The space between eyebrows represents the end of youth and the beginning of middle age - when the eyebrows are too close to each other, it means that you will have difficulties during this period of transition. These difficulties could arise concerning either your career or your family. Close-set eyebrows also tend to mean that you are very egocentric. As well, they indicate that you don't have a broad view of what you want to achieve in life, but instead tend to focus at the point immediately ahead of you without considering other alternatives. Happily, this intense concentration may bring you success from time to time.

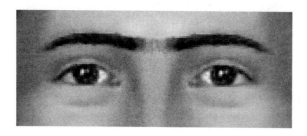

Widely spaced eyebrows

These are considered good fortune. Ideally, you should be able to put two fingers in the space between the two eyebrows. If so, you will have an open-mind, tending to accept other people's opinions rapidly. A wide space between your eyebrows also indicates that you will encounter success during your transition from youth to middle age, bringing you a bright future in your career.

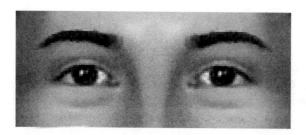

Eyes

The eyes reveal your intelligence and your attractiveness to other people. Large eyes are generally considered more favorable, according to the art of Chinese face reading.

Large eyes

Large eyes are associated with intelligence, astuteness, honesty and loyalty. An adventurous person, you dare to take on new assignments and are never afraid of a new challenge. You usually lead a very successful career which will bring you money and fame. Male or female, people with large eyes are very attractive to the opposite sex.

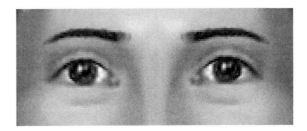

Small eyes

You tend to be inclined towards regulations and discipline. You would rather follow the rules set up by others than try to explore new territory. You concentrate on details, often to the extent that you miss the big picture. You dislike seeing other people succeed in your field and you will try hard to overtake them. Once you have made up your mind, you will do whatever is needed to reach your goal, even though you may sometimes head in the wrong direction.

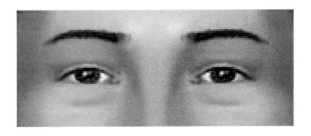

Upward-sloping eyes

These are considered a sign of highly intelligence. In dealing with others you are straight-forward and strong-willed. In Chinese face reading, these eyes are considered among the best. Whether you are male or female, these are the eyes of beauty. You are accustomed to success because you can get help from others effortlessly.

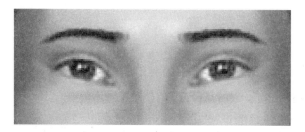

Downward-sloping eyes

It is not considered likely that you will encounter much success in life. Although you can be very wise in dealing with others, you lack the strong will necessary to achieve significant success.

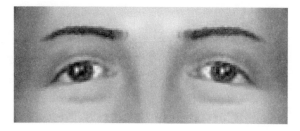

Triangular eyes

People with triangular eyes are usually very selfish and egocentric. You may be very successful in your early years, which will cultivate your seeds of arrogance, and as a result you will arouse jealousy in others. Very often you will ignore all of the rules in order to achieve your goal, considering only what is best for your own interests. Triangular eyes often indicate a strong appetite for sex and eroticism.

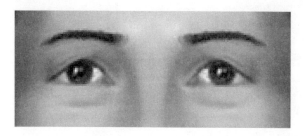

Nose

The nose is linked to personal wealth. Thus, by studying someone's nose, you can tell whether that person will be financially well endowed or not. It is also believed that the key to divining a man's sexual power is his nose.

Straight nose

A straight nose is linked with success in life. You will be the one who obtains great power or wealth in society. You are intelligent and wise and can easily obtain assistance in order to achieve your goals. Your success is practically assured. Male or female, your achievements are likely to bring you high social status.

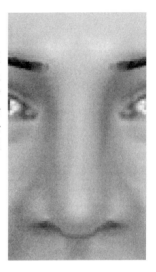

Curved nose

People with this kind of nose are usually characterized by courage and a sense of adventure. You dare to challenge authority and take on new assignments. You like to explore new ideas because of your adventurous spirit, usually leading to success in your career. Rather than taking over a half-finished project, you prefer to start something from scratch and carry it through yourself.

Fleshy nose

You are quite fortunate in life, always receiving help from others to boost you towards your goals. Whenever you are in trouble, help will appear to rescue you and lead you to success. As a result, your life will be easy and your difficulties slight. You may accumulate significant wealth during your career, and you try very hard to keep it. Still, you may occasionally show generosity toward others.

Bumpy nose

You will encounter more difficulties during your early years. You try hard to fulfill your dreams, but success is elusive, seeming always out of reach. It is difficult for others to change your views, despite the need to adapt to the changing world. During middle age, success is also difficult to attain - you will tend to meet more with failure than with success. Life will be exhausting for you and yet you will receive almost nothing in return.

A bumpy nose also means that you will encounter many problems in relationships with the opposite sex. Your relationships usually follow a bumpy road.

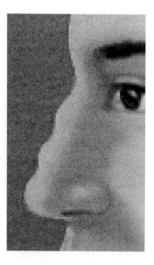

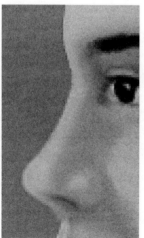

Snub nose

You start your career or business ventures alone, shunning help from others, preferring to do things your own way. You may meet with great success or with total failure during your middle years. It is difficult for you to hold onto wealth - you will find that money is a fleeting commodity. Man or woman, you have a strong appetite for sex.

Snub nose with a rounded tip

You have a kind and generous temperament. You are ready to help others even though this may sometimes require sacrificing your own interests - you will rarely refuse any request for help from others. You tend to accumulate great wealth during your existence, especially after middle age. The older you become, the richer you will be. Generally speaking, your destiny follows a favorable track to success in life.

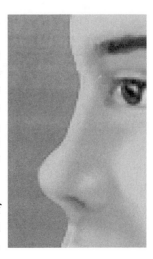

This nose shape is also a favorable sign in terms of your love life. You will tend to have many lovers in your life, thank to your willingness to help people. You are always welcomed by the opposite sex.

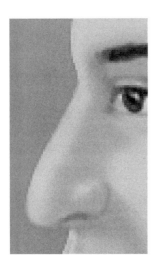

Aquiline nose

You may be selfish and egocentric, or even villainous. Even though you may accumulate wealth temporarily during your career, it will not last very long - you will see it disappear around middle age.

Curved and downward sloping nose

You tend toward aggressiveness. You always want to take on new challenges in your life and are always intent on winning. You do not shy from incurring more risks than you can afford. You may be quite successful during your early years, but starting around the middle of your life you will find your troubles multiplying. Eventually all of your fortune will disappear.

Cheeks

Your cheeks determine your fortune throughout your forties. Generally speaking, well-developed cheeks are considered best.

Round cheeks with high cheek bones

According to the Chinese art of face reading, high, round cheeks are a good sign. They show that you have plenty of energy and are usually self-confident, even to the point of arrogance. You dare to challenge anything that stands in your way, willing to try to whatever is necessary to clear it. Generally, high and round cheeks indicate a successful career during middle age - you will tend to advance very quickly during this period of time.

In Chinese culture, women with high cheeks are not considered good partners. High cheeks show that they will dominate over the rest of the family - their power will overshadow that of their husband, which is not an acceptable arrangement in oriental culture.

Flat cheeks

You are not likely to develop a successful career. You are not willing to work hard in order to succeed, and have a tendency not to challenge anything which may go against your will. You will tend to be financially unsuccessful. You lack the energy required to fulfill your dreams and usually abandon projects halfway through.

Mouth

The mouth belongs to the earthly region and determines your fate after the age of 50. This is a period during which your achievements on the earth are already well-established. Your mouth can reveal a lot about your wealth during this period of time, as well as your sexuality (especially if you are a woman).

Small mouth

You are usually considerate and charming. You do not talk much but are very sensitive and sensual at the same time. You are capable of achieving a great deal during your life and will always receive help from others in fulfilling your dreams. Generally speaking, you are able to accumulate wealth during your mid-life.

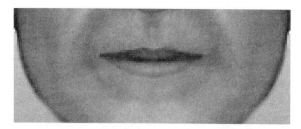

Large mouth with thick lips

You are favored to succeed in life. This mouth is a sign of shrewdness and intelligence. You tend to have your feet firmly planted on the ground and your dreams never exceed your reach. You will be able to amass great wealth in your life, never needing to worry about money. According to the Chinese art of face reading, a woman with large mouth are considered very erotic and sensual.

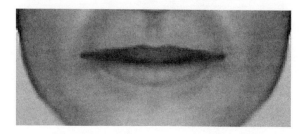

Upper lip is thicker than lower lip

A trust worthy person, you are very straightforward and never try to hide your intentions. You are also quite strong willed and tend to make decisions very fast. This mouth indicates that you are likely to lead a life of fame and wealth, especially toward the end of your career.

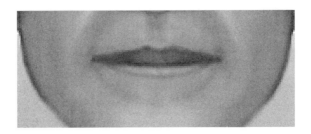

Lower lip is thicker than upper lip

This kind of mouth marks a loyal person, hidden under a facade of untrustworthiness. Although you may never be able to accumulate great wealth, you will always obtain the help required to fulfill your dreams, especially when you are in desperate situations. Luck is often your savior.

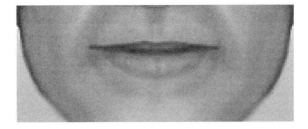

Mouth with turned-up corners

This is considered a sign of great power. You are very eloquent, you tend to be quick-witted and know how to make others accept your ideas. You can be very aggressive in your career and in business matters. You are willing to fight on every front in order to get what you want. Your intelligence and wisdom help you to achieve wealth and fame in life - generally you will lead a very fortunate existence.

You also have strong sex appeal, and tend to enjoy your sex life more than others. This is especially true for women.

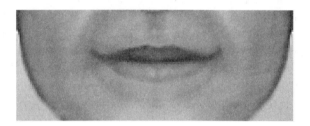

Mouth with turned-down corners

This is not usually considered very fortunate. You will tend to encounter problems in all aspects of your life, including your career, business or relationships with others. You usually have difficulty maintaining a long term relationship with a lover. You will have to work hard during your younger years to gain acceptance in society. Difficulties seem to arise from every corner you pass, but no help is forthcoming from others. You tend to live a lonely life. However, you may find the perspective on your career and relationships is better from your later years.

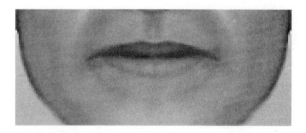

Chin

The chin also belongs to the earthly region and reflects your destiny beyond the age of 60. Generally speaking, a broad and rounded chin is most desirable, as it will bring prosperity to your old age.

Round, broad or double chin

A round or broad chin usually indicates a mild temperament. You are very generous in your dealings with others, and it is very rare that you will encounter conflicts with other people. This chin is usually considered good luck during old age, bringing you a very prosperous retirement. In some cases, it may even mark the start of a new life, especially if you have a less-developed celestial (upper) or human (middle) region. You may start a successful new venture during this period of time. A round or broad chin also signifies longevity.

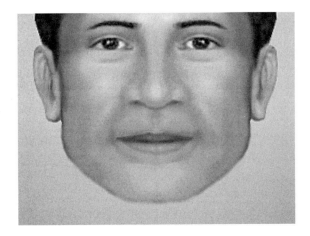

Pointed or narrow chin

A pointed chin indicates that you are very intelligent and usually excel in your work place. However, a pointed or narrow chin is usually considered a bad sign for your fortunes during old age. Although you may be very successful during your early and middle years, when you arrive at this period your good luck will dissipate. All of the wealth and fame which you have accumulated previously will slip away. Your late life will likely be lonely.

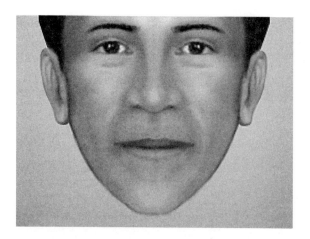

Square chin

You have plenty of energy and are not afraid of working hard to succeed in life. Once you make up your mind, you will stick with your plan and do whatever is necessary to fulfill your dream. You are characterized by a strong will and have a tendency toward stubbornness; this helps you to achieve success in most things you do. A square chin signifies a stable life during old age.

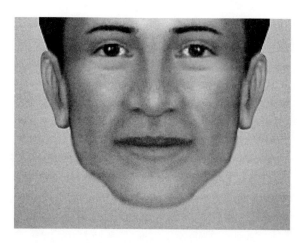

Long chin

A long chin is a sign that your luck will improve during old age, because it makes the earthly region longer than the others two regions. A hard-worker, you are very dedicated to your career. You may be less fortunate during your early and middle years, but upon reaching maturity you will have a better perspective. At this time you may also find wealth which had been absent previously. A long chin is also a sign of longevity.

Faces in general

1. Round face; long ears with large earlobes, flat against sides of head; large, high forehead; widely spaced eyebrows; straight nose; mouth with turned-up corners; round, wide chin; the three regions evenly divided.

Generally you have a mild, friendly personality. You are very generous toward other people. You don't like conflicts, so whenever they occur you are the one who tries to settle them. This is not to say that you are not an avid fighter, simply that you try to obtain your goals tactfully.

You are generally seen as clever and wise in business dealings, usually becoming a leader in your field. You often receive much help in fulfilling your goals - you sometimes find success knocking at the door without even making a concerted effort. You usually have a very solid finances thanks to success in your business or career.

Generally speaking, life is very generous towards you. You don't have to worry much about money; even if you are not always rich, you will always have enough to support your lifestyle. You will always receive help during difficult times and usually have a very comfortable old age.

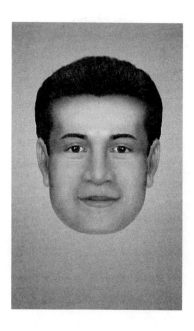

2. Rectangular face with high, round cheeks; straight nose; long ears; broad forehead.

Generally you have a clear, sharp mind. Your strong will sometimes turns to stubbornness. You are highly intelligent and have a strong sense of justice: you will try very hard to protect and defend the weak.

With your rectangular face, you tend to be more successful in politics and academics than in business. You rely more on your own efforts than on other people. Sometimes you can be very authoritarian and do not like accepting other people's opinions.

Generally speaking, you will meet often with success during your early years. Your childhood seems easy, as you receive plenty of support from your family. Your middle years also give you a good career perspective. Although you may encounter some difficulties around the forties, everything should smooth out to give you a bright pinnacle in your career. Life is also very good during your old age, possibly even leading to a new career which will bring wealth and fame.

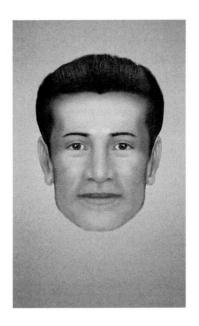

3. Square face with broad forehead; broad chin; well-developed cheeks; the three regions evenly divided.

Generally you have a good life waiting for you. Due to your broad forehead, you will have a very easy childhood, full of good fortune. During these early years your family will give you all of the support necessary to pave the way for success in later years.

You will start to harvest the fruit of your good luck during middle age. In this period, you may suffer some setbacks, but nothing serious - the reliable good luck of your human region will be there to protect you, helping you through difficult times.

Later years will also be very comfortable for you given the shape of your earthly region, providing you with a prosperous retirement. Generally speaking, with this face you will always have a comfortable financial situation; even if you do not accumulate great wealth, you will have more than enough to support your needs.

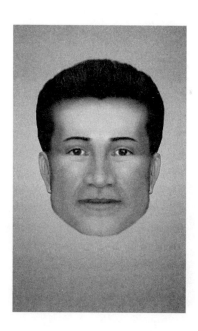

4. Long face; short forehead; human and earthly regions long; ears long but not thick.

You have a mild temperament, you are very flexible in dealing with others and you tend to readily accept the opinions of others. Generally you have a more difficult life in your early years, having to fight hard to obtain what you want. During childhood you will not be able to rely on others, not even your parents and family.

But upon reaching your middle years, your luck will change for the better. Life starts to smile upon you. The difficulties you endured during your younger age will give you a determination to succeed in life. You will be able to fulfill many of your dreams, possibly leading to a very successful career.

A long earthly region is an indication of longevity and a good life during old age. You may not have a prosperous retirement, but life is quite easy for you during this period. Financially speaking, you will always have enough to support yourself without too much worry.

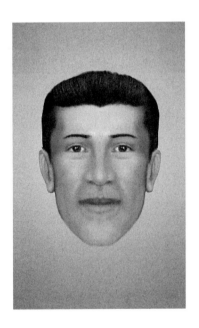

5. Narrow forehead; human and earthly region broad; well-developed cheeks.

Generally you will have a more difficult life during your early years. During this time you don't get enough support from your family, leaving you to struggle very hard in order to make your way. Your intelligence will not give you any help through these years, but your hard-working character will lead you go through the difficult time.

Upon reaching your middle years, you will gain a better perspective. You may even find help entering into ventures which will turn out to be highly successful. Because of the hardship that you have endured, you relish competition and fight hard to get what you want out of life. Generally you are capable of obtaining great success in your career.

You will also enjoy happiness during your old age. The broadness of your earthly region shows that life will be very generous with you during this time, and that great wealth could be within your reach.

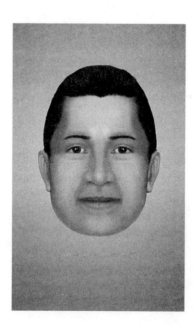

6. Broad, high forehead and narrow chin.

This shows that you are highly intelligent, passing a very easy childhood. During those years, everything is available to pave your way to success. You can have a very successful career starting in your thirties, your open-mindedness allowing you to readily accept other people's opinions. This will lead you to some very successful ventures.

You may start to notice a down-turn in your career during your forties. At this time, life will become more difficult, and the luck of the human region will not be of any help to you. There is more failure than success in your future, and you may have to work hard just to maintain a stable career.

During your later years, your luck will become even worse and you may encounter still more problems. You will receive no outside help and be forced to rely entirely on your own efforts. Generally your last years will be lonely, while all the wealth that you amassed during your youth disappears little by little. At the end, there will be nothing left for you.

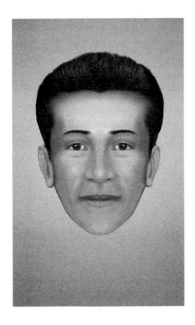